Praise for the previous editions of

QUICK ESCAPES®
San Francisco

"If you are in need of fast getaways to local adventures, Karen Misuraca's *Quick Escapes San Francisco* . . . is a good reference, listing interesting finds just outside the Bay Area's back door."
—*San Francisco Peninsula Parent* (Millbrae, Calif.)

"Misuraca's itineraries . . . are well organized and practical. Each day's journey has a sound plan, with workable directions—followed by listings of alternative events, places, restaurants, and lodgings . . . Misuraca managed to capture treasures of the area."
—*Napa Valley Appellation*

"The itineraries are quite detailed. . . . The presentation is affable, ever helpful, and informative—a fine book for San Franciscans and the rest of us as well."
—*Travelwriter Marketletter* (New York, N.Y.)

Help Us Keep This Guide Up to Date

Every effort has been made by the author and editors to make this guide as accurate and useful as possible. However, many things can change after a guide is published—establishments close, phone numbers change, facilities come under new management, etc.

We would love to hear from you concerning your experiences with this guide and how you feel it could be improved and kept up to date. While we may not be able to respond to all comments and suggestions, we'll take them to heart, and we'll also make certain to share them with the author. Please send your comments and suggestions to the following address:

> The Globe Pequot Press
> Reader Response/Editorial Department
> P.O. Box 480
> Guilford, CT 06437

Or you may e-mail us at:
> editorial@GlobePequot.com

Thanks for your input, and happy travels!

INSIDERS' GUIDE®

QUICK ESCAPES® SERIES

QUICK
ESCAPES®

San Francisco

GETAWAYS
FROM THE BAY AREA

SIXTH EDITION

KAREN MISURACA

INSIDERS' GUIDE®

GUILFORD, CONNECTICUT
AN IMPRINT OF THE GLOBE PEQUOT PRESS

INSIDERS' GUIDE ®

Copyright © 1993, 1996, 1999, 2001, 2003, 2006 Morris Book Publishing, LLC.

Insiders' Guide and Quick Escapes are registered trademarks of Morris Book Publishing, LLC.

Photo credits: Pp. 1, 5, 19, 67: courtesy Sonoma County Tourism Program; p. 56: courtesy Humboldt County Convention & Visitors Bureau; pp. 107, 111, 125: courtesy Santa Cruz Convention & Visitors Bureau; pp. 155, 188, 199, 211: courtesy Lake Tahoe Visitors Authority; p. 161: courtesy Sacramento Convention & Visitors Bureau. All other photos are by author.

Text design by Casey Shain
Maps by M. A. Dubé © Morris Book Publishing, LLC.

ISSN 1542-2526
ISBN 0-7627-3887-1

Manufactured in the United States of America
Sixth Edition/First Printing

Thanks to my traveling partner, golf guru, and tireless sherpa, Michael, for the best times of my life, on the road in California.

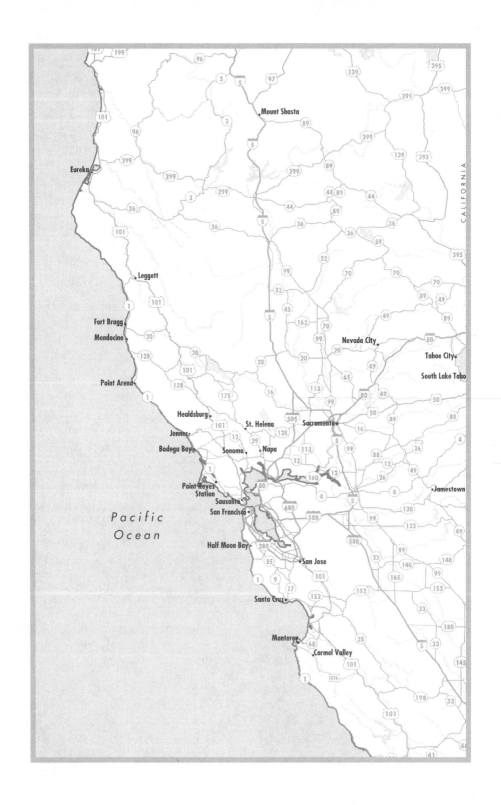

CONTENTS

The information listed in this guidebook was confirmed at press time. We recommend, however, that you call establishments before traveling to obtain current information.

INTRODUCTION

Twenty-one trips are described in this guidebook, with all the details and inside information you will need to know for a perfect getaway from San Francisco. Every escape is a driving tour, with sightseeing, recreation, restaurants, and lodging located and described. To give you a variety of activities from which to choose, each weekend itinerary is quite lively, packed with sights and side trips. Annual special events are listed, as are recommended restaurants and lodgings. There's More gives you reasons to return another time. For advance planning, check out the more than twenty-one maps and, listed under For More Information, the visitors bureaus.

If you favor weekends tucked away in one peaceful spot, use the chapters to book a quiet bed-and-breakfast inn, choose romantic restaurants, and read about what all the other tourists are doing.

Within easy distance are the Wine Country, '49er gold rush towns, redwood forests, villages by the sea, cabins in the Sierras, and houseboats on the Sacramento Delta. It's hard to avoid clichés when describing the wide choice of places to go within a few hours.

From the rocky shores of the Sonoma and Mendocino coastlines to the gleaming gem of Lake Tahoe, honky-tonk beach towns, and High Sierra wilderness trails, you can escape every weekend for a year and still have a hundred places to see.

For maximum enjoyment of your sojourns, take care to avoid heavy traffic times—Friday and Sunday afternoons and commuting hours. Keeping California's microclimates in mind, be prepared for weather changes throughout the year, particularly in the coastal and mountain regions. Fog, rain, or snow may not be what you expected, but discoveries made on a wintry weekend could turn you into a California lover, in more ways than one.

If you're looking forward to a particular bed-and-breakfast inn or a restaurant, be sure to call well in advance. And remember that in some resort communities, businesses may not be open every month of the year.

Most restaurants and lodgings listed are in the midrange pricewise; a few special places are expensive. Rates and prices are not noted because they can be counted on to change.

In this sixth edition, you will find more Web site addresses, reflecting the tremendous tide of information now available online, not to mention the benefits of browsing beforehand. Even the tiniest inn is likely to have a Web site, with a virtual tour of each room. Online, you can make restaurant and lodging reservations, get driving instructions, and print out maps to specific street addresses. Not like the old days, when we had to phone and write for brochures and maps!

If you have comments on how the escapes worked out for you, please drop me a note care of The Globe Pequot Press. Thanks to the travelers who made useful suggestions and contributions to this sixth edition of *Quick Escapes: San Francisco.*

It's a good idea to include the following items in your getaway bag:

- Jacket, long pants, and walking shoes for trail hiking and beachcombing in any weather.

- Binoculars (so as not to miss bald eagles circling and whales spouting).

- Corkscrew, a California necessity.

- Day pack or basket with picnic gear.

- Maps: The directions and maps provided here are meant for general information—you'll want to obtain your own maps.

- California State Park Pass: Most state parks charge a day fee of several dollars. Frequent visitors to the state parks will save money by purchasing an annual car pass and/or boat launching pass (discounts are available for seniors and those with a limited income). Call (800) 777–0369; www.parks.ca.gov.

- Golden Eagle Passport: For any person, and their accompanying private party, an annual pass is available to national parks and federally operated tourist sites for a $50 fee (888–467–2757; www.nationalparks.org).

For more information on northern California destinations, write or call the California Travel and Tourism Commission, P.O. Box 1499, Sacramento 94812-1499; (800) 862–2543; www.visitcalifornia.com.

NORTHBOUND
ESCAPES

Wine Road to the Sea

The Russian River Route, Healdsburg / 1 Night

In the mid-1800s tourists from San Francisco rode ferries across the bay and hopped onto a narrow-gauge railroad to reach summer resorts on the Russian River. The arrival of the motorcar and the decline of lumbering caused the towns along the river to fall into a deep sleep for a few decades. In the 1970s the tremendous growth of wineries began a new era of tourism. Now more than fifty Sonoma County wineries can be discovered on the back roads of the Russian River and Dry Creek Valleys.

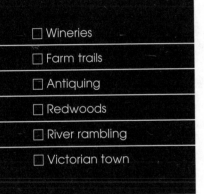

- ☐ Wineries
- ☐ Farm trails
- ☐ Antiquing
- ☐ Redwoods
- ☐ River rambling
- ☐ Victorian town

The Russian River winds through redwood canyons; past sandy beaches, orchards, and vineyards; sliding calmly all the way to the Pacific Ocean at Jenner. Rustic inns, casual cafes, leafy walking trails, great fishing holes, and magnificent redwood groves are reason to spend several weekends following its path.

Canoeing, kayaking, and tubing on the Russian are very popular activities. A good paddling route is the scenic 10-mile stretch from Forestville to Guerneville, where you find many beaches and stopping points for fishing and picnicking. It takes a half day, including rest stops. Ospreys, blue herons, deer, and turtles are some of the wildlife that accompany your trek. Bring plenty of water, secure your car keys with a safety pin in your pocket, and beware of sunburn on the top of your legs.

Your weekend begins in the Victorian town of Healdsburg. The westernmost destination of your Russian River Wine Road escape is the tiny town of Jenner, on a high bluff overlooking a marshy bird sanctuary at the mouth of the river.

Day 1 / Morning

Head north from the Golden Gate Bridge on U.S. Highway 101 to Healdsburg, about one and a quarter hours, taking the central Healdsburg exit into the center of town, parking on the **Healdsburg Plaza,** a lovely, tree-shaded Spanish-style plaza built when the town was established in 1867. Band concerts and outdoor festivals are held on the plaza green on many weekends.

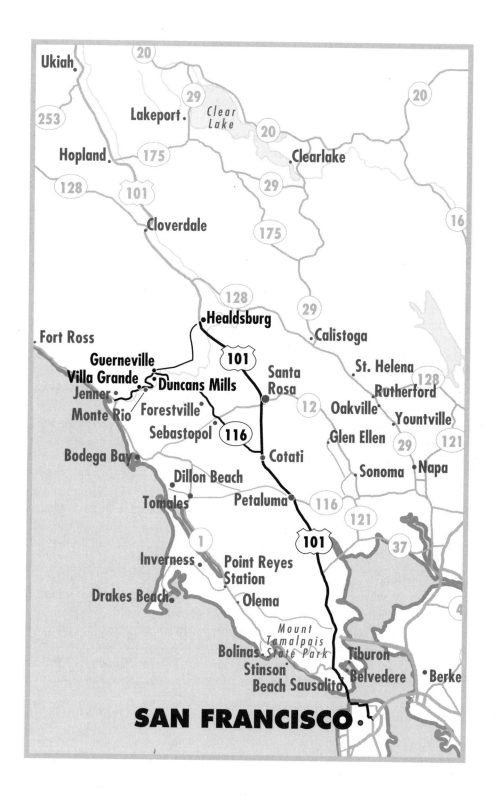

The plaza and surrounding streets are lined with shops, restaurants, bakeries, hotels, bed-and-breakfast inns, and more than a dozen winery tasting rooms, from Gallo of Sonoma to Todd Hollow Vineyards, to Thumbprint Cellars and Lounge. Between the Alexander and Dry Creek Valleys, at the top of the Russian River Valley, Healdsburg is the anchor town for this part of the wine country. On the east side by the river, **Front Street Five** on Front Street is a trendy complex of five separate tasting rooms. Here Camellia Cellars offers samples of reds from the nearby Dry Creek Valley. Sapphire Hill Vineyards features Russian River Valley wines, and Huntington Wine Cellars favors the Alexander Valley wines. Across the street, Davis Family Winery makes a luscious Pinot Noir.

The adjacent Dry Creek Valley is prime wine country, famous for California's finest Zinfandels, a hearty red of Italian heritage. At the **Russian River Wine Company,** 132 Plaza Street (707–433–0490), you can taste and collect wines from more than sixty wineries. Also nearby are the Healdsburg Public Library and the **Sonoma County Wine Library,** 139 Piper at Center Street (707–433–3772), and the **Healdsburg Historical Museum,** 221 Matheson (707–431–3325). Get a walking-tour map at the **Chamber of Commerce,** 217 Healdsburg Avenue (707–433–6935).

Among the shops on and nearby the plaza is **Options,** 126 Matheson Street (707–431–8861), where exceptional ethnic and American crafts are the main attractions. Fifty antiques dealers hold court in the big blue building at **Mill Street Antiques,** 44 Mill Street (707–433–8409).

At **Healdsburg Classics,** 226 Healdsburg Avenue (707–433–4315), are fourteen antiques shops selling everything from country pines to garden pieces, estate jewelry, and Native American artifacts.

The **Dry Creek Valley** west of town is top biking and wine tasting territory. A nice 20-mile loop on gently rolling hills starts at the town plaza, heads south to Mill Street, crosses under the highway, and joins Dry Creek Road going north. Endless vineyards and rows of low, forested mountains remain in view throughout the ride. At the old **Dry Creek General Store** (3495 Dry Creek Road; 707–433–4171), buy sandwiches and picnic here or take provisions in your bike basket.

Ferrari-Carano, at 8761 Dry Creek Road (707–433–6700; www.ferrari-carano.com), comes as a surprise in the valley, where most of the wineries are small, country places. Don and Rhonda Carano, second-generation Italian-Americans, re-created Tuscany on their winery estate. Voluptuous gardens surround the Villa Fiore tasting room, where the Mediterranean ambience echoes the character of the wines.

If Zinfandel is your passion, be sure to stop at **Quivira Winery,** 4900 West Dry Creek Road (707–431–8333; www.quivirawine.com), where picnic grounds overlook the valley.

Founded in 1876, **Simi Winery** (16275 Healdsburg Avenue; 707–433–6981) offers one of the most comprehensive and enjoyable tours in the valley; the shady terrace here is pleasant on hot days.

The Dry Creek Valley, kingdom of Old Vine Zinfandels.

On the south end of town on a bend of the Russian River, **Healdsburg Memorial Beach Park** (13839 Old Redwood Highway; 707–433–1625) is a popular place to sun and swim.

LUNCH: Bistro Ralph, 109 Plaza Street, Healdsburg; (707) 433–1380. Locally raised produce, meats, and poultry are used to create miracles: roasted garlic and polenta with baby lamb, Hog Island oysters, peach shortcake, crème brûlée. Ask for the Local Stash, a special wine list of older vintages from the Dry Creek and Alexander Valley wineries.

Afternoon

Proceed southwest out of town on Westside Road, stopping at the sharp left turn and driving through the arch to see **Madrona Manor,** 1001 Westside Road (707–433–4231), one of California's largest and finest Victorian masterpieces. Built in 1881, the huge manor is now an inn and restaurant surrounded by magnificent gardens. Walk in and ask for a tour of the museum-like rooms and outbuildings; depending on their bookings, it may or may not be possible but is definitely worth a try.

Mill Creek Vineyards, at 1401 Westside Road (707–433–5098), is a small, family-owned winery on a knoll overlooking the valley; it's fun to see their wooden mill wheel turning beside the creek. Two picnic areas offer panoramic views of the valley and beyond. Mill Creek Vineyards makes several wines, from a good "Old Mill Red" table wine to a superb Cabernet Sauvignon.

You'll be following the Russian River now, all the way to the ocean. Valley foothills become mountains, oaks give way to dark redwood and fir forests, and the roadsides become ferny and damp. Along the riverbank in freshwater marshes grow silvery gray-green willows and cottonwoods.

Take a left onto Wohler Road, passing more than a half dozen wineries on your way to River Road, then turn west. Stop at **Korbel Champagne Cellars,** 13250 River Road (707–824–7000), for a tour of the winery and the gardens. Founded in 1886 by Czech immigrants, the ivy-covered stone winery is a piece of Old Europe tucked into the rolling, vineyard-carpeted hills of the Russian River Valley. The guided winery tour, including museum, film, garden walk, and champagne tasting, is one of the most complete and enjoyable of all California wineries. In-depth garden tours show off antique roses and hundreds of spring bulbs. You can also taste Russian River Brewing Company beer at Korbel and choose from an astonishing variety of gourmet deli items in the market/deli/espresso bar.

You'll follow the river and the redwoods a few minutes farther down the road to the summer-vacation town of **Guerneville,** chock-full of souvenir shops, cafes, and art galleries. Johnson's Beach, below town, is a long stretch of sand with rentals of canoes, kayaks, paddleboats, tubes, umbrellas and beach chairs; there's also a snack bar (707–869–2022; www.johnsonsbeach.com). You can also launch your own watercraft here.

In the middle of town, turn north onto Armstrong Woods Road a mile or so to **Armstrong Grove Redwoods State Reserve** (707–869–2015), 750 acres of glorious redwood groves along Fife Creek. Easy paths lead to sunny picnic areas and old-growth trees up to 300 feet tall. For a half-day horseback ride into the wilderness bordering Austin Creek State Recreation Area, call the **Armstrong Woods Trail Rides and Pack Station** (707–887–2939). Even beginning riders will love the lunch ride, which meanders gently out of the redwood forest through a variety of wildlife habitats to ridgetops overlooking the Russian River Valley.

Accessed from Armstrong Grove, the **Austin Creek Recreation Area** (707–869–2015) is 4,200 acres of hills, canyons, and river glens that campers, hikers, and horseback riders love to explore. Wildflowers in the spring, deep forests, good birding, bluegill and black bass fishing in Redwood Lake, and primitive camping sites are a few of the attractions. It is hot and dry in summer, glorious in spring with blooming wild azaleas, rushing creeks, and maples, ash, and alder in full leaf.

LODGING: Applewood Inn, 13555 Highway 116, Guerneville; (707) 869–9093; www.applewoodinn.com. An elegant 1920s California Mission Revival mansion in the redwoods, featuring a heated swimming pool, and acres of glorious gardens and forest, a secluded hideaway. All the romantically decorated rooms have down comforters and garden views; some have fireplaces, Jacuzzis, double showers, and balconies or verandas. A gourmet picnic basket can be put together for your day-tripping, and in-room massage is available. A noted Italian chef conducts a popular small-group cooking school here, La Buona Forchetta. Ask about special packages. You could forget the sightseeing and just settle in here.

DINNER: Applewood Inn. Candlelight gourmet dinners by the fireplace. Think about sea bass with chive and quinoa crust, and roasted chicken with bing-cherry mustard reduction.

Day 2 / Morning

BREAKFAST: Brie omelets, eggs Florentine, and more fresh, hot entrees in the beautiful dining room at Applewood Inn.

Ten minutes west of Guerneville, bear left across the bridge onto Moscow Road and through the tiny burg of Monte Rio to **Villa Grande,** a small river-bend village that's changed little since the 1920s, when it was built as a summer encampment for vacationers from San Francisco. There is a beach here and a delightful array of early Craftsman-style cottages.

Back on the main road, it's not far to **Duncans Mills,** where a dozen or so shops nestle in a Victorian-era village, another 1880s railroad stop. Take a look at the only remaining North Pacific Coast Railroad station.

The **Duncans Mills General Store** (707–865–1240) stocks fishing gear, groceries, and antiques. The **Gold Coast Coffee Co. Cafe and Bakery,** Steelhead Boulevard (707–865–1441), offers a selection of freshly baked goods from their wood-fired brick oven. Shops in Duncans Mills sell everything from fishing gear and fine jewelry to top-notch wildlife art. A worldly surprise in this bucolic village, the aromatic, elegant **Sanctuary** shop (25185 Main Street; 707–865–0900) specializes in beautiful Asian imports.

Farther west, the Russian River meets the sea at Bridgehaven, the junction of Highways 116 and 1. In winter, ocean waves and the river clash here in a stormy drama. In summer the mouth of the river is cut off from the ocean by temporary dunes.

Fabulous, easily accessible beaches are located just to the north and the south, off Highway 1. Have a picnic on the beach or head back to Duncans Mills for lunch.

LUNCH: Cape Fear Cafe, 25191 Highway 116, Duncans Mills; (707) 865–9246. African tribal masks are dramatic accents at this charming little place. The North Carolinian chefs turn out wonderful fresh seafood dishes, homemade pasta, and vegetarian specialties.

Afternoon

Drive back on Highway 116 to Guerneville, turning south on 116 past Forestville to **Kozlowski Farms,** 5566 Gravenstein/Highway 116 (707–887–1587), for luscious berries, jams, fresh fruits, and pies—the ultimate Sonoma County farm store. Pick up a **Sonoma County Farm Trails** map at Kozlowski's to locate the many produce outlets and nurseries in these verdant rolling hills. This is Green Valley, a sylvan triangle of the Russian River Valley between Sebastopol, Occidental, and Guerneville. Misted by the nearby Pacific Ocean, gloomy redwood groves live in rocky canyons and creekbeds and march across wild, windy hilltop ridges. Until a couple of decades ago, this was the "Gravenstein Apple Capital of the World." Apples and old-time agriculture are celebrated at the annual Apple Blossom Festival in April, when the orchards are floating clouds of white. At the festival and at farmers' markets and roadside stands, apples, berries, artisan cheeses, olive oils, nuts, and other locally produced foodstuffs are for sale, along with pies, ciders, and jams.

As vineyards gradually overtake the farms, the noble burgundy grape, Pinot Noir, has become king; small, premium wineries are scattered on the back roads. On a lovely country lane, Martinelli Road, a redwood, bay, and maple forest is the backdrop for split-rail fences and vintage farmhouses, where vineyards have been cultivated by the Martinelli family since the late 1800s. **Martinelli Vineyards** welcomes visitors to their historic red hop barn on River Road, where Muscat the cat holds court in a retail shop crowded with old-fashioned china and cottage trinkets (3360 River Road; 707–525–0570; www.martinelliwinery.com).

Chardonnay and Pinot Noir are created with Spanish flair at **Marimar Torres Estate Winery** (11400 Graton Road; 707–823–4365; www.marimarestate.com). In a tile-roofed, golden-toned hacienda on the hilltop, the winery resembles a Catalan farmhouse—an elegant one—decorated inside with antiques and ceramics from Spain, where the owners family, the House of Torres, is the largest independent producer of wines in Spain.

A narrow, oak-lined byway, Ross Station Road crosses a bridge and coils up a hill to a spectacular view of the Green Valley, the Sonoma and Mayacamas ranges, and Mount St. Helena. On the grounds of **Iron Horse Ranch and Vineyards**, palm and olive trees and stepped gardens surround the restored 1876 Carpenter Gothic family home of the winery owners (9786 Ross Station Road, Sebastopol; 707–887–1507). Iron Horse sparkling wines have been served at state dinners in the Reagan, Clinton, and both Bush White Houses.

Developed on an old railroad bed, several miles of the **West County Millennium Community Trail** is paved for walking and bicycle riding. The trail runs through Green Valley from Occidental Road near Graton north to Forestville between farms and vineyards; an unpaved equestrian trail runs alongside.

Between Sebastopol and Highway 101 are dozens of antiques shops on Gravenstein Highway. Proceed south on Highway 101 and back to the Golden Gate Bridge.

There's More

Canoeing. Trowbridge Canoes, 13840 Old Redwood Highway, Healdsburg; (707) 433–7247.

Burke's Canoe Trips, 8600 River Road, Forestville; (707) 887–1222; www.burkes canoetrips.com.

Fishing. An excellent map to fishing access in the entire Russian River area is available from the Russian River Chamber of Commerce & Visitor Center, P.O. Box 255, Guerneville 95446; (707) 869–9000.

Jimtown Store, 6706 Highway 128, a few miles northeast of Geyserville, just north of Healdsburg off Highway 101; (707) 433–1212; www.jimtown.com. A destination in itself, this is an upscale general store/souvenir and antiques shop/gourmet deli/refreshment stand.

Northwood Golf Course, 19400 Highway 116, Monte Rio; (707) 865–1116; www.northwoodgolf.com. Eighteen holes in a spectacular redwood grove. There is a pleasant cafe here with a shady deck overlooking the fairways.

Western Hills Rare Plants, 16250 Coleman Valley Road, Occidental; (707) 874–3731. Just west of Occidental, on three densely planted acres, the mother of all the legendary West County nurseries. A footpath ambles over whimsical wooden bridges through a woodland and an organized jungle of rare plants, primarily Mediterranean and Australian varieties thriving in this coastal climate. A native of Lancashire, England, Maggie Wych is the owner and keeper of this green cathedral. Ask her to show you the rare Kashmir cypress. Spring and summer blooming creates a riot of color that brings many sightseers. The Royal Horticultural Society in London, the most distinguished of all garden clubs, has bestowed upon Western Hills the Award of Garden Merit.

Special Events

January. Winter Wineland, Healdsburg; (800) 723–6336. A weekend of tasting, live entertainment, and celebrity events at the wineries.

March. Russian River Wine Road Barrel Tasting; (800) 723–6336.

April. Passport to Dry Creek, Healdsburg; (707) 433–3031. Wine tastings, winery and vineyards tours, food pairings, entertainment at several wineries.

May. Memorial Day Weekend Antiques Fair, Healdsburg; (707) 433–4315. An extravaganza of antiques displays and sales.

September. Russian River Jazz Festival; (707) 869–3940. Huge crowds at the beach in Guerneville; big-name performers.

November. Russian River Wine Road; (800) 723–6336; www.wineroad.com. Open houses at about fifty wineries in the Russian River Valley; wine, food, music, and fun.

Other Recommended Restaurants and Lodgings

Forestville

Topolos at Russian River Vineyards, 5700 Gravenstein/Highway 116, Forestville; (707) 887–1562. Greek and California cuisine in a circa 1870 estate home, in the dining room by the wood-burning stove or outside on the garden patio. Local seafood, duckling in black currant Madeira sauce, souvlaki, spanakopita, seasonal specialties; adjacent to Russian River Vineyards.

Healdsburg

Belle de Jour Inn, 16276 Healdsburg Avenue; (707) 431–9777; www.belledejour inn.com. On a hilltop on six acres, white garden cottages have king or queen beds, fireplaces, whirlpool tubs, refrigerators, and country charm.

Costeaux French Bakery and Cafe, a block from the plaza at 417 Healdsburg Avenue; (707) 433–1913. Award-winning breads and pastries, scrumptious sandwiches, and picnic items to stay or to go; breakfast and lunch.

The Haydon Street Inn, 321 Haydon Street; (707) 433–5228. A 1912 Queen Anne Victorian on a quiet, tree-shaded street. French and American antiques, down comforters, designer touches. Claw-foot and Jacuzzi tubs, full breakfasts, air-conditioning. Separate two-room cottage.

Healdsburg Charcuterie, 335 Healdsburg Avenue; (707) 431–7213. An upscale restaurant where locals love the eccentric, pig-inspired decor and the dazzling Provence-inspired food: bouillabaisse, monkfish soup with artichokes, rabbit Provençal, house-cured pork, rib-eye steak in roasted garlic sauce, and more rib-sticking, fabulous food; including the best hamburger in the Wine Country. Lunch and dinner.

Healdsburg Inn on the Plaza, 110 Matheson Street; (707) 433–6991 or (800) 431–8663. Victorian bed-and-breakfast with ten antiques-chocked rooms, private baths, fireplaces, afternoon wine and tea, full breakfast.

Honor Mansion, 14891 Grove Street; (800) 554–4667; www.honormansion.com. One of the most luxurious and gorgeous small inns on the planet. Each room, cottage, and suite is very private and loaded with romance, from a million pillows to antiques, fireplaces, whirlpool tubs, private gardens, shady porches, sumptuous breakfasts, wine/appetizer service. Tennis, pool, putting green, boccie, croquet—

with a winery down the street, you never need to leave. A place for honeymoons, anniversaries, and unforgettable encounters.

Hotel Healdsburg, 25 Matheson Street, off Healdsburg Avenue; (707) 431–2800. With the arrival of Hotel Healdsburg on the square, the town has achieved a level of chic unmatched in the Wine Country. Ask for a room on the third floor overlooking the town square. The hotel offers a full-service spa and complimentary continental breakfast from Dry Creek Kitchen, off the lobby.

Madrona Manor, 1001 Westside Road; (707) 433–4231 or (800) 258–4003. California cuisine, French and Italian classic dishes; a much-heralded restaurant in one of the most elegant Victorian mansions in California. Reservations absolutely necessary. Twenty elaborately decorated inn rooms in the mansion, plus stunning traditional decor, large rooms and suites in a carriage house, and other cottages. Swimming pool, fireplaces, private baths.

Oakville Grocery, 124 Matheson Street; (707) 433–3200. In the old city hall, an upscale market and deli with scrumptious take-out food, local wine, and cheese from around the world.

For More Information

Healdsburg Chamber of Commerce, 217 Healdsburg Avenue, Healdsburg 95448; (707) 433–6935 or (800) 648–9922; www.healdsburg.com.

Redwood Empire Association and North Coast Visitor Center, 2801 Leavenworth, San Francisco 94133-1117; (415) 394–5991; www.redwoodempire.com. Brochures and information on the Wine Country, the North Coast, and Redwood Country.

Russian River Chamber of Commerce and Visitor Center, 16209 First Street, Guerneville 95446; (707) 869–9212.

Sonoma County Tourism Program, 520 Mendocino Avenue, Santa Rosa 95401; (707) 565–5383 or (800) 380–5392; www.sonomacounty.com. Free sixty-five-page visitors guide to the entire county.

Sonoma Valley

On Country Roads / 2 Nights

Between the rugged Mayacamas Mountains and the Sonoma Mountains, the 17-mile-long Sonoma Valley is a patchwork of vineyards and rich farmlands. Two-lane roads meander along rivers and creeks, through oak-studded meadows and foothills to country villages and to towns with sites on the National Register of Historic Places. The Victorian and early California Mission eras come alive in museums and in hundreds of restored homes, inns, and buildings all over the valley.

☐ Early California history

☐ Wineries

☐ Shopping

☐ Hiking, biking, golf

☐ Cheese, wine, produce

☐ Mountain and valley parks

Dozens of premium wineries are located here, the birthplace of the California wine industry. Their production facilities and tasting rooms, in many cases, are of significant architectural and historical interest. Thousands of acres of vineyards create a tapestry of seasonal color and texture that cascades across the hills and streams out onto the valley floor.

Moderate climate and rich soil produce world-famous gourmet foods—cheeses, sausages, foie gras, orchard fruits and berries, nuts, and sourdough French bread. California Wine Country cuisine, a gastronomic genre all its own, attracts diners and chefs from afar.

Exploring the Sonoma Valley on quiet back roads by car, foot, or perhaps bike, you'll enjoy the landscape and discover some of old California. After a day of wine tasting, browsing in the shops, gourmet dining, and maybe a round of golf, a cozy bed-and-breakfast inn will be a welcome refuge.

Day 1 / Morning

From the Golden Gate Bridge, drive north on U.S. Highway 101 to the Highway 37/Napa/Vallejo exit, driving east to the Highway 121/Sonoma left turn. Drive north on this road to Schellville (four-way stop) and continue to the Arnold Drive right turn; stay on Arnold for 8 miles to the foresty village of Glen Ellen.

This is the **Valley of the Moon,** named by its most famous (sometimes infamous) resident, Jack London, author of the classic adventure tales *Call of the Wild* and *The Sea Wolf*. You'll pass the **Jack London Bookstore,** 14300 Arnold Drive

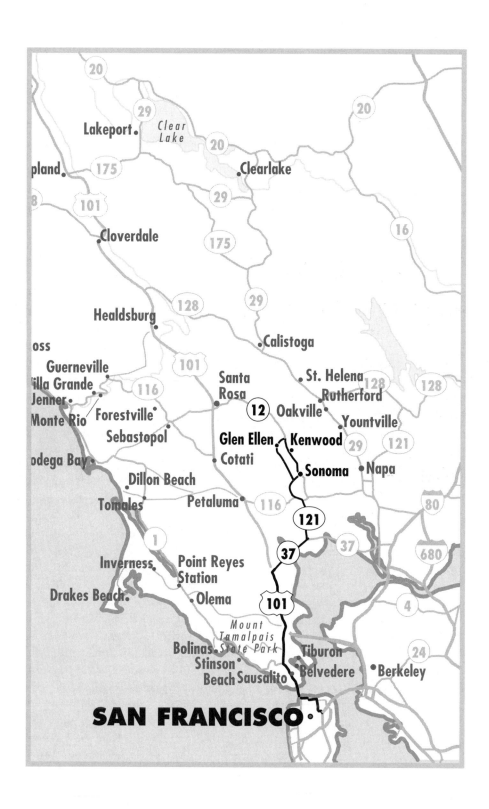

(707–996–2888), across the road from a wonderful old gristmill, still creaking slowly over a rushing creek.

Near the gristmill in the rustic Jack London Village complex, you can sip and swirl at the **Eric Ross Winery** tasting room (707–939–8525), which is in the same pleasant space as a gourmet deli cafe. Next door, the **Olive Press** sells olive oils, packaged foodstuffs, linens, and ceramics from Provence; you can watch the fruit being pressed at harvest time in December (707–939–8900). Behind the building, the new **Folk Art Traditions** gallery and gift store is a gorgeous environment for paintings, ceramics, retablos, carvings, mirrors, toys, and more vividly colored things from Mexico, expertly chosen and reasonably priced by longtime importer Suzanne da Rosa (707–780–3300; www.folkarttraditions.com). The decks and gardens overlooking the creek and forested hillside are just what you came to Glen Ellen to enjoy. Look for a new wine bar and restaurant in this complex.

When you see the large **London Lodge** banner, you've arrived in Glen Ellen, just a few blocks long. Turn left at the lodge, driving 1 mile up into dense oak forests to **Jack London State Historic Park** (707–938–5216). Once London's home ranch, the park is 800 magnificent acres of walking trails through groves of oaks, madrones, Douglas fir, redwoods, ferns, and explosions of wildflowers. There are shady picnic sites, mountain and valley views, a romantically spooky ruin, and a museum. Remnants of **Wolf House,** London's gigantic stone mansion, lie deep in a forest glade, at the end of a delightful short path through the trees (wheelchair accessible by golf cart). Only walls and chimneys remain of the elaborately decorated and furnished home, which burned to the ground before London and his wife, Charmian, could enjoy it. Filled with London memorabilia and most of the original furnishings, his smaller home, the **House of Happy Walls,** is open to visitors daily except holidays. You can view the exhibits free of charge.

On the way back to Glen Ellen, make a wine-tasting and -touring stop at **Benziger Family Winery,** 1883 London Ranch Road (707–935–3000). Beautiful valley oaks and gardens, an art gallery, and picnic grounds are here, in addition to the tasting room. This is the only winery in the valley to offer a motorized tram tour of the vineyards. Call ahead for reservations.

In Glen Ellen, cross the stone bridge, bear left, and turn left onto Warm Springs Road for a 6-mile drive. First you'll see **Glenelly Inn,** 5131 Warm Springs Road (707–996–6720), a peach-and-white confection built in 1916 as a railroad inn for summer train passengers who came to gambol at nearby mineral springs resorts. Feeling lazy and warm? Stop at **Morton's Sonoma Springs Resort** (707–833–5511) for a picnic on sweeping lawns or a swim in one of three heated pools. Just beyond, you'll come into Kenwood, a tiny, overgrown hamlet of cabins and rustic homes. A Southern Pacific train station from 1888 to 1936, the **Kenwood Depot** is an architectural gem in the Richardsonian Romanesque style. Around the corner,

Kenwood Plaza is a nice little park fronting the white-steepled Kenwood Community Church, anchoring the village as it has since 1888.

From here connect with Highway 12 and turn left.

LUNCH: Cafe Citti, 9049 Sonoma Highway, Kenwood; (707) 833–2690. A deli cafe with tables outdoors under the trees. Fresh, fabulous salads are ready to take out, or you can stay here and enjoy homemade pasta entrees and a glass of wine.

Afternoon

Just north on Highway 12 is **Sugarloaf Ridge State Park** (707–833–5712), a 3,000-acre green and golden jewel of mountains, redwood groves, creeks, wildflower-strewn meadows, and views. You may take a short walk or a hike, picnic in the pines, park your RV overnight, or camp out in your tent.

R eturning toward Kenwood, make a pilgrimage to **Chateau St. Jean** for their highly rated, vineyard-designated wines (707–833–4134; www.chateaustjean.com). Cinq Cépages—"Five Varieties"—was named in 2003 as one of the best wines in the world. Surrounding the 1920s-era mansion, formal gardens and a redwood-shaded picnic area make this a nice stop.

Just beyond, watch for the **Family Wineries of Sonoma Valley**, the tasting room for seven fine small wineries (9200 Sonoma Highway; 707–833–5504). You can lounge here on the grass or have a picnic.

DINNER: Kenwood Restaurant, 9900 Sonoma Highway, Kenwood; (707) 833–6326. On the vineyard-surrounded terrace or in the cool, elegant dining room, go for the top-drawer Petaluma duck with brandied cherries, Bodega Bay bouillabaisse, or a hearty Kenwood burger; save room for fresh berry cobbler. The wine list will not disappoint. R eservations absolutely necessary, lunch and dinner.

LODGING: Kenwood Inn and Spa, 10400 Sonoma Highway, Kenwood; (707) 833–1293; www.kenwoodinn.com. A complex of vine-covered, Tuscan-style villas for romantics. Around walled courtyards are gorgeous antiques-filled suites with featherbeds and fireplaces, balconies, and vineyard views; two swimming pools, Jacuzzis, herb and flower gardens. Sumptuous breakfasts, all-day guest-only dining, wine bar, and an in-house Caudalíe® spa with beauty and body treatments—a place for honeymoons and luxurious getaways. Privacy and luxury are to be expected. *Food and Wine* magazine says it's the best in the California Wine Country.

Day 2 / Morning

BREAKFAST: Kenwood Inn and Spa.

Highway 12 runs south and becomes West Napa Street, meeting the **Sonoma Plaza,** a typical Spanish town square, the largest and one of the oldest in California, laid out by Gen. Mariano Guadalupe Vallejo in 1834. The site of many annual festivals and historical events, it's a National Historic Landmark, and a beautiful one—

huge bay and eucalyptus trees, a meandering stream with chattering ducks, a playground, picnic tables, and the monolithic stone **City Hall,** which houses the **Visitors Bureau,** 453 First Street East (707–996–1090). If you are here on a Tuesday, be sure to take a walk through the plaza during the Farmer's Market in the early evening, when locals get together to picnic and purchase their weekly veggies and fruits, baked goods, cheeses, flowers, honeys, and more, all locally produced.

Surrounding the plaza, and for several blocks around, are many historic buildings, including the **Mission San Francisco Solano de Sonoma,** circa 1841, the last of the California missions built, with a beautiful small chapel and museum. The commandant who held sway in the Sonoma area when Mexico owned California, Gen. Mariano Vallejo constructed a barracks compound for his soliders, which is now a state park and a museum on the plaza (707–938–1519). Thick-walled adobes, Victorians, and Classic Revival and Mission Revival structures line the plaza and adjacent streets. Park your car, get out your camera, and explore the plaza and the streets and alleyways for a block or so in each direction. The visitors bureau has good walking-tour maps.

Not to be missed on the plaza: **The Wine Exchange of Sonoma,** at 452 First Street (707–938–1794), to taste and buy the wines of almost every winery in the Sonoma and Napa Valleys, and **Kaboodle,** 447 First Street (707–996–9500), a feminine fairyland of country French gifts and accessories.

On the corner, in a historic building topped by a dome, **The Corner Store** is upscale and delightfully crowded with European and Wine Country accessories and gifts, from Italian ceramics and pewter to fine linens, bath products, and French posters. In the store is a popular wine-tasting bar (498 First Street East; 707–996–2211; www.sonomacornerstore.com).

Look for the replica of a San Francisco cable car for a free ride around the plaza and to **Sebastiani Vineyards,** a few blocks away. Behind the winery are shaded picnic tables with vineyard and hillside views (707–933–3230).

The **Spirits in Stone Gallery** at 452 First Street displays dramatic African Shona stone sculpture, and there are interesting large photographs of Africa and a video to watch (707–935–6254). At **Artifax International,** 450 First Street, take a look at African and Asian carvings, masks, jewelry, and doodads of great color and variety in an exotic incensed environment (707–996–9494).

LUNCH: At a sweet yellow manor house a couple of blocks from the plaza, relax on the tree-shaded patio to enjoy creative Wine Country cuisine at **Deuce** (692 Broadway, Sonoma; 707–933–3823; www.dine-at-deuce.com). Locals know this is one of the best restaurants in the region. Choose from a wide array of wines by the glass and a full bar. Try the crispy calamari; roasted quail; diver scallops; savory, seared duck breast with arugula fig salad and blackberry vinaigrette; or the hearty caramelized pork chop, fresh fish, or a steak. Amazing soups and stews and a cozy atmosphere in the wintertime. In a hurry? Eat at the bar.

Afternoon

Even if you're not interested in wine tasting, you'll want to walk, bike, or drive 1.5 miles (take East Napa Street south to Lovall Valley Road, then go left onto Old Winery Road) from the plaza to the **Buena Vista Winery** (707–938–1266), an enchanting Wine Country estate with vine-covered stone buildings, ancient trees, and rampant flower gardens. Tasting rooms are stocked with guidebooks, artwork, and museum-quality antiques. Buena Vista's Hungarian founder, Count Agoston Haraszthy, engaged in friendly wine-making competition with General Vallejo in the mid-1800s. The interconnected small roads on this eastern outskirt of town are pretty and quiet for walks, drives, and bike rides to several other wineries.

Also in this area, **Ravenswood** winery is perched above a quiet, winding road that is a perfect 1-mile walking route through vineyard lands. Ravenswood's low-slung, stone tasting room is one of the most interesting for souvenir and wine shopping. They vow, "No wimpy wines allowed," and their famous Zinfandel and spicy Early Harvest Gewürztraminer prove the point. Weekend gourmet barbecues at the winery are held on a leafy terrace; reservations are not necessary (18701 Gehricke Road; 888–669–4679; www.ravenswood-wine.com).

Another paved path for walking and biking, accessed near the plaza, winds 1.5 miles, east-west, from Fourth Street East to Highway 12, passing by parks, playing fields, and the historic Vallejo Home. A block from the plaza on the walking path, **Depot Park** has a playground, barbecue grills, and picnic tables under the trees, a good choice when the plaza is crowded. If you are hooked on local history, visit the small **Depot Park Museum** to see a restored stationmaster's office, re-creations of Victorian households, and photos of early Sonomans (707–938–1762).

Near the walking path at 315 Second Street East, the **Vella Cheese Company** is one of the best of the great Sonoma County cheese makers (800–848–0505). In this stone building, jack, blue, and cheddar have been made since 1931. Try the pepper jack and the garlic cheddar. Across the street look for **The Patch,** a vegetable stand beside a huge garden, where produce is picked fresh every day.

Accessible by the walking path and by car, the **General M. G. Vallejo Home** is a classic Yankee-style, two-story Gothic Revival shipped around the Horn and erected in 1851 (707–938–1519). You can tour the home, which is called *Lachryma Montis,* meaning "Tears of the Mountain." Original and period furnishings in every room re-create the days when Vallejo and his daughters lived here. The glorious garden has huge magnolia, fig, and oak trees and a fish pond with turtles and koi. The home is part of the state park property, so one admission ticket is good at the mission, the barracks compound, and the Vallejo home.

DINNER: Della Santina's, 133 East Napa Street, East Sonoma; (707) 939–1266. The fireplace creates a cozy atmosphere for fancifully prepared fresh seafood from both coasts; intimate in winter, popular and fun on the patio in summer.

LODGING: Inn at Sonoma, 630 Broadway, Sonoma; (707) 939–1340 or (888) 568–9818; www.innatsonoma.com. New in a small chain of upscale small inns, a block or so from the plaza. Eighteen very comfy, plush rooms, each with fireplace, armchair sitting area, high-tech amenities; most have private balconies or patios. Full breakfast, afternoon wine and hors d'oeuvres; complimentary bikes, rooftop hot tub. One of Sonoma's best restaurants is across the street.

Day 3 / Morning

BREAKFAST: Inn at Sonoma. For a second late breakfast, try the **Basque Boulangerie Cafe**, 400 First Street East, Sonoma; (707) 935–7687. At a sidewalk table or indoors in the tiny, busy cafe on the plaza, enjoy luscious European pastries, quiche, coffee drinks, and light breakfasts, plus snacks and sandwiches all day.

Leaving Sonoma, head south from the plaza on Broadway/Highway 12 for less than 1 mile, then turn left onto Napa Road, another view-filled country byway. If you're extending your trip to the lower Napa Valley (see Northbound Escape Three), turn left at the Highway 121 junction; otherwise, turn right at the junction. Go straight on through the Schellville–Highway 121 intersection and down the road to **Schug Carneros Estate** (707–939–9363), a winery tucked up against a low range of hills, a lost little corner of the valley. German-owned Schug makes a traditional California Chardonnay, a sparkling red wine, and a German-style Gewürztraminer, unusual for this area.

Continue on Highway 121 south at a slow pace along a 10-mile stretch of rolling hills. You can take a scenic ride in an antique biplane at **Aero-Schellville** (707–938–2444). Turn right at the **Gloria Ferrer Champagne Caves** sign and drive up toward the hills to the tile-roofed Spanish hacienda built by the largest sparkling wine company in the world—Freixenet, based in Spain—at 23555 Highway 121 (707–996–7256). Gloria Ferrer has a luxurious tasting salon with a fantastic view. Many annual events are scheduled here, such as Catalan cooking classes and fireside concerts.

Back on Highway 121 heading south, a vine-draped arbor leads to **Viansa Winery and Marketplace** (707–935–4700), a red-tiled, terra-cotta–colored Italian winery on a hill above the highway. There is much to enjoy at Viansa besides their unusual Italian wine varieties. Sangiovese, Vernaccia, Nebbiolo, Aleatico, Trebbiano, and Chardonnay are the grapes blended into their traditional wines. At the huge gourmet delicatessen and Italian marketplace you can buy a sandwich, a salad, packaged gourmet foods, cookbooks, ceramics, and waterfowl-related gifts. Barbecues and special events open to the public are held here in the summertime.

Viansa has restored the ninety-acre wetlands below the winery, one of the largest private waterfowl preserves in the state; more than 10,000 birds have been spotted in a single day. For a two-hour guided wetland tour, February through May, call (707) 935–4717.

The Sonoma Valley, birthplace of the California wine industry.

At the junction of Highways 121 and 37, head west toward Marin County and take US 101 south to the Golden Gate.

There's More

Balloon rides. Aerostat Adventures Hot Air Ballooning; (800) 579–0183; www .aerostat-adventures.com. Fly over the Sonoma County vineyards.

Air Flambuoyant; (800) 456–4711.

Bike rental. Sonoma Cyclery in Sonoma; (707) 935–3377.

Horseback riding. Sonoma Cattle Company; (707) 996–8566.

Sugarloaf Ridge State Park; (707) 833–5712.

Ramekins Sonoma Valley Culinary School, 450 West Spain Street, Sonoma; (707) 933–0450; www.ramekins.com. For adventurous home cooks, an annual schedule of more than 300 hands-on classes presented by renowned chefs from around the country, from traditional Provençal recipes to wine and food pairing, Southwestern and California cuisine, artisan bread baking, and much more. Upstairs are six lovely bed-and-breakfast rooms with views of the surrounding hills. This is a beautiful "rammed earth" building with a Spanish adobe look.

Sonoma Valley Regional Park, Highway 12 between Arnold Drive and Madrone Road, near Glen Ellen; (707) 539–8092. A mostly flat, paved path winding a mile one-way through an oak forest, with a pretty creek along the way. You can bike and picnic; dogs must be leashed.

Sonoma Overlook Trail, north of the plaza, just as First Street West turns uphill; parking lot next to the cemetery. Wide views of the Sonoma Valley are dazzling from the upper meadows of this 3-mile loop of trails on wooded hillsides. Blue lupine and flax, wild roses, and California poppies are rampant; buckeye, live oak, and manzanita trees create shady hideaways. After a hard rain, you may need to ford a small creek.

Sonoma Golf Club, 17700 Arnold Drive, Sonoma; (707) 939–4100; www.sonoma golfclub.com. One of Northern California's oldest and most beautiful parkland courses, tough enough for the annual Charles Schwab Cup on the PGA Champions Tour; semiprivate. Spectacular new clubhouse, pro shop, and restaurant; luxe locker room with massage, steam, and whirlpools; swimming pool and tennis. Need a lesson? Ask for Chris Moe, teaching pro extraordinaire.

Sonoma Valley Museum of Art, 551 Broadway, Sonoma; (707) 939–7862; www.svma.org. Near the plaza, a new, airy space for a variety of changing exhibitions.

Valley of the Moon Winery, 777 Madrone Road, Glen Ellen; (707) 996–6941; www.valleyofthemoonwinery.com. Just south of Glen Ellen, award-winning Cabernets, Chardonnays, and more varieties are made in a nineteenth-century stone building on the creekside. In the visitor center, tall paned windows frame the gardens and an old Zinfandel vineyard, while wine lovers browse the chock-full gift shop and sip wine; a 300-year-old bay tree stands in silent splendor.

Special Events

March. Heart of the Valley Barrel Tasting, Sonoma; (707) 996–1090.

Cinema Epicuria; (707) 933–2600; www.cinemaepicuria.org. In the vintage theater on the plaza and at a few other venues, a wildly popular schedule of celebrity appearances; independent and short films and documentaries, food and wine.

Cornerstone Festival of Gardens, 23570 Highway 121; (707) 933–3010; www.cornerstonegardens.com. A quirky complex of garden-related art, from a forest of red bamboo poles to a startling tree made of bright blue balls. A plant nursery, a cafe, and a garden accessory store, too.

April. "Barreling into Spring" annual barrel tasting of Family Wineries of Sonoma Valley; (707) 833–5504. Two days of tastings, meet the wine makers, gourmet food, live entertainment.

June. Ox Roast, Sonoma Plaza; (707) 996–1090. Visitors are welcome at this locals' fund-raising event. Scrumptious beef barbecue, wine and beer, live entertainment.

July. Salute to the Arts, Sonoma Plaza; (707) 938–1133; www.winery.com/salute. The biggest and best of the annual art festivals in the plaza, with two days of displays and sales of some of the highest-quality art, fine crafts, and gift items by county artisans; plus wine tasting, concerts, and lots of food.

Fourth of July Parade, Sonoma Plaza; (707) 996–1090. The mother of all hometown parades, with every kid in town, antique cars, fire engines, the town band, cops on bikes, and more. Food, live music, and art in the plaza all day, and evening fireworks.

Sonoma Valley Wine Festival, Sonoma; (707) 996–1090.

July through August. Jazz Series, Bartholomew Park Winery; (707) 935–9511. At a beautiful outdoor winery site, top-notch jazz performers in concert.

August. Wine Country Film Festival; (707) 935–FILM; www.winecountryfilm fest.com. For nearly two decades, indoor and outdoor venues for film nights, celebrity tributes, food, wine, and entertainment.

September. Valley of the Moon Vintage Festival, Glen Ellen; (707) 996–1090.

Sonoma Valley Harvest Wine Auction Fairmont Sonoma Mission Inns, Boyes Hot Springs; (707) 935–0803; www.sonomavalleywine.com.

December through February. Sonoma Valley Olive Festival—blessing of the olives at Sonoma Mission; tastings, dinners and luncheons, wine events, tours, olive oil production, hikes, classes, art, workshops, food, wine, and music.

Other Recommended Restaurants and Lodgings

Glen Ellen

Fig Cafe and Winebar, 13690 Arnold Drive; (707) 938–2130; www.thefigcafe.com. To eat here in a casual bistro setting or to take out, thin-crust pizza, pot roast, salads, duck confit, seafood, lavender crème brûlée. Fine cheese plates, risotto, stews, grilled meats and poultry, made with all-local products. Dinner nightly and weekend brunch. No corkage fee.

Gaige House Inn, 1354 Arnold Drive; (800) 935–0237; www.gaige.com. An Italianate Victorian on the outside, a mix of styles and periods within. Gorgeous inn rooms with luxe bedding, some canopy beds, fireplaces, and whirlpool tubs; big swimming pool, lovely gardens, lots of privacy. Newly added are Japanese-style spa suites inspired by the Ryokan inns of Kyoto, with double soaking tubs above Calabasas Creek; glass walls, private gardens. Big breakfasts; spa treatments.

Sonoma

Breakaway Cafe, 19101 Highway 12 in the Albertson's shopping plaza on the west end of Sonoma; (707) 996–5949. Relax in a big booth and dig into an all-American breakfast of omelets, platter-size hotcakes, or sausage and eggs. This is a popular locals' place for breakfast, lunch, and dinner. Come back later for pork chops and mashed potatoes, roasted chicken, burgers and salads, comforting soups, veggie specials, luscious desserts, and smoothies; full bar.

Brick House Bungalows, 313 First Street East; (707) 996–8091; www.brickhouse bungalows.com. Five vintage cottages around a private courtyard, each with garden, kitchen, TV, leather sofas, and luxury decor. A block to Sonoma Plaza.

El Dorado Kitchen, 405 First Street West; (707) 996–3030; www.eldorado kitchen.com. From the owners of Auberge du Soleil in the Napa Valley, new and trendy on the plaza, this stunning contemporary country-style dining room with bar, fireplace lounge, and tree-shaded patio features seasonal Mediterranean-inspired cuisine by chef Ryan Fancher, veteran of the venerable French Laundry. Try the Caesar Provençal and the hearty saddle of lamb; top-notch wine list, including a generous menu of still and sparkling wines by the glass. Be prepared for a high noise level.

El Pueblo Inn, 496 West Napa Street; (707) 996–3651 or (800) 900–8844; www .elpuebloinn.com. In a superconvenient location on Highway 12, a newly renovated motel with heated pool, courtyard garden, and rooftop Jacuzzi; some rooms have fireplaces, minirefrigerators, and two queen beds. Complimentary continental breakfast; rental bicycles. Ask for a room away from the road.

Fairmont Sonoma Mission Inn and Spa, 18140 Highway 12; (888) 270–1118; www.fairmont.com. A pink and white, 1920s style extravaganza of a hotel guarded by tall palms and surrounded with lush gardens. An elegant lobby with cushy furnishings and a huge fireplace greets guests. Rooms in the historic building are beautiful but small; rooms and suites in the annex buildings are spacious and luxurious, some with fireplaces and terraces. A fabulous $20 million spa is world famous, offering exotic and traditional treatments and pampering beauty and health regimes, including weight loss. Ayurvedic "revitalizers," grape seed body polishes, and special couples programs are popular. The glassed-in, elegant Grille dining room overlooks a beautiful swimming pool terrace; the cafe, located on the highway, is a casual place for California cuisine and spa food. Ask about spa and golf packages; the resort owns the Sonoma Golf Club.

The Girl and the Fig, 110 West Spain Street; (707) 938–3634; www.thegirlandthe
fig.com. On the plaza, sharing a charming historic building with the Sonoma Hotel;
one of the region's most highly rated restaurants. Country French cuisine in a vibrant,
artful setting with a garden patio. The menu is always seasonal and local-product
based; exceptional cheese and charcuterie platters, Dungeness crab cakes, rabbit pap-
pardelle, morel and spring pea risotto, rib-eyes, pork, creative veggies. Memorable
brunches, lunches, and dinners. Sip an aperitif or a local wine at the antique bar.

Hotel Eldorado, 405 First Street West; (800) 289–3031; www.hoteleldorado.com.
With French doors and balconies overlooking the plaza or the courtyard, twenty-
seven airy, contemporary hotel rooms with four-poster beds, luxe bedding, flat-
screen TVs. Two bungalows are wheelchair-accessible. Heated lap pool, health club
passes; day spa across the street. Top-notch restaurant/bar downstairs.

Lodge at Sonoma, 1325 Broadway; (707) 935–6600; www.thelodgeatsonoma.com.
A large luxury hotel within a few blocks of the plaza with spacious rooms and
suites, some with sitting areas, fireplaces, whirlpool tubs. Swimming pool terrace
and quite a nice full-service spa with comfy fireplace lounge; fitness facility with
outdoor mineral pools. In the spa, the private Raindance Suite has a fireplace,
sauna, shower, and whirlpool tub. Cool, contemporary atmosphere in the award-
winning Carneros Bistro; open kitchen, California and Mediterranean cuisine, and
a huge wine list. On the sofa or in armchairs by the fireplace, the cozy lobby bar is
a great place to relax.

MacArthur Place, 29 East MacArthur Street; (800) 722–1866; www.macarthur
place.com. Anchored by a smashing 1850s main house and surrounded by gardens
and a clutch of large cottages with plush accommodations, MacArthur Place is a
full-service spa with bicycles to borrow and a large swimming pool; plus, Saddles,
a dinner house.

Nonna's Eastside Market, 1190 East Napa Street; (707) 933–3000; www.nonnaseast
sidemarket.com. On the east end of town, a Wine Country deli, gift shop, gourmet
grocery, and wine shop. Stop here for picnic goodies: sandwiches, salads, soups,
stews, and daily entrees. On the property, four quaint cottages with kitchens, bikes;
(707) 933–0340; www.cottagesofoldsonoma.com.

Schellville Grille, 22900 Broadway; (707) 996–5151. In a "historic shack" 3 miles
from the plaza on the way to the Bay Area; grilled meats, poultry, and fish; breakfast and lunch; dinner Thursday.

Sonoma Creek Inn, 239 Boyes Boulevard; (888) 712–1289; www.sonoma
creekinn.com. Five minutes from the plaza, new and really nice; an alternative to
pricey accommodations in town. Sixteen sleek, simple rooms decorated with handcrafted accessories and original artwork; some rooms with private patios or porches
and fountains; all with refrigerators, queen beds, and high ceilings.

Thistle Dew Inn, 171 West Spain Street; (800) 382–7895. Five antiques-filled rooms and a suite, garden hot tub, fireplaces, private decks and private entrances, lovely gardens, gourmet breakfast, afternoon refreshments; free use of bicycles. Book well in advance.

Victorian Garden Inn, 316 East Napa Street; (707) 996–5339. A dream of a century-old home a block from the plaza; pool, fireplaces, and full breakfast.

For More Information

Bed and Breakfast Association of Sonoma Valley; (800) 969–4667.

Sonoma County Tourism Program, 520 Mendocino Avenue, Santa Rosa 95401; (800) 576–6662; www.sonomacounty.com.

Sonoma Reservations; (800) 576–6662. Motels, inns, spas, homes.

Sonoma Valley Visitors Bureau, on the plaza, 453 First Street East, Sonoma 95476; (707) 996–1090; www.sonomavalley.com.

Lower Napa Valley

Napa, Yountville, and Rutherford / 1 Night

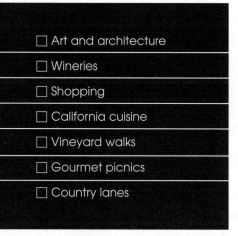

- ☐ Art and architecture
- ☐ Wineries
- ☐ Shopping
- ☐ California cuisine
- ☐ Vineyard walks
- ☐ Gourmet picnics
- ☐ Country lanes

Thirty miles long, just one-sixth the size of Bordeaux, the Napa Valley is home to the densest concentration of wineries in North America and to some of the state's most highly regarded California-cuisine restaurants, championship golf courses, charming bed-and-breakfast inns, and scenery reminiscent of southern Italy and France.

Your escape begins in the town of Napa, with a day in Yountville and a meander down the Silverado Trail. Stretching from Napa 35 miles north to Calistoga, the trail winds along the foot of high mountain ridges. Sprinkled along the way are wineries and champagne cellars, gargantuan mansions, small stone cottages, luxurious hotels, and quaint inns, each in its own idyllic corner of the Wine Country.

Day 1 / Morning

From the Oakland Bay Bridge, drive forty-five minutes north on Interstate 80, *past* the Napa/Highway 37 exit, to the American Canyon exit a few miles north of Vallejo, turning west and connecting with Highway 29 north into Napa; you'll be on Soscol Avenue. From Soscol take a left onto Third Street, crossing the Napa River, and park a few blocks down, across from a bright blue Victorian at 1517 Third Street.

BREAKFAST: Alexis Baking Company, 1517 Third Street, Napa; (707) 258–1827. Inventive breakfasts, the best pastries and desserts in the county, cappuccino, local color.

Just behind the bakery cafe, charming Victorian neighborhoods are bounded by Franklin, Division, Elm, and Riverside Drives; for just a peek, behind the bakery, drive up Franklin and down Randolph.

A red-and-green trolley trundles along the revitalized Riverfront District at the south end of Main Street, transporting visitors to historic buildings that are now retail and restaurant complexes. Within the Hatt Market and the Napa Mill

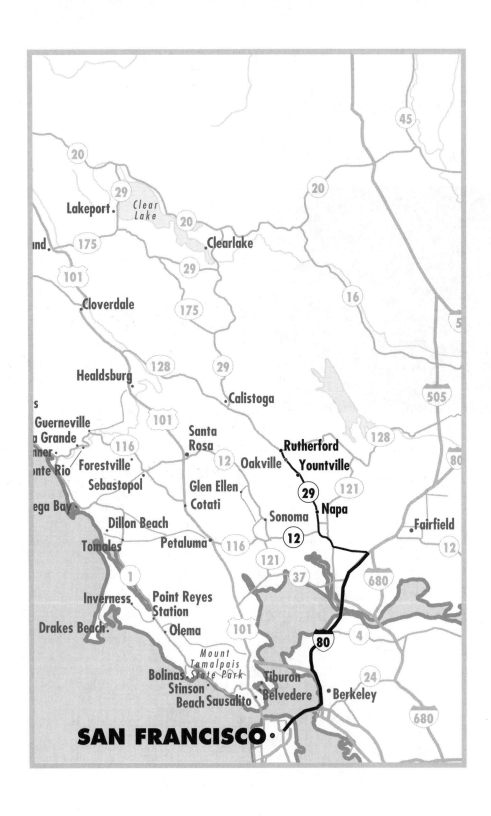

are cafes, a luxury hotel, a wine bar, a general store, a day spa, a bakery, and an outdoor stage. Rooms at the upscale **Napa River Inn** open onto verandas over the river (877–251–8500; www.napariverinn.com).

As fancy as a decorated wedding cake, the 1879 **Napa Opera House** on Main Street, which opened in 1880 with a production of Gilbert and Sullivan's *HMS Pinafore,* is now the venue for a lively schedule of top-notch concerts, drama, jazz, symphony, and cabaret (707–226–7372; www.napavalleyoperahouse.org).

Foodies flock to the Napa farmers' markets on Tuesday and Saturday mornings at COPIA, on the east end of First Street (707–252–7142).

Connect again with Highway 29 and head north to a left onto Redwood Road, then 6.5 miles through redwood and oak forests to **Hess Collection,** 4411 Redwood Road, Napa (707–255–1144). A large and important European and American contemporary art collection resides here in a historic winery building. Take the self-guided tour and enjoy the gardens, the views, and the wine.

Back on Highway 29 head north for ten minutes to **Yountville.** Park at Vintage 1870, 6525 Washington Street, in the middle of town. The few streets of this tiny town are lined with vintage cottages in overgrown country gardens. On Washington, the main drag, a blizzard of shops, restaurants, and inns makes this a popular Wine Country destination.

The landmark building in Yountville is **Vintage 1870,** a huge former winery sheltering a big toy store, import and clothing shops, outdoor cafes, and more (707–944–2451; www.vintage1870.com). Behind the building, with outdoor tables overlooking the green, **Cucina a La Carte** offers homemade soups, salads, and sandwiches with a Franco-Italian, and sometimes an Asian, twist; wine and beer, desserts, and espresso drinks. All for here or to go (707–944–1600).

LUNCH: Pacific Blues Cafe, in front of Vintage 1870, Yountville (707–944–4455). Indoors or on the deck, gourmet burgers and sandwiches, veggie specialties, fresh seafood, homemade soups, big salads; microbrews on tap.

Afternoon

Take a rest on a garden bench at Vintage 1870, or rush the stores! **The Toy Cellar** is a treasure house of dolls and games, with a toy train zipping around the ceiling (707–944–2144). In the **Vintage 1870 Wine Cellar,** more than one hundred locally produced wines are available to taste; (707) 944–9070 or (800) 946–3487.

Other shops sell Victorian gewgaws, gourmet cooking accessories, fashions, art—more than enough to wear the numbers off your credit cards.

Near Vintage 1870, the **Overland Sheepskin Company** (707–944–0778) has sheepskin coats, leather jackets, and Western hats. **Blue Heron Gallery,** 6526 Washington (707–944–2044), has for more than three decades displayed the best of local artists' works. **Raspberry's,** at Beard Plaza, 6540 Washington (707–944–9211), is one of the loveliest art-glass galleries you will ever see. My favorites are the vibrantly glowing, handblown, foot-long tropical fish that are "swimming" in the window.

At the north end of town, **Yountville Park** is a grassy, oak-shaded commons with a fantastic children's playground and picnic tables. For a 3-mile round-trip walk or bike ride, go east from the park through the fascinating old cemetery to Yount Mill Road and follow it north to Highway 29 and back. Running along a tributary of the Napa River, the road is shady and bedecked with lovely views of the mountains and vineyards. Watch for a plaque about George Calvert Yount, the first white settler in the valley. Yount wangled from Mexico the huge land grant of Rancho Caymus in the 1850s—comprising much of the heart of the valley, including Yountville—and built grist- and sawmills on the river. You will see the remains of one of his large wooden barns.

From the intersection of Yount Mill and Yountville Cross Roads, you can head east a couple of miles to connect with the Silverado Trail. On Yountville Cross Road at the bridge, the **Napa River Ecological Reserve** is a place to walk beside the river under oaks and sycamores. You can wade and fish here, too.

Few people know that you can take an easy, pleasant walk on paved paths around the grounds of the old **Yountville Veterans Home,** on the west side of Highway 29 from Yountville (707–944–4600). It's a veritable botanical garden, with magnificent, huge trees that were planted well before the turn of the twentieth century.

On the grounds of the Yountville Veterans Home is an architectural surprise, the new **Napa Valley Museum** of contemporary art, winemaking, and the history of the valley, with indoor and outdoor exhibits and a garden terrace (55 Presidents Circle; 707–944–0500; www.napavalleymuseum.org).

Just below the museum, off Highway 29, **Domaine Chandon** is a French-owned sparkling-wine cellar where you can wander the oak-studded grounds and learn about *méthode champenoise* winemaking. A flute of champagne awaits in the tasting salon; try the Blanc de Noirs, a blossomy pink bubbly. The airy, contemporary-design restaurant here is one of the most celebrated in the valley, headed by a distinguished chef who produces miracles of California and French cuisine.

Arrive at your lodgings in time to enjoy the gardens and perhaps a dip in the pool before dinner.

DINNER: For a snazzy, upscale atmosphere and renowned California cuisine, try **Mustard's** (707–944–2424), two minutes north of Yountville on the highway. Go for inventive pastas, grilled and spit-roasted poultry and meats, and the supercolossal wine list. This is a very popular, fun place; you may need to make reservations several days ahead.

LODGING: Villagio Inn and Spa, 6541 Washington Street, Yountville; (800) 351–1133; www.villagio.com. A 112-room luxury garden hotel; elegant, spacious rooms with fireplaces, spa baths; 60-foot lap pool, tennis, buffet breakfast. A stroll on the grounds turns up fanciful murals and replicas of ancient Greek and Roman statuary, lush gardens, stone walls, and sunny terraces. Weekends by the pool are lively, with a barbecue and live music; reserve a private cabana. The complimentary hot breakfast buffet is sumptuous, complete with champagne, smoked salmon, and mountains of fresh fruits, cheeses, egg dishes, and pastries. At the full-service luxury spa, enjoy a grape-seed body polish or a mud wrap, massage, and beauty treatments; relax in the outdoor whirlpool and the sauna; take a yoga, aerobics, or spinning class, a tennis lesson, or a guided walk. Although all the rooms are commodious, ask for a room away from Highway 29—and away from the pool area if you seek privacy; ask about the new spa suites. The concierge may be able to snag a reservation for you at Yountville restaurants that are booked up for weeks, if not months, in advance.

Day 2 / Morning

BREAKFAST: Villagio Inn. After breakfast head north on Highway 29. Just past Oakville Cross Road, stop at the **Oakville Grocery** (707–944–8802) for the makings of a French country picnic: pâtés, baguettes, quiches, *fromages,* charcuterie, baby vegetables, salads. There are hundreds of northern California wine selections and specialty foods from this region and around the world; fresh, rustic hearth breads; and the famous oversize cookies.

If you have time for only one winery visit (say it isn't true), this is the one (1991 St. Helena Highway, Rutherford; 707–968–1100; www.niebaum-coppola .com). In addition to making dazzling wines, **Niebaum–Coppola Estate Winery** has a Hollywood connection. Renowned moviemaker Francis Ford Coppola restored one of the oldest winery estates in the valley (Inglenook) to its former glory and had his Hollywood designers create an extravaganza of a winery, gift store, museum, and park. Drive down a long allée between vineyards and trees to his spectacular park modeled after the Luxembourg Gardens, complete with bubbling fountains, promenades, and lawns. The elegant Mamarella Cafe is a cozy wine and cigar bar. Walk from the cafe through cool caves, where wine is stored behind iron bars, into high-ceilinged rooms full of Wine Country–style home accessories, clothing, art and books, and the main wine-tasting bar. Notice the gleaming exotic woods, huge stained-glass windows, and the glamorous, curving main stairway leading to the museum. Ever see real Oscars up close? Here they are: Coppola's golden beauties, along with photos and other cool stuff from his movies, including the *Tucker* auto, the boat from *Apocalypse Now,* costumes from *Bram Stoker's Dracula,* and charming artifacts from his family history. Italian opera music drifts through the winery.

Up the road at **St. Supery Vineyards and Winery,** 8440 St. Helena Highway, Rutherford (707–963–4507), you can walk through a demonstration vineyard, see an art show, tour a lovely Queen Anne Victorian farmhouse, and enjoy elaborate exhibits about grape growing and winemaking. And taste wine, too.

Drive to the Silverado Trail and turn left; then turn right up the hill to **Auberge du Soleil Resort** (180 Rutherford Hill Road, Rutherford; 707–963–1211 or 800–348–5406; www.aubergedusoleil.com), where you'll feel as though you've dropped suddenly into an olive grove in the south of France. Wisteria-draped arbors and riots of flowers beckon you past fat stucco walls into a tile-floored entry, flooded with light from the terraces where beautiful people dine al fresco on California cuisine. Enjoy the heartstopping view, take a look at the sculpture garden, and ask to see a villa, for future getaways. This is one of the most luxurious and beautiful resorts in the Wine Country, if not the world. Rooms and suites have huge, elegant, comfortable furnishings; French doors opening onto private terraces; giant, fabulous bathrooms; and amenities galore. *Gourmet, Travel and Leisure,* and *Condé Nast Traveler* call it one of the world's best and most romantic small resorts.

LUNCH: Picnic under the oaks at **Rutherford Hill Winery;** (707) 963–1871; www.rutherfordhill.com. Just up the hill from Auberge du Soleil, with the same panoramic view, this winery has 40,000 square feet of cool, underground caves, seen on thirty-five-minute tours. Enjoy your Oakville Grocery picnic at tables under the oaks or in the olive grove.

A little south of Rutherford Hill, **Mumm Napa Valley,** at 8445 Silverado Trail (707–963–1133), is a French-American sparkling-wine cellar with a tasting terrace, vineyard views, and a great gift shop.

Pine Ridge Winery, at 5901 Silverado Trail (707–253–7500), is a small but top-notch winery where you can tour the caves, taste medal-winning Chardonnay, and picnic in a grassy grove under tall pines. There are swings for the kids and a nice walking trail through the vineyards and along the ridge overlooking the winery.

Eighteen-foot-tall, golden columns topped with capital bulls announce **Darioush**, one of the most unusual wineries in the state, if not the country. Inspired by the architecture of Persepolis, the ancient capital of Persia, the Darioush family erected a temple to Persian culture and premium Napa Valley wine (4240 Silverado Trail; 707–257–2345; www.darioush.com). Pale-gold travertine blocks from the Middle East clad the visitor center, where waving palms, formal Mediterranean gardens, and indoor and outdoor water features create a setting fit for royalty. In the sleek tasting room, guests wander the polished floors, sipping Bordeaux varietals such as Viognier, Shiraz, and a luscious late-harvest Sauvignon Blanc.

Afternoon

Watch for the left turn to the **Silverado Country Club and Resort,** 1600 Atlas Peak Road, Napa (707–257–0200), a 1,200-acre resort famous for its two eighteen-hole Robert Trent Jones golf courses. Towering eucalyptus, palm, magnolia, and oak trees line the drive leading to a huge, circa 1870 mansion. A curving staircase and period chandeliers grace the lobby; a terrace bar overlooks sweeping lawns, waterways, and gardens. Silverado has several restaurants and one of the largest tennis complexes in northern California. Scattered about the lush gardens and quiet courtyards are condominium units and cottages, some with fireplaces; nine swimming pools, and a glamorous new beauty and fitness spa. Popular with nongolfers at the spa is the "Golf Widow"—three hours of massage, facial, manicure, and pedicure. Golfers like the hydromassage, with a hundred air and water jets, and the old-fashioned Swedish massage.

Take tea in the lounge, then head south to Napa and back to the Bay Area.

There's More

Ballooning. Floating silently in a hot-air balloon is an unforgettable way to see the Wine Country. Always scheduled for the early morning, balloon trips are usually accompanied by champagne, breakfast, and much revelry. Rates average $185 per person.

Adventures Aloft, P.O. Box 2500, Yountville 94599; (707) 255–8688.

Balloons Above the Valley, P.O. Box 3838, Napa 94558; (707) 253–2222 or (800) 464–6824; www.balloonrides.com. Departs from Domaine Chandon Winery in Yountville.

Bonadventura Balloon Company, P.O. Box 78, Rutherford 94573; (800) FLY–NAPA; www.bonadventuraballoons.com.

Napa Valley Balloons, P.O. Box 2860, Yountville 94599; (707) 253–2228 or (800) 253–2224; www.napavalleyballoons.com. Launches at sunrise from Domaine Chandon Winery.

Biking. The Napa Valley can be divided into three moderately strenuous bike trips: a circle tour around the spa town of Calistoga, a midvalley tour in and around St. Helena and Yountville, and a third tour in the Carneros region. The mostly flat Silverado Trail, running along the east side of the valley, is a main biker's route. Crisscrossing the valley between Highway 29 and the Silverado Trail are myriad leafy country roads. You can arrange to have the bike rental company deliver bikes to your hotel and pick up you and your bikes at a winery or other destination.

Bicycle Trax, 796 Soscol Avenue, Napa; (707) 258–8729.

Napa Valley Cyclery, 4080 Byway East, Napa; (800) 707–BIKE. Pickup service, scheduled and private tours, rentals.

COPIA, the American Center for Wine, Food and the Arts, 500 First Street, Napa; (888) 51–COPIA; www.copia.org. On the banks of the Napa River, cuisine- and wine-related exhibits, classes, demonstrations, tastings, winery events, and tours by famous chefs, food/wine experts and authors; special events for kids. Vintage and foreign movies; live musical performances on the lawn. The restaurant, Julia's Kitchen, is inspired by the late culinary diva; also a casual cafe/wine bar; a fabulous retail shop and extensive gardens. Gardeners, cooks, and food and wine lovers make pilgrimages here.

Di Rosa Preserve, 5200 Carneros Highway, Napa; (707) 226–5991; www.dirosa preserve.org. Call well ahead to see a fantabulous contemporary art collection, one of the largest and most valuable ever assembled in California, in a nineteenth-century manor house beside a lake, outdoors, and in a big gallery.

Golf. Chardonnay Club, 2555 Jameson Canyon, Napa; (707) 257–8950; www .chardonnayclub.com. On the south end of Napa, twenty-seven semiprivate holes in a challenging landscape of ravines, hills, and vineyards; predictably windy.

Eagle Vines Golf Club, 580 South Kelly Road, Napa; (707) 257–4471; www .eaglevinesgolfclub.com. At the south end of the Napa Valley, Johnny Miller's new design is draped over low rolling hills, challenged by prevailing winds off the top of San Francisco Bay, carpets of vineyards, and overhanging oak trees.

J. F. Kennedy Municipal Golf Course, just north of Napa; (707) 255–4333. Eighteen challenging holes, water on fourteen; reasonable rates.

Yountville Golf Course, 7901 Solano Avenue, Yountville; (707) 944–1992; www .yountvillegc.com. A walkable nine-holer in a beautiful site at the foot of Mount Veeder. Giant redwoods loom along fairways dotted with young trees and watered by a small creek and ponds. Pleasant indoor/outdoor dining.

Napa Valley Wine Train, 1275 McKinstry Street, Napa; (707) 253–2111 or (800) 427–4124; www.winetrain.com. Elegant restored dining and observation cars, a relaxing way to see the valley; lunch and dinner; no stops on the slow, three-hour chug from Napa to St. Helena and back.

Skyline Park, East Imola Avenue, Napa; (707) 252–0481. Hilly woodlands and meadows for hiking, horseback riding, picnicking, and RV and tent camping. Great for winter mushroom expeditions and springtime wildflower walks; find the water-falls for a summer splash.

Wine education. Robert Mondavi Winery's three-and-a-half-hour tour and wine essence tasting is one of the most comprehensive of the free educational tours offered by wineries. For reservations call (707) 226–1395, ext. 4312. Located at 7801 St. Helena Highway (Highway 29) in Oakville.

Merryvale Vineyards holds a beginner's wine-tasting seminar in the cask room on Saturday mornings. For reservations call (800) 326–6069. Located at 1000 Main Street in St. Helena.

Franciscan Winery has a hands-on blending seminar. Call (707) 963–7111.

Special Events

January through April. Napa Valley Mustard Festival; (707) 944–1133; www .mustardfestival.org. Celebrating the blooming of the mustard in the vineyards, a series of food, art, and wine events that gets bigger every year. Kicks off with a grand event at the Culinary Institute of America (CIA) with auctions, live music, art, food, and wine. Also on the schedule are recipe, art, and photo competitions; a huge showcase and marketplace at COPIA; and a grand finale party with music and dancing. Special events throughout the valley with celebrity winemakers, chefs, musical performers, and artists.

June. Napa Valley Wine Auction; (707) 963–5246; www.napavintners.com. Wine aficionados from all over the world come for three days of parties, barrel tastings, and events at wineries; auction benefits local hospital.

August. Music in the Vineyards, Napa Valley wineries; (707) 578–5656. Noted chamber music artists from across the country assemble to play in beautiful winery settings; wine tasting, too.

September. River Festival, Third Street Bridge, Napa; (707) 226–7459. Napa Valley Symphony performs at the riverside.

October. Yountville Days Festival; (707) 944–0904. Parade, music, entertainment, food.

November. Napa Valley Wine Fest; (707) 253–3563.

December. Napa Valley Jazz Festival, Yountville; (707) 944–0310.

Other Recommended Restaurants and Lodgings

Napa

Bistro Don Giovanni, 4110 Howard Lane (visible from Highway 29), five minutes north of Napa; (707) 224–3300. Rub elbows with the beautiful Wine Country people in a lively cafe atmosphere. Country Italian cuisine, risotto, wood-fire roasted chicken, eclectic pasta, one of the valley's best wine lists. A little noisy but never boring.

Blackbird Inn, 1755 First Street; (888) 567–9811; www.foursisters.com. Built as a private residence in 1910, the inn is a virtual gallery of California's Arts and Crafts period. Hallways and public areas are lined with early California landscape art. Guests meet for wine and hors d'oeuvres, then again for a hearty country breakfast. Eight rooms with fireplaces and private decks.

The Carneros Inn, 4048 Sonoma Highway; (707) 299–4900; www.thecarneros inn.com. An upscale hostelry on an idyllic site above rolling hills surrounded by vineyards and meadows where horses and cows graze. One- and two-bedroom guest cottages have between 975 and 1,800 square feet of indoor/outdoor space; wood-burning fireplaces, flat-screen TVs; private, heated patios; and gorgeous bathrooms, some with indoor/outdoor showers and soaking tubs; each with a private, fenced patio. The large swimming pool and full-service spa are open to the glorious view. There is a fitness center and a lobby "living room" with fireplace and games. The sleek dining room serves sophisticated, French-inspired lunches and dinners with a view, or you can order room service. Just down the hill, the casual Boon Fly Cafe serves breakfast and lunch; and there are boccie and croquet courts.

La Residence, 4066 St. Helena Highway, on the north end of Napa; (707) 253–0337. A romantic inn in a French barn and a circa 1870 mansion surrounded by gardens on two oak- and pine-studded acres. Rooms are elaborately decorated with antiques, designer fabrics and linens, and four-poster beds and have fireplaces, patios, and verandas. Full breakfast, wine and hors d'oeuvres, swimming pool.

Oak Knoll Inn, 2200 East Oak Knoll Avenue; (707) 255–2200. In the middle of 600 acres of Chardonnay vines, four huge, elegant guest rooms with private entrances, fireplaces, king-size brass beds, hot tub, swimming pool. Full gourmet breakfast, wine and cheese in the evening.

Pasta Prego, 3206 Jefferson Street; (707) 224–9011. A best-kept secret, one of the best casual restaurants in the area: 1990s-style Northern Italian cuisine, like polenta with mushroom sauce, smoky grilled veggies, rich risottos, fresh local fish, poultry, meats, and many pastas. Noisy and fun, patronized by the "in crowd" of local winery families. Dining is indoors in the small dining room, at the counter, or on the heated patio.

Soda Canyon Store, 4006 Silverado Trail; (707) 252–0285. At Soda Canyon Road just north of Napa, a great place to stop for a quick picnic or to pick up yummy provisions for lunch or snacks on the road. Locals start the day with breakfast burritos, smoothies, pastries, and espresso drinks. Gourmet deli sandwiches, cheeses, homemade salads, and a nice selection of local wines; packaged condiments make nice gifts.

Rutherford

Rutherford Grill, 1880 Rutherford Road; (707) 962–1782. Go for the smoky baby back ribs, mountains of feathery onion rings, grilled and spit-roasted poultry and meats, garlic mashed potatoes, and jalapeño corn bread. Big booths inside, umbrella tables and a wine bar outside. The bad news: It is a very popular place, and you may have to wait on weekends. The good news: The attractive patio where you wait has a wine bar and a bubbling fountain.

Yountville

Bistro Jeanty, 6510 Washington Street; (707) 944–0103. An upscale French country bistro with wonderful, hearty dishes prepared by a famous Frenchman.

Bouchon, 6534 Washington Street; (707) 944–8037. The $1 million interior resembles an elegant Parisian brasserie, with a stunning bar and ceiling fixtures from Grand Central Station. Owned by the legendary Thomas Keller (see French Laundry), this may be the best bistro outside France. Next door, the incredible breads and pastries made for the French Laundry and Bouchon are available at the Bouchon Bakery, a country-style *boulangerie*. With your latte, have an apricot spice scone, a *pain au chocolat,* or a lemon tart.

Compadres, next to Vintage 1870; (707) 944–2406. Delightful outdoor patio under giant palms and oaks, zowie margaritas, good Mexican food.

The French Laundry, 6640 Washington Street; (707) 944–2380; www.french laundry.com. Said to be one of the best restaurants in the world, a veritable temple of country French and California cuisine, so revered and desired it has no sign out front (reserve weeks, even months, in advance). In a vine-covered stone building in a garden, as if in the south of France. The food, the service, and the wine list are astounding.

Gordon's Cafe and Wine Bar, 6770 Washington Street; (707) 944–8246. In a former stagecoach stop, the small, noisy, popular place for exotic picnic fare to go and casual, quick meals here. Breakfast (cinnamon buns!) and lunch every day, prix fixe dinner on Friday.

Maison Fleurie, 6529 Yount Street; (707) 944–1388 or (800) 522–4140; www .foursisters.com. An ivy-covered stone inn with the look of southern France; lush gardens and a swimming pool, bountiful breakfasts, afternoon wine, bikes. Thirteen guest rooms have vineyard views; some have fireplaces and spa tubs.

Napa Valley Lodge, 2230 Madison Street; (707) 944–2468 or (800) 368–2468; www.napavalleylodge.com. In a great location near the city park, with a heated pool on a sunny terrace, this upscale, Mediteranean-style lodge with recently renovated, spacious rooms and suites with balconies or patios in a garden setting; an extravagant champagne breakfast buffet is complimentary. Sauna, fitness center.

Ristorante Piatti, 6480 Washington Street; (707) 944–2070. One in an upscale chain of Northern Italian places in northern California. It's fun to watch the chefs in the open kitchen prepare pastas, roasted and rotisseried poultry and meats, and vegetable specialties galore. Outdoors under the arbor is the place to be.

Wine Garden Restaurant and Wine Bar, 6476 Washington Street; (707) 945–1002; www.napawinegarden.com. Creative small plates made with local ingredients and inspired by a variety of cuisines, from oysters to Dungeness crab, duck tamales to *carnitas* and hush puppies. Intimate, casual; indoors or in the gardens. Lunch and dinner.

For More Information

Napa Valley Conference and Visitor Bureau, 1310 Napa Town Center, Napa 94559; (707) 226–7459; www.napavalley.com.

Napa Valley Reservations Unlimited, 1819 Tanen, Suite B, Napa 94559; (707) 252–1985 or (800) 251–6272; www.napavalleyreservations.com.

Yountville Chamber of Commerce, 6795 Washington Street, Yountville 94599; (707) 944–0904; www.yountville.com. In Washington Square Center, north end of town.

Upper Napa Valley

Heart of the Wine Country / 2 Nights

"Up valley," as the northern half of the Napa Valley is called, is anchored by Calistoga, a hot springs resort town founded in the 1840s. Steam rises from 200-degree mineral springs at a dozen or so health resorts. Some are scatterings of historic clapboard cottages with simple facilities; others are Roman-style spas with luxurious lodgings. This is the place for rest and rejuvenation, for massages, mud baths, beauty treatments, and slow swims in warm pools. The mud-bath experience must be tried at least once; be warned that après mud bath you won't feel like moving for quite a spell.

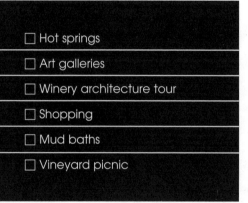

- ☐ Hot springs
- ☐ Art galleries
- ☐ Winery architecture tour
- ☐ Shopping
- ☐ Mud baths
- ☐ Vineyard picnic

As you drive to Calistoga, through the valley bordered by the Mayacamas Range on the west and the Howell Mountain Range on the east, the tremendous variety of Napa Valley soils and microclimates becomes evident. It's fun to try the diverse wines produced from grapes grown on the dry hillsides, those from the valley floor, and especially the wines from grapes grown on the "benches," the alluvial fans of soil and rocks eroded down from the mountainsides into triangles of rich bedding for vineyards whose grapes have produced wines besting the best in France.

Besides wine tasting and hot-bath soaking "up valley," there's tons of shopping to do in St. Helena, plus biking, hiking, golfing, and ballooning; perhaps you'll be forced to return for another weekend or two.

Day 1 / Morning

From the Golden Gate Bridge, drive north on U.S. Highway 101 to the Napa/Highway 37 exit, connecting with Highway 121 east to Highway 29 at Napa, then driving thirty minutes north to **St. Helena**—about ninety minutes altogether.

BREAKFAST: Gillwoods, 1313 Main Street, St. Helena; (707) 963–1788. Unique breakfast specialties and all-American favorites.

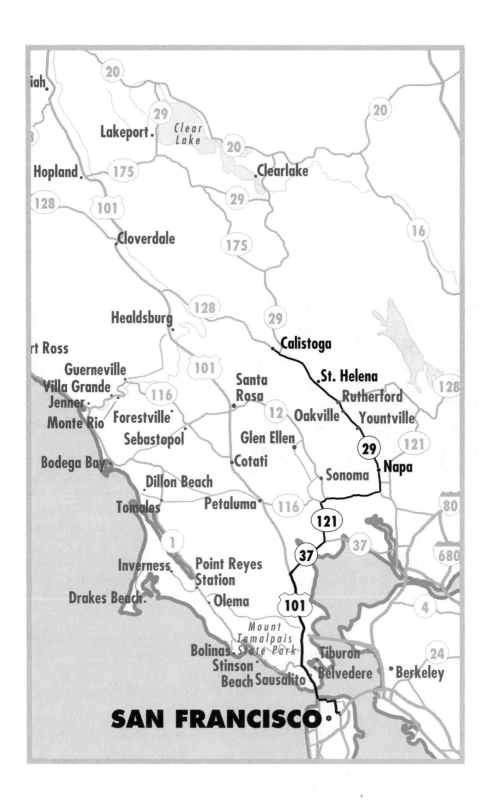

Enjoy the plethora of specialty shops on Main. **Main Street Books,** 1371 Main (707–963–1338), is stocked with regional guidebooks. The **Gallery on Main Street,** 1359 Main (707–963–3350), shows the best of local artwork.

Showplace North at 1350 Main (707–963–5556) is worth a stop to see the beautiful stone-walled interior hung with tapestries and the view out the back through wavy windows to the mountains on the east side of the valley. European-style feather comforters ride high over custom-designed pine and iron beds.

The **St. Helena Wine Center,** 1321 Main (707–963–1313), will ship mixed cases of local wines, from Schramsburg Blanc de Blanc to Marilyn Merlot. They sell fine cigars, too.

Get your pet a rubber frog, a doggie futon, or some gourmet biscuits at the ultimate dog and cat store, **Fideaux** (1312 Main Street; 707–967–9935).

Anchoring the north end of town on Main Street is tiny Lyman Park, for almost a century a grassy spot for reclining under the oaks, with a gazebo and a stone water fountain for dogs and horses. Across the street at 1429 Main, **Vanderbilt and Company** is a huge store with ceramics, linens, glassware, and myriad accessories from France and Italy (707–963–1010).

If you're a Robert Louis Stevenson aficionado, you'll find 8,000 pieces of his memorabilia at the **Robert Louis Stevenson Museum,** 1490 Library Lane (707–963–3757). Next door, the **Napa Valley Wine Library** (707–963–5145) houses 6,000 books, tapes, and reference materials on the art of wine making and the history of the valley.

A block off the main drag, take a step back in time at the retro **Big Dipper** old-fashioned ice-cream parlor, decorated with old Coke signs and other fun relics. Have a thick shake or a banana split, or some penny candy (1336A Oak Avenue; 707–963–2616).

Driving north from St. Helena, you'll see redwood forests grow darker and deeper. Maples and oaks crowd closer to the roadside, creating canopies of leaves and branches overhead, brilliant canyons of color in the fall. Watch for **Beringer Winery's Rhine House** on the left, built in 1883 as a reminder to the winery founder of his family home in Germany. This is a good place to take a full winery tour, which includes the huge cellar caves carved into the hillside by Chinese laborers more than a hundred years ago.

LUNCH: Wine Spectator Greystone Restaurant, just north of Beringer on Highway 29 in St. Helena; (707) 967–1010; www.ciachef.edu/greystone. A massive stone landmark guarded by towering palms, Greystone was built as a winery in 1889 with 22-inch-thick, hand-cut volcanic stone blocks. Today it houses the West Coast annex of the prestigious culinary college, the Culinary Institute of America (CIA). Visitors interested in fine food and wine history like to browse in the gourmet store and the food and wine museum. You can wander paths through aromatic herb gardens and arrange to tour the state-of-the-art teaching kitchens in the upper reaches of the building.

The stunning Mediterranean (rather noisy) restaurant turns regional cuisine into high art. The outdoor dining terrace overlooks an ancient oak forest and rolling vineyards.

Afternoon

Two minutes north of the CIA on Highway 29 at the Freemark Abbey sign, turn right into the parking lot and go into the **Hurd Beeswax Candle Factory and Store** (707–963–7211) to see wild and colorful handmade beeswax candles of every description being created for shipment worldwide.

Just up the road, **Bale Grist Mill State Park** (707–963–2236) is a wooded glade with a 36-foot waterwheel beside a rushing creek. Walk from here into **Bothé–Napa Valley State Park** (707–942–4575) to find a lovely campground in Ritchie Creek canyon, a swimming pool, and shady picnic sites under redwoods and firs along the creek. Both of these parks are home to the endangered spotted owl. You can take a one- or two-hour guided horseback ride along Ritchie Creek and up along the ridges overlooking the valley. Call **Napa Valley Trail Rides** at (707) 996–8566.

Proceed another ten minutes to Calistoga and have a predinner glass of wine at the trendy **Hydro Bar and Grill,** 1403 Lincoln Avenue (707–942–9777). The exotic bistro menu here changes daily and may include red wine–fennel sausage with potato and artichoke hash or roasted mushroom and goat cheese lasagna. The wine and microbrew list is extensive.

DINNER: All Seasons Cafe, 1400 Lincoln, Calistoga; (707) 942–9111. A classically trained chef holds forth in the kitchen, inventing American versions of Mediterranean food with all locally grown and produced ingredients. Home-smoked salmon and chicken, grilled Petaluma duck breast, pizzettas, pasta, fresh fish, killer pies. Salads are tops here, such as warm spinach with smoked chicken and lemon dressing.

LODGING: Scott Courtyard, 1443 Second Street, Calistoga; (707) 942–0948. Private, roomy suites (some with full kitchens) in circa 1940 bungalows surrounded by lush gardens. Swimming pool, hot tub, library with fireplace, fully equipped art studio, separate video/TV room. Full breakfasts served in a bistro setting; evening wine and cheese.

Day 2 / Morning

BREAKFAST: Scott Courtyard.

Set off on a walking tour of town, a compact grid of tree-shaded streets. The architecture is an eclectic conglomeration of Victorian, Art Deco, 1950s funky, Craftsman, and Greek and Mission Revival. Get a map and some orientation at the **Sharpsteen Museum,** 1311 Washington (707–942–5911), where an elaborate diorama re-creates the 1800s resort town. Exhibits are lifelike and colorful, and a huge collection of old photos recalls the people who came here more than a hundred years ago to "take the waters." Ben Sharpsteen was one of Walt Disney's original animators, and you can see his Oscar in the museum.

Just off the main street on Cedar, the green oasis of **Pioneer Park** on the Napa River has lawns, a gazebo, and a great kids' playground. Next door to the park, **The Elms,** 1300 Cedar (707–942–9476), is a bed-and-breakfast inn in a fanciful French Victorian mansion.

Lee Youngman Galleries, at 1319 Lincoln (707–942–0585), displays large collections of well-known California artists' works.

The **Evans Ceramics Gallery,** at 1421 Lincoln (707–942–0453), sells one-of-a-kind, fine ceramic art. Don't miss **Ca'Toga Galleria d'Arte,** where a noted Venetian artist and muralist showcases his fabulous glazed ceramics, painted furniture, and garden sculpture, which have been *faux* painted to echo ancient Pompeian, Roman, and sixteenth-century Venetian originals. The beautiful building itself and the spectacular ceiling mural inside are worth a special visit (1206 Cedar Street; 707–942–3900).

The work of some of the best artisans in northern and southern California is shown and sold at the **Artful Eye:** jewelry, wine glasses, ceramics, glass, clothing, and more (1333A Lincoln; 707–942–4743). **Zenobia** (1410 Lincoln Avenue; 707–942–1050) has everything from Z to A: jewelry, glass art, folk art, clothing, and metal artwork—anything that is colorful and bright. If you are a wine aficionado and want to add to your wine book collection or pick up guidebooks to the Wine Country, stop in at the **Calistoga Bookstore,** 1343 Lincoln (707–942–4123).

LUNCH: Wappo Bar Bistro, 1226B Washington Street, Calistoga; (707) 942–4712. A small cafe with patio tables beside a fountain, serving ethnic-inspired inventions such as Middle Eastern pomegranate-glazed pork, Ecuadorean *hornada,* Central American duck *carnitas,* Asian noodle salads, and homemade ice cream. Choose from a 600+ label wine list; a wine bar with appetizers is open all day and evening. Try to arrive either before or after the traditional mealtimes, or you may wait for a table.

Afternoon

A restored 1868 Southern Pacific train station on Lincoln houses the visitors bureau and the **Calistoga Wine Stop,** 1458 Lincoln Avenue (707–942–5556), where you can choose from more than 1,000 Napa and Sonoma Valley wines and arrange for them to be shipped.

Spend the rest of the day at one of Calistoga's health resorts being herbal-wrapped, enzyme-bathed, massaged, and soaked in mineral-rich mud; expect to feel like warm Jell-O when it's over.

Calistoga Spa Hot Springs, at 1006 Washington Street (707–942–6269), is one of the largest. You come for the day or stay overnight in spacious motel units equipped for light housekeeping. Float blissfully in three large, naturally heated mineral pools and take advantage of full spa services.

One of the oldest resorts in town, founded in 1865, **Indian Springs Hot Springs Spa and Resort,** at 1712 Lincoln Avenue (707–942–4913), has an old-fashioned air about it, but it offers all the spa treatments that the newer resorts do. Built in 1913 and still restoring the spirits of bathers is the Olympic-size pool filled with mineral water from three natural geysers, heated to 92 degrees in summer and 101 in winter. From a studio cottage to a large house, accommodations are simple and comfortable, including gas fireplaces, soft terry robes, and air-conditioning. Amenities include a clay tennis court, bicycles and bike surreys, croquet, hammocks, and barbecue grills.

The elegant **Lavender Hill Spa** (1015 Foothill Boulevard at Hazel; 707–942–4495) specializes in treatment for couples, offering everything from massage to acupressure, aromatherapy, and "Vibra Sound" in addition to the traditional mud baths.

Not in the mood for mud and massage? Take a hike in **Robert Louis Stevenson State Park,** 7 miles north of Calistoga on Highway 29, or on the **Oat Hill Mine Trail,** a historic landmark that starts at the junction of Lincoln Avenue and the Silverado Trail. Mountain bikers, horseback riders, and hikers like this rocky, rigorous, 5-mile climb to China Camp.

DINNER: Stomp Restaurant, in the **Mount View Hotel and Spa** at 1457 Lincoln Avenue, Calistoga; (707) 942–8272. Watch the passing parade through a wall of windows while choosing from an elaborate, California cuisine–Mediterranean menu—from steak tacos with truffles to seared ahi tuna, freshwater prawns with watermelon and black radishes, bouillabaisse, artisan cheeses, fig bread pudding, and more inventive dishes created from locally produced ingredients. The sprawling interior is retro '60s, with an open grill; 350 choices on the wine list, and lots of advice for pairing.

Rooms at the Mount View overlook the town or the palm-shaded courtyard; room decor may be Art Deco or Victorian. There is a heated outdoor pool, a whirlpool filled with mineral water from the inn's own hot springs, and an upscale spa facility with beauty and health treatments. Ask about the private spa rooms with double-size Jacuzzis (707–942–6877).

LODGING: Scott Courtyard.

Day 3 / Morning

BREAKFAST: Scott Courtyard.

Proceed a few minutes north on the Silverado Trail, north of Calistoga to **Château Montelena,** 1429 Tubbs Lane (707–942–5105), at the foot of Mount St.

Helena. Secluded in a piney wood, the winery is a spectacular castle built of French limestone brought around the Horn in 1880, enchantingly poised above a small lake surrounded by gardens and weeping willows, with a vineyard view. A Chinese junk floats serenely, and red-lacquered gazebos provide private places for conversation and sipping of the renowned estate-grown Cabernets and Reislings, available only here. In 1972 a Château Montelena Chardonnay exploded the myth that French wines are best by winning a blind tasting against France's finest.

Head south on the Silverado Trail. To commemorate the founding of the Calistoga Mineral Water company and to have some fun, a larger-than-life sculpture was erected on the trail near Calistoga—a great photo op. At six tons, 14 feet tall, and 35 feet long, it is an oversized version of the 1926 truck that the company founder and his dog, Frankie, drove over narrow dirt roads to the California State Fair in Sacramento, where his water won gold medals year after year. Today, Calistoga Water is one of the most popular bottled waters in the world.

Proceed south and (turn right) onto Dunaweal Lane to **Clos Pegase** (707–942–4982), a russet-colored, postmodern extravaganza of a winery, the result of an international architectural competition. Besides wine tasting here, you'll enjoy the vineyard views, sculpture garden, frescoed murals, and a slide show about the history of winemaking.

A minute farther on Dunaweal, the sparkling white Moroccan aerie of **Sterling Vineyards** (800–726–6136) floats like an apparition high on a hilltop. For a small fee, a tram will take you on a gondola ride to a sky-high terrace with valley views. The winery tour is self-guided, and there are outdoor tables up here for picnicking with your own provisions, or you can buy simple deli items on-site.

Back on the Silverado Trail, continue south through the valley to a left onto Meadowood Lane for a stroll on the grounds of the **Meadowood Napa Valley** (707–963–3646), a posh country lodge reminiscent of the 1920s, residing regally on a rise overlooking 250 densely wooded acres, a golf course, and tennis and croquet courts. The full-service health and beauty spa is luxurious, offering traditional and exotic treatments. Spacious, very private cottages and suites nestle in an oak-and-pine forest. The restaurant and bar here are quite pleasant, overlooking a secluded valley. Meadowood is the home of the annual Napa Valley Wine Auction, a spectacular four-day event attended by deep-pocket bidders and wine lovers from all over the world.

In an oak woodland off the Silverado Trail, **Joseph Phelps Vineyards** offers an in-depth, sophisticated wine tasting and educational program (200 Taplin Road; 707–963–2745; www.jpvwines.com). Call ahead, and plan to settle in here for an hour or so. An innovator, Joseph Phelps introduced Insignia, the first Bordeaux-style blend produced in California under a proprietary label, and one of the first California-style Syrahs, followed by an entire family of Rhône-style wines. If you decide to picnic under the oaks, a staff member will pair the perfect bottle of wine with your menu.

LUNCH: The Grill, on the terrace at Meadowood. Or, for a picnic lunch, take a right onto Zinfandel Lane, crossing over to Highway 29, and head south a few minutes to Oakville, stopping for gourmet goodies at **Oakville Grocery** (707–944–8802), at Oakville Cross Road.

Or try **V. Sattui Winery,** at 111 White Lane south of St. Helena (707–963–7774), which has a pretty, shady picnic grove on two acres of lawn around a stone-walled 1885 winery. The gourmet deli sells literally hundreds of varieties of cheeses and meats, fresh breads, and juices and drinks. Disadvantages here are the sight of the busy highway and the arrival of tour buses. Don't be concerned if you miss the wine tasting here; there are better choices for wine.

Afternoon

Head south to the Bay Area.

There's More

Biking. Getaway Adventures, 1117 Lincoln Avenue, Calistoga; (707) 942–0332; www.getawayadventures.com. Guided biking and hiking day trips and overnights in the Napa Valley, with gourmet picnics and wine tasting. Try the thrilling Downhill Cruise guided bike descent from the top of Mount St. Helena, with stops on the way down for photo ops and catching your breath. It's perfectly safe, even for kids nine years old and older and for toddlers in bike trailers.

Las Posadas Bike and Hike Trail: Drive 6 miles up Deer Park Road to Angwin, go right on Cold Spring Road, and take the left onto Las Posadas Road to the parking area. Cruise on your bike or stroll on a leafy trail through dense redwood and oak groves, a cool place to be on a hot day.

Palisades Mountain Sports, 1330B Gerrard Street, Calistoga, behind the fire department; (707) 942–9687. Rentals. Mountain bike specialists, rock climbing equipment.

St. Helena Cyclery, 1156 Main Street, Street, Helena; (707) 963–7736. From here you can bike out Spring Street to White Sulfur Springs on a level, quiet paved road.

Spring Mountain Road: Bike on Madrona for 3 blocks, west of Main Street in St. Helena; then turn right on (paved) Spring Mountain for a steep ride up (about an hour) and a fast ride down.

Old Faithful Geyser, 1299 Tubbs Lane, Calistoga; (707) 942–6463. Blows its top every fifteen minutes.

Safari West, 3115 Porter Creek Road, Santa Rosa; (707) 579–2551 or (800) 616–2695; www.safariwest.com. Giraffes in Napa? Yes, at the far northern end of the valley on open grasslands and rolling hills in a wildlife preserve with more than 400 exotic animals and birds, and African plains animals, including zebras, elands, endangered antelope, giraffe, impala, and Watusi cattle. Private half-day tours in safari vehicles. A once-in-a-lifetime expedition; advance reservations required. Many animals at Safari West are either members of an endangered species or are already extinct in the wild.

Spas. Calistoga Village Inn and Spa, 1880 Lincoln Avenue, Calistoga; (707) 942–0991; www.greatspa.com. Complete spa facilities in a country setting with vineyard views.

Golden Haven Hot Springs, 1713 Lake Street, Calistoga; (707) 942–6793; www .goldenhaven.com. Complete spa facilities, mineral pool.

Health Spa Napa Valley, 1030 Main Street, St. Helena; (707) 967–8800; www.napa valleyspa.com. In the town center, a full-service, very pretty day-use beauty and fitness spa offering complete skin and body care, ayurvedic treatments, and massage and couples packages; a lap pool, whirlpool, steam, and more.

Lincoln Avenue Spa, 1339 Lincoln Avenue, Calistoga; (707) 942–5296; www.lincoln avenuespa.com. Mud baths, body and beauty treatments, pools.

Roman Spa, 1300 Washington Street, Calistoga; (707) 942–4441; www.romanspa hotsprings.com. Mineral pools, beauty treatments, mud baths, enzyme baths, saunas; rooms around a tropical garden.

White Sulphur Springs Resort and Spa, 3100 White Sulphur Springs Road, St. Helena; (707) 963–8588; www.whitesulphursprings.com. The oldest hot springs resort in the state, in a wooded canyon with hiking trails, with a warm outdoor sulfur soaking pool; a nice swimming pool; museum; hammocks; and barbecues. Creekside cottages and inn rooms have simple decor; complimentary continental breakfast. There is a full-service spa with beauty and health treatments; spa guests are welcome to enjoy the facilities along with inn guests.

Special Events

September. Hometown Harvest Festival, Oak Street, St. Helena; (707) 963–4456. Dancing, parade, arts and crafts, music, food, wine.

October. Old Mill Days, Bale Grist Mill State Park; (707) 963–2236. Costumed docents grind grain and corn on the millstones and make bread; demonstrations of traditional trades and crafts, games, entertainment.

Other Recommended Restaurants and Lodgings

Calistoga

Cafe Pacifico, 1237 Lincoln Avenue; (707) 942–4400. A Mexican motif is the backdrop for incredible breakfasts, lunches, and dinners. Try the blue-corn buttermilk pancakes and chili rellenos.

Calistoga Inn, 1250 Lincoln Avenue; (707) 942–4101. In a charming circa 1880 building with a splendid outdoor dining terrace on the Napa River. Breakfast, lunch, and dinner. Hearty country fare: chili, burgers, huevos rancheros, crab cakes, fresh fish, and award-winning home-brewed beers and ales. Also eighteen comfortable rooms.

Calistoga Ranch, 580 Lommel Road; (800) 942–4220; www.calistogaranch.com. Very new, very luxe, in a secluded pine and oak forest, forty-seven spacious, contemporary cedar lodges, each with indoor/outdoor living room, fireplace, outdoor shower. Absolutely beautiful "bathhouse" full-service spa and fitness facility; boccie, hiking trails, wine cave; dining room and bar; swimming pool, lake.

Carlin Country Cottages, 1623 Lake Street; (707) 942–9102. Nice, simple cottages in a wide courtyard, with Shaker-style furnishings. Some have Jacuzzi tubs; some have one or two separate bedrooms. Spring-fed swimming pool.

Cottage Grove Inn, 1711 Lincoln Avenue; (707) 942–8400 or (800) 799–2284. One of the most commodious, private, and romantic of Wine Country accommodations; separate cottages with luxurious furnishings, fireplaces, deep whirlpool tubs, front porches with wicker rockers, and perfectly wonderful breakfasts, all within a short stroll of town.

Palisades Market, 1506 Lincoln Avenue; (707) 942–9549. Looks like an old grocery store on the outside—gourmet surprises await within. Market and deli with miraculous sandwich and salad combinations, wonderful fresh produce, and myriad locally made packaged foodstuffs.

St. Helena

Cantinetta Tra Vigne (at Tra Vigne); (707) 963–8888. Cozily residing in a nineteenth-century sherry distillery, an Italian deli, market, and wine bar. Fresh pizzettas, salads, sandwiches, sweets, house-brand oils and vinegars. Eat here or take out.

Dean and DeLuca, 601 Highway 29; (707) 967–9980. Huge gourmet market, wine shop, produce mart, and deli—offshoot of the famous New York store. Incredible variety of cheeses and meats, rotisserie chicken, and wonderful salads and entrees to go, plus packaged foodstuffs of all kinds, from fig balsamic vinegar to olive oil pressed in the most obscure orchard in Tuscany. Enjoy sandwiches, fresh-fruit smoothies, and espresso drinks in the back on the sunny patio. Expensive and worth it.

El Bonita, 195 Main Street; (707) 963–3216 or (800) 541–3284. Hidden behind the original 1930s Art Deco motel are two-story motel units with private balconies looking into the trees and over the gardens. Large, two-room suites have microkitchens. Small pool, sauna; reasonable rates.

Harvest Inn, 1 Main Street, just south of town; (707) 963–9463; www.harvest inn.com. Antiques, four-posters, elaborate furnishings in luxury rooms and suites surrounded by acres of lush English gardens, a labyrinth of shady pathways, lawns, and bowers. Private balconies, fireplaces, two pools. Expanded continental breakfast.

Inn at Southbridge, 1020 Main Street; (800) 520–6800. A small inn with spacious, luxurious rooms with fireplaces, sitting areas, private balconies with vineyard views, down comforters, and more amenities.

Pinot Blanc, 641 Main Street; (707) 963–6191. Exotic French and California cuisine prepared by one of the country's young star chefs in a luxe country bistro, with a smashing wine list.

Taylor's Refresher, 933 Main Street on the south end of town; (707) 963–3486. A roadside stop with picnic tables, serving burgers and dogs, tacos, fish-and-chips, garlic fries, Mexican food; Double Rainbow ice cream in the fabulous shakes, floats, and malts.

Terra, 1345 Railroad Avenue; (707) 963–8931. In a historic stone building, warm and romantic; exotic California cuisine with French and Italian accents, miraculous wine list. Chef Hiro Sone made a name for himself at Spago in Los Angeles.

Tra Vigne, 1050 Charter Oak Avenue at Highway 29; (707) 963–4444. At stone-topped tables under the trees and umbrellas, keep your eyes peeled for movie stars and winery owners. It's easy to imagine you are at a villa in the Italian countryside. The terra-cotta–toned stone walls are rampant with vines, and a glimpse through iron-framed windows discloses a vibrantly painted, high-ceilinged bar and restaurant. A rich balsamic vinegar game sauce blankets roasted polenta; house-cured prosciutto melts in your mouth. Exciting varieties of homemade ravioli, roasted poultry rubbed with exotic spices, and more. Can't get a reservation? Stop in here at Cantinetta Tra Vigne for luscious gourmet picnic fare, snacks. PBS and Food Channel star and cookbook author Michael Chiarello founded the restaurant, which continues to express his vivacious style and savvy knowledge of Italian cuisine.

Tra Vigne Pizzeria, 1016 Main Street; (707) 967–9999. In a charming pizza house with booths, plasma TVs and billiards entertain while you wait for luscious brick-oven-baked, Cal-Ital style pizza. Besides traditional favorites, you can order the Benito (fennel sausage, hot coppa salami, smoked pork), the Ducati (roasted onions, broccoli rabe, smoked mozzarella, and chicken-and-apple sausage), or the Clam Pie (garlic paste and fresh chopped clams); or create your own.

For More Information

Bed and Breakfast Inns of the Napa Valley; (707) 944–4444.

Calistoga Chamber of Commerce, Old Depot, 1458 Lincoln Avenue, Calistoga 94515; (707) 942–6333; www.calistogafun.com.

St. Helena Chamber of Commerce, 1080 Main Street, St. Helena 94574; (707) 963–4456; www.sthelena.com.

The Redwood Route

Seacoast Towns, Path of the Giants / 2 Nights

On your drive up U.S. Highway 101 to the seaside logging town of Eureka, stop along the way to see the redwoods and play on the Eel River. California's coastal redwoods are the world's tallest living things. Walking beneath a 300-foot forest canopy among these silent giants from the age of the dinosaurs is an unforgettable experience.

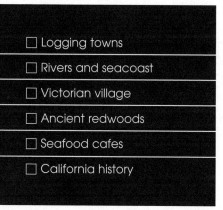

□ Logging towns

□ Rivers and seacoast

□ Victorian village

□ Ancient redwoods

□ Seafood cafes

□ California history

Eureka and smaller coastal towns look much as they did in their Victorian heyday—streets lined with gracious old homes and elaborate gingerbread-trimmed hotels. Settled during the California gold rush in the mid-1800s, the county's founding coincided with the birth of Victorian architecture, and in every town are glorious examples of the era.

From partaking of bed-and-breakfast inns, fresh seafood, logging and Indian history, wildlife sanctuaries, and sea air to fishing for the mighty salmon, biking on forest paths, and going river rafting or beachcombing, you'll find more than a weekend's worth of enticements here. In addition, Humboldt County is home to nearly 8,000 artists—more artists per capita than any other county in California. Named the "Number One Best Small Art Town in America," Eureka is a uniquely creative community, as demonstrated in many art-, music-, and culture-related events, festivals, and galleries. Take note of the flamboyant murals around town; ask for a mural walk map at the chamber of commerce.

Expect foggy mornings, even in summer, and winter rains December through March. These tremendous northern woods are true rain forests, thriving on drizzle and damp. But don't let drippy weather keep you at home. Fishing is best from October through March; Eureka is misty and romantic then, too.

Day 1 / Morning

Begin the 280-mile trip at the Golden Gate Bridge, going north on US 101.

Between Cloverdale and Leggett you'll share the road with logging trucks as the highway winds along the rugged, forested spine of the Coast Range. Above

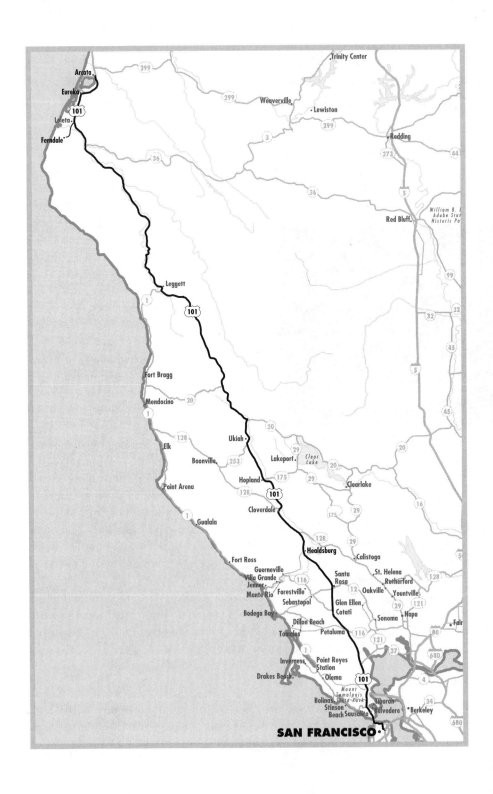

Leggett, watch for the **Redwood Tree House,** a fun tourist trap with a good collection of guidebooks and maps. The vestibule is formed from the burned-out shell of a giant sequoia; the tree, however, is still alive and thriving.

Twenty-three miles north of Leggett, the four-Diamond-Rated **Benbow Inn,** built in 1925, is a Tudor-style monolith overlooking a twenty-six-acre summer lake and glorious gardens (445 Lake Benbow Drive, Garberville; 707–923–2124 or 800–355–3301; www.benbowinn.com). You can stay at the historic inn in antiques-filled rooms, some with fireplaces, and have afternoon tea and scones in the parlor. The excellent restaurant overlooks the lake, and there is a nine-hole golf course across the road. Here you can fish and rent a canoe; for a refreshing side trip, go with the park rangers (707–946–2263) on a one-hour interpretive canoe tour to absorb some natural history and see ospreys, turtles, herons, and belted kingfishers in the springtime.

Now on to the **Avenue of the Giants,** a world-famous 33-mile scenic drive, bypassing the highway. Turnouts and parking areas access short loop trails into spectacular redwood groves along the Eel River in **Humboldt Redwoods State Park** (707–946–2263). These are the biggest of the 2,000-year-old beauties remaining in a 30-mile-wide belt of coastal redwoods stretching from Monterey to Oregon.

Pick up picnic goodies at one of the small groceries along the first few miles of the avenue; then begin your tour at the **Humboldt Redwoods Visitor Center** (707–946–2263), about 4 miles from the south end of the avenue. Here you'll get oriented by a movie, exhibits, and trail maps. Ask for advice on the lengths and types of walks and drives you'd like to take in the park. Docents will show you a special binder of trail maps, pointing out new trails and those that may be closed due to weather or maintenance.

Not to be missed is the **Rockefeller Forest** in the **Big Trees** area, a 5-mile drive on Mattole/Honeydew Road. Tiptoeing along boardwalks and spongy pathways in the damp, cool stillness at the foot of these magical giants, you'll hear only the bustle of chipmunks. Under a fragrant green canopy hundreds of feet above your head, the shade on the forest floor is deep, even on a hot summer's day. Wildflowers—trillium, wild iris, and redwood orchid—spring from a carpet of moss and fern, while brilliant blue Steller's jays flash through the branches overhead. A spooky rush of air signals the flight of a black raven; the shiny and silent 2-foot-long ravens are aggressive guardians of their thousand-year-old forest. A short trail leads to a sandy riverbank, for sunbathing, wading, picnicking, and fishing.

LUNCH: Have your picnic here or at Bull Creek Flats.

Afternoon

Returning toward the highway on the Mattole/Honeydew Road, watch for the sign to **Bull Creek Flats,** a sunny pebbled beach and picnic area at a lovely bend in the river; wild lilacs bloom here in great purple clouds in spring. In the rainy season the river runs with salmon and steelhead. Summer fishing—carp and eels—is for fun, not for food.

One hundred miles of trails in Humboldt Redwoods State Park are for walkers, backpackers, bikers, and horseback riders. Meanderings will turn up old homesteaders' cabins and a plethora of campgrounds. Apple blossoms bloom in orchards planted by early settlers. In the fall big-leaf maples, alders, and buckeyes turn red and gold. In the farthest outback are bobcats, black-tailed deer, foxes, ring-tailed cats, and even black bears.

Reaching Eureka by day's end, you'll be warmly welcomed in the lobby of the Hotel Carter with wine and hors d'oeuvres before the fireplace.

DINNER: Restaurant 301, Hotel Carter, 301 L Street, Eureka; (707) 444–8062 or (800) 404–1390. At your table beside sky-high windows overlooking Old Town, try fresh Humboldt Bay oysters with teriyaki/wasabi crème fraîche, sesame-seared salmon, portobello chèvre lasagna, or perfectly fresh seafood, local poultry, and game dishes; seasonal produce is featured, including the vast array of veggies from the kitchen gardens. Special dinners with top winemakers are popular occasions booked well in advance. The wine list was chosen by *Wine Spectator* as one of the world's best; oenophiles make pilgrimages here to taste the rare vintages. In spite of it all, the atmosphere is comfortable, welcoming, and understated.

LODGING: Carter House Inns, 301 L Street, Eureka; (707) 444–8062 or (800) 404–1390; www.carterhouse.com. A stunning four-building complex in Old Town: a magnificent replica of a San Francisco Victorian, the Bell Cottage, and the Hotel Carter, each housing plush, ultracomfortable accommodations. Marble fireplaces, whirlpool tubs, four-poster beds, cushy armchairs and couches, and spacious parlors. No lacy kitsch here, just understated elegance and top personal service, enjoyed by such notables as Steven Spielberg and Rene Russo and their families. Named the "Best B&B/Small Hotel in Northern California," the restaurant and the lodgings here are exceptional in their ambience and comfort.

Day 2 / Morning

BREAKFAST: A sumptuous breakfast at the Hotel Carter. Take time to browse the kitchen gardens, one of the most extensive at any inn on the West Coast; guests are often invited to join in the daily harvest.

With an architectural/scenic walking-tour map, explore the surrounding Victorian neighborhood, between C and M Streets and about 5 or 6 blocks south of Second Street, ending up under the gaslights in Old Town. For a short waterfront stroll, park at the Carson Mansion on the north end of town, enjoy glimpses of the mansion gardens, then walk a block south on Second Street and turn right into the Adorni Center parking lot. A paved path extends in both directions along the waterfront for beautiful views of the bay and boats. On the waterfront, home port to more than 500 fishing boats, are several blocks of 1850 to 1904 Queen Anne, Eastlake, and Classic Revival buildings. The Victoriana is enhanced by parks, fountains, playgrounds, and shaded benches for resting between shopping, photo snapping, and museum discoveries along the brand-new Eureka Boardwalk, extending 4 blocks along the bay from G to C Streets.

Not to be missed are the nautical art and artifacts, collectibles, and unique gifts at **Many Hands Gallery,** 438 Second Street; (707) 445–0455. **Gallery Dog** shows and sells work by more than 150 artists, jewelers, furniture makers, and ceramicists (214 E Street; 707–444–3251; www.gallery-dog.com). The **Humboldt Bay Maritime Museum** displays nautical relics, old navigation equipment, an early radar unit, a lighthouse lens, and fragments of wrecked ships; admission is free (122 First Street; 707–444–9440). The **Clarke Historical Museum,** at Third and E Streets (707–443–1947), a 1920s Italian Renaissance–style former bank with a glazed terra-cotta exterior, houses an extraordinary collection of Indian basketry, antique weapons, maritime artifacts and photos, furniture, and memorabilia of early Humboldt days. **Humboldt's Finest** displays fine art glass, sleek woodwork and furnishings, and a variety of other locally produced home accessories and gifts; not craftsy or cute, simply elegant (405 Second Street; 707–443–1258). The **William Carson Mansion,** at Second and M Streets, said to be the most photographed home in America, is a wedding cake of an Italianate/Queen Anne mansion built in the 1880s by a lumber baron; it's a private club, and the interior is off-limits to the public.

L U N C H : **Cafe Waterfront Oyster Bar and Grill,** 102 F Street at First, Eureka; (707) 443–9190. On the waterfront with a water view, fresh seafood for breakfast, lunch, and dinner. Fish burgers, clam and oyster specialties, lively bar, casual Victorian decor, and jazz on weekends. Or, for a picnic lunch, go to **Sequoia Park,** Glatt and W Streets, in fifty-two acres of virgin redwoods with a zoo, a kids' playground, formal gardens, walking paths, and a duck pond.

Afternoon

From June through September, a seventy-five-minute cruise of the bay, departing from the foot of L Street, can be had on the **MV *Madaket*** (707–444–9440), a wooden steamer built in the 1920s. You'll get a narrated tour of historical and natural sights around the bay, passing oyster farms, aquatic birds, and the third largest colony of harbor seals in the West. If it's a clear, mild day, try the cocktail cruise, leaving at 4:00 P.M. Another choice for touring the bay is at **Hum Boats,** at Woodley Island Marina, where on weekends you can rent kayaks and sailboats or go on a guided wildlife ride by water taxi in the bay (707–444–3048; www.hum boats.com).

One of the magical places in Eureka is the **Blue Ox Millworks and Historic Park** (800–248–4259; www.blueoxmill.com), an old mill at the foot of X Street.

This museum-like job shop and sawmill makes custom trim for Victorian buildings, using the same machines that were used to create the originals. Take a self-guided tour on catwalks above the workers, or call ahead for a guided tour. A loggers' camp, a blacksmith shop, a gift shop, a bird sanctuary, and other attractions make this a worthy stop.

DINNER: Sea Grill, 316 E Street, Eureka; (707) 443–7187. Voted "Best Seafood Restaurant" in the county for several years, Sea Grill is a noisy, popular place. Come early to avoid the crowds and enjoy choosing from a huge seafood menu; great salad bar, steaks, and luscious desserts, too. Reservations are usually necessary; lunch and dinner.

LODGING: Carter House Inns.

Day 3 / Morning

BREAKFAST: The Samoa Cookhouse, on the Samoa Peninsula, Eureka; (707) 442–1659. Reached by the Highway 255 bridge on the north edge of Old Town, this is the last surviving lumber camp cookhouse in the West. At long oilcloth-covered tables with charmingly mismatched chairs, giant American breakfasts are served from 6:00 A.M., including biscuits with sausage gravy, platters of pancakes, and scrambled eggs. Lunch and dinner are served family-style: Huge loaves of bread, cauldrons of soup, big bowls of salad and vegetables, baked ham, and roast beef are followed by wedges of homemade pie. Prices are quite reasonable, and kids four and younger eat free.

Even if you don't eat here, stop in to see the delightful museum of logging equipment, artifacts, and fantastic photos of early days. A short walk from behind the cookhouse is a quiet bayside village and a nice playground. From here you can walk or bike along the edge of Humboldt Bay for 6 miles north to Arcata. Bird life is extraordinary, from marbled godwits to curlews, dowitchers, falcons, and many more.

From the Samoa Cookhouse, drive scenic Highway 255 north fifteen minutes around Humboldt Bay to **Arcata,** home of Humboldt State University. This is another old logging town with unique attractions, such as the **Historic Logging Trail** in Arcata's 600-acre **Community Forest,** Fourteenth Street and Union (707–822–7091). On foot, take Nature Trail #1 on the west side of the parking lot and follow signs and a map to see logging sites and equipment from a century ago.

Arcata Marsh and Wildlife Sanctuary, 600 South G Street in Arcata (707–826–2359), is a bird-watcher's mecca. Spend a couple of hours here on 4.5 miles of quiet footpaths in a stunning bayside setting, with freshwater ponds, a salt marsh, tidal mudflats, and winding water channels alive with birds and ducks. This is also a good place to jog or have a picnic; leashed dogs are allowed. You would never guess this is a wastewater reclamation project and, in fact, a model for the nation. Stop at the interpretive center here for maps and information about birding walks throughout the region, and ask about guided walks at the marsh. In April, Godwit Days, the annual spring migration bird festival, is a big event, bringing birders from across the country (800–908–WING; www.godwitdays.com). For daily bird sightings call (707) 822–LOON.

Another area for good walking and biking is **Arcata Bottoms,** just west of town, bordered by Humboldt Bay and Lamphere-Christensen Dunes Preserve.

At the **HSU Natural History Museum and Store** are million-year-old fossils, live tidepools and native animals, and exhibits about the natural history of the region (1315 G Street; 707–826–4479). If you visit Trinidad north of here, stop in at the Humboldt State University Marine Lab and Aquarium (570 Ewing Street, Trinidad).

Twenty-two miles north of Arcata and stretching for more than 40 miles, **Redwood National Park** is a World Heritage Site encompassing three state parks: **Prairie Creek Redwoods, Del Norte Coast Redwoods,** and **Jedediah Smith Redwoods.** The National Park Visitor Center (707–464–6101) is between the park entrance and the town of Orick. You will need to get a (free) permit to drive the steep, 17-mile road to Tall Trees Grove, where a 3-mile round-trip walking trail leads to the world's first-, third-, and fifth-tallest redwoods. There are more than 300 developed campsites in the park, shoreline trails, and swimming beaches in the Smith River and Redwood Creek.

For an afternoon of antiquing and a walk in the country, drive 22 miles south of Eureka and take the Ferndale exit, driving 5 miles west across the Eel River through flat, green dairylands to **Ferndale.** Just two long streets of glorious Victorian buildings, the entire tiny town is a State Historic Landmark. Art galleries, antiques shops, ice-cream parlors, and cafes abound. The **Gingerbread Mansion,** at 400 Berding Street (707–786–4000; www.gingerbreadmansion.com), is one of the premier Victorian masterpieces on the West Coast. Dressed in bright yellow and peach with cascades of lacy white trim and surrounded by whimsical formal gardens, the gigantic hundred-year-old beauty is ½ block long. Nine elaborately decorated rooms have claw-foot tubs (one room has two tubs, toe to toe), and the mansion has four parlors.

It will take a couple of hours to stroll Main Street, take pictures of the old buildings, and browse in the shops. (On the way into town, watch for a large, light green building with striped awnings and a red door: the **Fernbridge Antiques Mall,** a veritable bazaar of forty dealers selling everything from estate jewelry to Victorian furniture, at 597 Fernbridge Drive; 707–725–8820.)

At **Golden Gait Mercantile** (421 Main Street; 707–786–4891), time is suspended in the 1850s with barrels of penny candy, big-wheeled coffee grinders, and glass cases lined with old-fashioned restoratives and hair pomades. Step into the **Blacksmith Shop** to see the largest collection of modern-day iron accessories in the West, including fanciful chandeliers, lamps, and furnishings (445 Main Street; 707–786–4216).

Main Street in the Victorian village of Ferndale.

Take a peek at the **Ferndale Museum** to see a small but mighty exhibit of the history and the agriculture of the "Cream City," with complete room settings, an operating seismograph, and a blacksmith shop (Shaw and Third Streets across from Main; 707–786–4466). Keep up your energy with a shake or an ice-cream soda, or pick up a game of pool, at **Candy Stick Fountain and Grill**, which is also open for lunch and dinner (351 Main Street; 707–786–9373).

At the **Kinetic Sculpture Museum** are strange, handmade, people-powered machines that travel over land, mud, and water (393 Main Street; 707–845–1717; www.kineticsculpturerace.org). These were driven in the World Championship Great Arcata to Ferndale Cross-County Kinetic Sculpture Race, which is held annually in

May. Called the "triathlon of the art world," the three-day event is great fun to watch, as the fantastical contrivances are driven, dragged, and floated over roads, sand dunes, Humboldt Bay, and the Eel River. Among the machines in past races were "Nightmare of the Iguana" and "Tyrannosaurus Rust," which was powered by cavemen.

Ferndale sparkles all over and decorates to the max at Christmastime. The lighting of the tallest living Christmas tree in America, a parade, a Dickens Festival, and concerts are among the blizzard of holiday activities.

LUNCH: Curley's Grill, 400 Ocean Street in the Victorian Inn, Ferndale; (707) 786–9696. California cuisine, homemade soup and foccacia, local fresh fish, grilled sandwiches, and more, indoors in an old-fashioned dining room or on the patio; lunch and dinner.

Afternoon

On the south end of Main, go left onto Ocean Street to **Russ Park** to stretch your legs in a 110-acre closed-canopy spruce-and-redwood forest with more than 3 miles of wildflower trails.

On the edge of the Eel River Delta, a resting point on the Pacific Flyway, Ferndale is within minutes of great bird-watching and some nice walks. Running 5 miles west out of town, Centerville Road leads to the beach, where a wide variety of bird life and animals can be seen on walks north and south—swans, geese, sandpipers, pelicans, and cormorants, as well as seals and whales.

On the east side of town are country lanes leading to the Eel River Estuary, great routes for walking and biking, and you can launch canoes and kayaks here in quiet waters or take a guided boat tour of the estuary (Camp Weoh Guide Service; 707–786–4187). Loons, cormorants, harriers, egrets, and more than 150 feathered species live in or pass through these wetlands. Where the Eel meets the sea, watch for sea lions, seals, and river otters.

Head back to the Bay Area, stopping along the way to walk again under the great redwoods.

There's More

Beachside Camping. Big Lagoon County Park, off US 101, 34 miles north of Eureka; (707) 445–7652. A 3-mile-long protected lagoon, a popular destination for beachcombing, swimming, sailing, windsurfing, kayaking, parasailing, and boating. Campsites in a Sitka spruce forest on the lagoon and the shore. Dogs welcome; no reservations required; no showers or hookups.

Clam Beach County Park, off US 101, 7.5 miles north of Arcata; (707) 445–7652. A long stretch of shoreline for beachcombing, clamming, fishing, picnicking, and surfing. Vehicles, bonfires, and horses are allowed, keeping in mind the posted information about the nesting snowy plover, an endangered shorebird.

Gold Bluffs Beach Campground, Prairie Creek Redwoods State Park; (707) 464–6101. In the dunes on a stunning 10-mile beach, tent and RV sites (less than 24 feet long); no reservations required; restrooms, solar showers. Exposed to wind, rain, and fog, sites are between the ocean and a forested bluff. Best weather is fall and spring—summer can be cool. Leashed pets allowed. Easy walk to enchanting Fern Canyon.

Patrick's Point State Park, Trinidad, 25 miles north of Eureka; (707) 677–3570; www.parks.ca.gov. More than a hundred sites at Abalone, Penn Creek, and Agate Beach campgrounds, each with table, stove, and cupboard; restrooms, showers.

Bigfoot Rafting Company, P.O. Box 729. Willow Creek 95573; (800) 722–2223; www.bigfootrafting.com. The largest and most experienced white-water outfitter in the Klamath-Trinity region; guided day trips, multiday campouts; Class IV and V wilderness trips; raft and inflatable kayak rentals; steelhead and salmon fishing.

Humboldt Bay National Wildlife Refuge, 1020 Ranch Road, Loleta, just south of Eureka; (707) 733–5406. Take the Hookton Road exit from US 101 and drive 1.2 miles to the Hookton Slough trailhead, a 1.5-mile path along the south edge of Humboldt Bay. Thousands of birds and ducks migrate through these beautiful grasslands, freshwater marshes, and mudflats, including 25,000 black brants that fly from their nesting grounds in the Arctic to Baja. Look for herons, owls, ospreys, mallards, egrets, terns, and more. Restrooms.

Humboldt Lagoons State Park, 40 miles north of Eureka on US 101; (707) 488–2041; www.parks.ca.gov. A marshland habitat for myriad birds and other animals, wonderful for boating, fishing; 6 miles of beach and a 3-mile coastal trail. Picnic areas near the visitor center at the north end of Stone Lagoon on the beach.

Loleta Bottoms. For an easy walk or bike ride on quiet, coastside roads, drive or bike from Loleta (just south of Eureka) west on Cannibal Island Road to Crab Park, at the mouth of an arm of the Eel River. You can scramble around the edge of the estuary and walk back east on the quiet road, watching for plovers, tundra swans, and curlews. Go right on Cock Robin Island Road, where mudflats attract masses of shorebirds. Continue back to your car or on toward Loleta, where the Loleta Cheese Factory (800–995–0453) is a good place to stop for sandwiches, snacks, and cheese tasting (fabulous organic cheese). There is a network of two-lane roads in this area, between the highway and the ocean.

Morris Graves Museum of Art, 636 F Street, Eureka; (707) 442–0278; www.hum boldtarts.org. Newly renovated and spectacular, a stunning library building donated to the town by Andrew Carnegie early in the twentieth century is now an exceptional art museum showing a wide variety of works in seven galleries. Call ahead for information on musical and theatrical performances held here.

Prairie Creek Redwoods, 50 miles north of Eureka on US 101, a World Heritage Site; (707) 488–2171. Twelve thousand acres of magnificent coastal redwoods, mountain biking and hiking trails, Roosevelt elk, museum, beaches, campgrounds, Fern Canyon.

Richardson's Grove State Park, 8 miles south of Garberville on US 101; (707) 247–3318. Walk or bike on 10 miles of trails to see old-growth redwoods along the south fork of the Eel River. Swim, fish, picnic, and camp; three leafy, pretty campgrounds are near the river.

Special Events

April. Redwood Coast Dixieland Jazz Festival, Eureka; (707) 445–3378; www.red woodjazz.org. Put on your zoot suit and kick up your heels to big band, Dixieland, zydeco, and swing music from some of the top bands in the country; all over town and on the waterfront. Arrive a day early for the Taste of Main Street, when twenty area restaurants show off their specialties.

Rhododendron Festival, Eureka; (707) 442–3738. Home and garden tours, parade, and more.

Dolbeer Steam Donkey Days, Fort Humboldt State Historic Park; (707) 445–6567. Logging competition; operation of steam donkeys, locomotives, and equipment; rides.

May. Bebop and Brew, Arcata; (707) 826–6059. Big-name jazz and twenty-five microbrew varieties; food, too.

June. Scandinavian Festival and Barbecue, Main Street, Ferndale; (707) 444–8444. Dancing, food, a parade, and festivities for descendants of Scandinavian lineage; for visitors; food, music, and fun.

August. Humboldt County Fair and Horse Races; (707) 786–9511.

September. Festival on the Bay, Eureka; (707) 443–7252. Boat tours, carriage rides, arts and crafts, food, music, and live entertainment.

November. Humboldt County's Coastal Christmas celebrations begin, two months of festivites; (800) 346–3482.

December. Truckers' Parade, downtown Eureka; (707) 443–9747. Some 150 big rigs decorated in Christmas lights; logger-style floats. You've never seen anything like this parade.

Other Recommended Restaurants and Lodgings

Arcata

Abruzzi's, in historic Jacoby's Storehouse on the town plaza, 780 Seventh Street; (707) 826–2345. Homemade pasta and Italian specialties in an upscale atmosphere; make reservations for lunch and dinner. Stained-glass glows, and brick and old beams create ambience in a circa 1850 building. Contemporary and traditional Italian housemade pasta and veal dishes, steak and wonderful fresh fish; try the sweet potato crab cakes and the blackened salmon.

Bon Boniere Ice Cream, 215 F Street in the Jacoby Building; (707) 822–6388. Since 1898, a famous place for homemade ice cream, caramel popcorn, and other sweets. They also have soup, salad, and sandwiches (another site is located in Old Town Eureka on F Street).

Larrupin Cafe, 1658 Patrick's Point Drive, 2 miles north of Trinidad; (707) 677–0230. In a two-story yellow house in the country is an art-filled space with masses of fresh flowers and a fireplace; California cuisine and seafood, barbecued oysters, Cajun ribs; dinner only.

Plaza Grill, 780 Seventh Street in Jacoby's Storehouse; (707) 826–0860; www .abruzzicatering.com. A casual cafe with a fireplace and town views. Terrific burgers, sandwiches, and fish platters; lunch and dinner.

Eureka

Campton House, 305 M Street; (707) 443–1601 or (800) 772–1622. A charming Craftsman-style cottage with three spacious, comfortable bedrooms; two baths; parlor; dining room; and a kitchen—perfect for a big family or a family reunion. You can also book just one room. Across the street from the Carson Mansion and within walking distance of all the sights and restaurants in town. A plain continental breakfast and afternoon tea are included, as are use of the pool and sauna at the adjacent motel.

Cornelius Daly Inn, 1125 H Street; (707) 445–3638 or (800) 321–9656; www.daly inn.com. A beautiful bed-and-breakfast mansion built in 1905, with elegant antiques; three rooms, one with fireplace; and two suites, each very private and very pretty. Full breakfast.

Elegant Victorian Mansion, 1406 C Street; (707) 444–3144. Perhaps the finest of Eureka's great treasure trove of Victorian bed-and-breakfast inns, built in 1888, it's an extravagantly antiques-filled Queen Anne surrounded by a garden of 150 antique roses; there are four large, comfortable rooms, plus croquet, vintage movies, fireplace chats, and a library of guidebooks.

Eureka Inn, 518 Seventh Street; (707) 442–6441 or (800) 862–4906; www.eureka inn.com. A fabulous English Tudor–style, half-timbered hotel built in the 1920s. In the lobby before the huge fireplace, guests loll in cushy leather couches and armchairs during the week and dance their socks off when swing bands play on the weekends. Red leather booths are cozy in the Rib Room dinner house; the Bristol Rose casual cafe and a poolsidedining area serve exceptional California cuisine, American comfort food, and plenty of fresh seafood; the extensive wine list, featuring some of the best California and European wines, gets top marks from serious wine buffs. A lively pub and a cocktail lounge are popular gathering spots. Christmastime is festive, when a towering, glittering tree is the backdrop for nightly live entertainment. Rooms are spacious, with traditional decor.

Lost Coast Brewery, 617 Fourth Street; (707) 445–4480; www.lostcoast.com. At this friendly microbrew pub, try some AlleyCat amber ale or a rugged glass of Downtown Brown; hearty pub food at lunch and dinner. Owned by a woman who was one of the first females to found a microbrewery in the United States.

Loleta

Southport Landing, 444 Phelan Road; (707) 733–5915; www.northcoast.com/southport. Once a haven for ship captains, Southport Landing is a historic landmark beside the Humboldt Bay National Wildlife Refuge in a quiet, idyllic country setting. Seven charming, smallish bedrooms with garden and water views, bikes to borrow for exploring the surrounding countryside, kayaks to borrow for paddling the bay; a pool table, table tennis, games, and a library; sumptuous breakfast.

For More Information

Arcata Chamber of Commerce, 1635 Heindon Road, Arcata 95521; (707) 822–3619; www.arcata.com/chamber.

Greater Eureka Chamber of Commerce, 2112 Broadway, Eureka 95501; (800) 356–6381; www.eurekachamber.com. Visitor center has an extensive display of local information.

Humboldt County Convention and Visitors Bureau, 1034 Second Street, Eureka 95501; (800) 346–3482; www.redwoodvisitor.org. Call for a copy of *Destination Redwood Coast,* an excellent guide to the area.

Redwood Empire Association, 1925 Thirteenth Avenue, Oakland 94606; (510) 536–8828; www.redwoodempire.com.

Victorian Village of Ferndale, 248 Francis Street, Ferndale 95536; (707) 786–4477; www.victorianferndale.org/chamber.

Bodega Bay to Elk

A Weekend at the Coast / 2 Nights

From the fishing village of Bodega Bay, along the rocky coastline to the tiny burg of Elk, there is much to fill a weekend. Some of the warmest and most beautiful of the northern California beaches are found near Bodega Bay, where sea lions, boats, sailboarders, and birds share a harbor. On up the Sonoma/Mendocino coast, the wild shoreline is studded with jewel-like beaches, the outlets of several rivers, a harbor or two, and a few old seagoing towns where fishermen and loggers have lived since the nineteenth century.

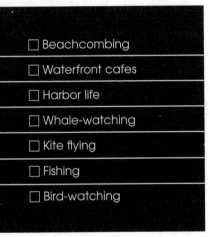

- ☐ Beachcombing
- ☐ Waterfront cafes
- ☐ Harbor life
- ☐ Whale-watching
- ☐ Kite flying
- ☐ Fishing
- ☐ Bird-watching

Tourism, some agriculture, and the works of resident artists and craftspeople are what fuel the economy today in this magical kingdom between the misty sea and the dark forests. Spring means breezy, clear days; wildflowers and lambs in roadside meadows; and the migration of the great gray whale, easily viewed from the entire coastline. Summers are foggy and busy with visitors, fairs, and festivals. The warm, bright fall is the best time; most tourists are gone and the weather is perfect, each beach a postcard view. Winter is for lovers; magnificent storms turn every sandy cove into a treasure chest of driftwood, shells, and other discoveries washed up the crashing surf, while cozy fireplaces beckon from bed-and-breakfast inns.

Day 1 / Morning

Drive north from the Golden Gate on U.S. Highway 101 to Santa Rosa, then head west on Highway 12 through Sebastopol, 6 miles farther, to where the Bohemian Highway crosses Highway 12 at Freestone. At the roadside store, nip into **Wild Flour Bread** for legendary sticky buns, artisan breads, and other treats made from organic grains and seeds and baked in a eucalyptus-fired oven; pizzas, too. (140 Bohemian Highway, 707–874–2938; open Friday through Monday). They hand-knead everything right in front of your eyes, and the baking goes on all day.

Drive into Freestone, just 0.1 mile, to the **Wishing Well Nursery,** 306 Bohemian Highway (707–823–3710), like no other nursery. Surrounding a

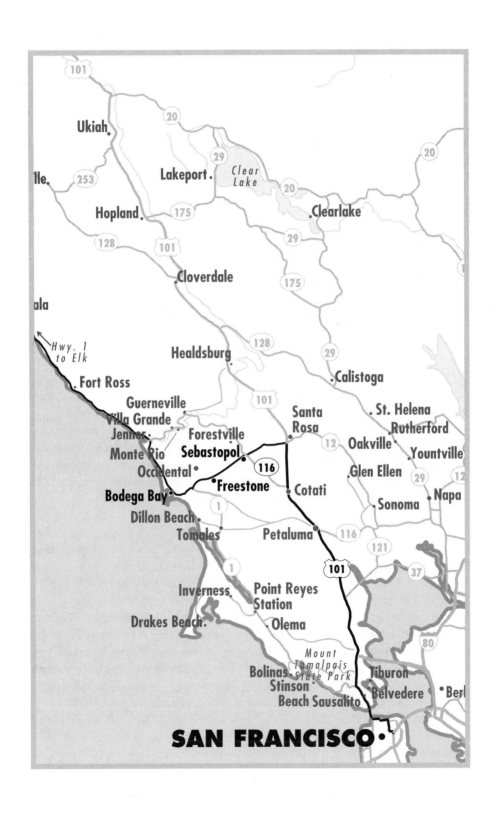

200-year-old hotel are acres of fabulous plants and flowers, outdoors and in green-houses. Exotic birds, fancy chickens, ducks, swans, peacocks, and pheasants twitter in cages, glide on ponds, and strut around as if they owned the place. Decorating the grounds are statuary remnants of the century-old Palace of Fine Arts in San Francisco.

Take a morning walk in **Doran Beach Regional Park** (707–875–3540), a 2-mile curve of beautiful beach separating Bodega Bay and Bodega Harbor. Clamming in the tidal mudflats and sailboarding in the harbor waters are two popular activities. The combination of freshwater wetlands, salt marshes, and the open sea attracts a great variety of shorebirds and waterfowl; you may even see pond turtles, harbor seals, or sea lions. RV and tent camping sites are breezy (707–875–3540).

LUNCH: **The Tides Wharf and Restaurant,** 825 Highway 1, midtown Bodega Bay; (707) 875–3652. Dine at a sunny window table overlooking the action of the wharf and the harbor. Fresh local seafood: clam chowder, Dungeness crab, salmon, mussels, sand dabs—the list goes on. Breakfast, lunch, and dinner; snack bar. Shop for gizmos at the small souvenir shop.

Afternoon

Whale-watching cruises and deep-sea fishing party boats leave from the wharf, head-quarters for Bodega Bay's harbor and the home port for northern coast fishing vessels. Fishermen unload their catch, and shoppers choose from local and imported fresh seafood. It's crab in fall, herring in spring, salmon in summer—and rock and ling cod all year. Mingled with weathered clapboard houses are a handful of seafood restaurants along with a few shops and motels scattered around the edges of the large, protected harbor where pleasure boats from all over the world come to anchor away from the open sea.

On the north end of town, turn left onto Eastshore Road, then right onto Westshore Road, circling the bay. Fishing boats and sailboats are lined up at **Spud Point Marina** (707–875–3535), and there's a long fishing pier where you can try your luck. Adjacent to the docks, at **Spud Point Crab Company,** (707–875–9472) you can get coffee, breakfast and lunch, chowder and sandwiches, and sit at an outdoor table watching the boating activity; get some home-smoked salmon to take away. At **Westside Park** (707–875–2640), you can picnic, dig for clams and bait, and launch a boat. Most days sailboarders flit like butterflies in the harbor breezes. Every April, thousands of visitors come to the park for the **Bodega Bay Fisherman's Festival** to see the blessing of the fleet and a decorated boat parade and to enjoy a big outdoor fair with food and entertainment, arts and crafts (707–875–3422).

At the end of the road, park and get out onto the bluffs of **Bodega Head** (707–875–3483), a prime whale-watching site. Footpaths from here connect to 5 miles of hiking and horseback-riding trails in grassy dunes.

Back on Eastshore Road near the highway, stop in at **Branscomb's Inn and Art Gallery,** 1588 Eastshore Road (707–875–3388). There are three floors of galleries with sea views, featuring local and internationally known artists, wildlife etchings, seascapes, and vineyard scenes; one of the best galleries in gallery-rich Sonoma County. At **Candy and Kites,** 1415 Highway 1 (707–875–3777), get you-know-what for your beach walks. The **Ren Brown Collection,** 1781 Highway 1 (707–875–2922), features works from California and Japan—wood blocks, etchings, silkscreens—the largest collection of contemporary Japanese prints in California. The only wine-tasting room on the Sonoma Coast, **Gourmet Au Bay** features wines by the glass as well as fine crafts and gifts (913 Highway 1; 707–875–9875; www.gourmetaubay.com). The shop is owned by Grammy-winning record producer Ken Mansfield (ask him about the Beatles) and his wife, Connie. You can choose here from more than 1,000 bottles of Sonoma County wines.

The **Bodega Bay Surf Shack** is headquarters for rentals, maps, and advice on biking, beachcombing, kayaking, surfing, and sailboarding, with lessons and guided tours available; plus beachwear. Go to the Web site for fascinating satellite reports, maps, and forecasts about waves and weather (Pelican Plaza; 707–875–3944; www.bodegabaysurf.com).

From Bodega Bay north to Bridgehaven, the **Sonoma Coast State Beach** (707–875–3483) is 13 miles of sandy beaches and coves accessible in a dozen or so places; dramatic rocky promontories and sea stacks, tidepools, and cliffsides make this a thrilling drive. You can camp at **Wright's Beach** or **Bodega Dunes** (800–444–7275). On the north end of the Bodega Bay area, the Bodega Dunes comprise more than 900 acres of huge sand dunes, some as high as 150 feet. There is a 5-mile riding and hiking loop through the dunes and a hiking-only trail to Bodega Head. In a spectacular show of color, thousands of monarch butterflies flock to a grove of cypress and eucalyptus trees adjacent to the dunes every October through February. There are restrooms here and a campground.

For rock fishing and surf fishing, **Portuguese Beach** is a good choice; for beachcombing and tidepooling, try **Shell Beach.** Across Highway 1 from Shell Beach, a pretty 0.5-mile trail runs up and over the hills to a small redwood forest. Also from Shell Beach, the **Kortum Trail** winds nearly 5 miles, an easy path through wildflowery meadows and gullies along the headlands, north to the beach at Goat Rock.

Surf fishing is good at **Salmon Creek Beach** (campsite reservations: 800–444–7275), a beautiful dune area planted with European grasses. At the north end of the beaches, **Goat Rock,** a notoriously dangerous place to swim, is popular for seashore and freshwater fishing at the mouth of the Russian River; seals like it, too.

DINNER: **Duck Club** at Bodega Bay Lodge, Highway 1 on the south end of Bodega Bay, near Bodega Harbour Golf Links; (707) 875–3525. Fresh Sonoma County seafood, poultry, artisan cheeses, and produce on a California cuisine menu.

LODGING: Bodega Bay Lodge and Spa, 103 Highway 1, Bodega Bay; (707) 875–3525 or (800) 368–2468; www.bodegabaylodge.com. Among pines and grassy, landscaped dunes overlooking the Pacific, Doran Beach, bird-filled marshes, and the bluffs of Bodega Head. Spacious, deluxe rooms and luxury suites with views, terraces, or decks; comforters; Jacuzzi tubs; robes; fireplaces. The lobby has a giant stone fireplace and two 500-gallon aquariums filled with tropical fish. Sheltered swimming pool with sea view; spa; fitness center; bikes; golf packages.

Day 2 / Morning

BREAKFAST: Complimentary continental breakfast in the Duck Club restaurant at Bodega Bay Lodge.

Drive north on Highway 1, about forty-five minutes, to Fort Ross.

From the parking lot at **Fort Ross State Park,** 19005 Highway 1 (707–847–3286), walk down to the small, protected beach below the fort. As you breathe in fresh sea air before starting your explorations of the fort, think about the Russians who arrived in 1812, accompanied by Aleut fur hunters. They came to harvest otter and seal pelts and to grow produce for their northern outposts. Their small settlement of hand-hewn log barracks, blockhouses, and homes, together with a jewel of a Russian Orthodox church, was protected with high bastions and a bristling line of cannons, just in case the Spanish decided to pay a call. At the visitor center are exhibits, films, and guidebooks. Inside the restored buildings are perfectly preserved rifles, pistols, tools, furniture, and old photos.

Back on the highway, if you're ready for a snack, stop at the **Fort Ross Store and Deli** (707–847–3333) for an ice-cream cone. Then go on to **Salt Point State Park** (707–847–3221), 6,000 acres of sandy beaches, tidepools, high cliffs, sunny meadows, and hiking and biking trails: a good place to beachcomb, scuba dive, or get a little exercise. Campground sites on both sides of the road are private and protected. The dense forestlands of Salt Point are inhabited by gnarly pygmy pines and cypress, their ghostly gray, mossy trunks tickled by maidenhair ferns. Seven miles of coastline are characterized by long, sandy beaches; rocky coves with tidepools rich in wildlife; and many breeding and nesting locations for birds, such as at **Stump Beach,** where a large number of cormorants reside. On both sides of the highway, a wide variety of weather-protected campsites are available: developed and primitive tent sites and biker/hiker sites, RV sites for up to 31-foot vehicles, and walk-in sites (800–444–7275).

Near the park, **Salt Point Lodge Bar and Grill** (23255 Highway 1; 707–847–3234) is a wonderful spot for casual dining, indoors or outdoors, with an ocean view. It specializes in mesquite-grilled fresh fish and a big salad bar. **Salt Point Lodge** here has comfortable rooms, a hot tub, and voluptuous gardens.

Just north of Salt Point, off Highway 1 at Milepost 43, **Kruse Rhododendron State Park** (707–847–3221) should not be missed in the months of April, May,

A quiet stretch of sand on rugged Sonoma coastline.

and June, when wild rhododendron glades up to 15 feet high are brilliant with bloom under redwood, oak, and madrone branches. There's a 1-mile dirt road into the park; a trail sign shows 5 miles of easy and challenging hikes through quiet forest and over picturesque bridges straddling fern canyons and streams.

LUNCH: Sea Ranch Lodge, 60 Sea Walk Drive off Highway 1, Sea Ranch; (707) 785–2371 or (800) 732–7262; www.searanchlodge.com. From your table, enjoy wide ocean views—and the sight of whales in wintertime. California cuisine and comfort food for breakfast, lunch, and dinner: sandwiches, salads, homemade soups, lots of fresh fish, pasta, pizza and steaks, and an award-winning wine list. The lounge bar has a big fireplace.

Nestled in grassy meadows on headlands above the ocean, the small lodge and nearby rentable homes are headquarters for coastal getaways. You can access several beaches (Shell, Pebble, and Black Point Beaches are the best) and walk easy paths on the bluffs. Twenty upscale lodge rooms have ocean views, some have fireplaces and hot tubs; without a view, one room has a fireplace and a hot tub; breakfast is complimentary. A general store stocks gifts and home accessories, toys, games, snacks, and books by local authors.

With an ocean view from eighteen holes, the beautiful **Sea Ranch Golf Links** course is laid out on the bluffs and in the meadows and forests above the highway (707–785–2468). Ask about play-and-stay packages.

Afternoon

On up Highway 1 about 12 miles, when you see the lace curtains and wooden porches of the century-old **Gualala Hotel**, you are in the village of Gualala, a one-time logging center, now an art colony and fishing headquarters. Shops and several art galleries in the Seacliff Center, on the south end of town, are worth browsing. The **Top of the Cliff** restaurant here serves up gourmet seafood and cocktails with ocean views and legendary sunsets (39140 South Highway 1, 707–884–1539).

The **Dolphin Gallery,** a showplace of local fine arts and crafts (39225 Highway 1; 707–884–3896), houses the Redwood Coast Visitor Center. Prowl around town a bit to find antiques shops and more art galleries.

At the mouth of the Gualala River, **Gualala Point Regional Beach Park** has a mile-long, driftwood-strewn beach and grasslands, habitat for bird life, including great blue herons, pygmy owls, and seabirds (42401 Coast Highway 1, 707–785–2377). You can camp here and hike on a coastside trail to the Sea Ranch. Stop in the visitor center to view displays of early California, Native American, and logging history and to get trail maps.

DINNER: Gualala Hotel, 39301 Highway 1, Gualala; (707) 884–3441; www.the gualalahotel.com. In a landmark 1903 building; family-style Italian dinners, homemade cioppino on Friday night, country-fried chicken with biscuits and gravy, thirty-ounce steaks, fresh crab and seafood, all in a lively, friendly, casual environment. Come in early for a tall one at the long bar, where fisherman and tourists rub elbows beneath a museum-like array of photos of early days; or come in late for billiards and jukebox music. Hotel rooms are small, simple, and nicely furnished with antiques; rates for rooms with private or shared bath are reasonable.

LODGING: Whale Watch Inn, 35100 Highway 1, 5 miles north of Gualala in Anchor Bay; (800) 942–5342; www.whalewatchinn.com. In contemporary-design buildings on a cliff above the ocean, stained-glass windows, lush gardens, eighteen luxurious suites and rooms with whirlpool tubs, fireplaces, and private ocean-view decks. The common lounge has big fireplaces, leather sofas, and a telescope for whale- and sunset watching. Full breakfast, beach with tidepools and a waterfall. No TV, phones, or clocks—bliss!

Day 3 / Morning

BREAKFAST: Sumptuous breakfast at the Whale Watch Inn.

Drive north to **Point Arena.** At the south end of the main street, turn west onto Port Road, following it to the **Point Arena Public Fishing Pier,** which thrusts 330 feet out into the water from the edge of a cove seemingly protected by high cliffs on either side. The original wooden pier was dramatically smashed to pieces in 1983, along with all of the buildings in the cove. In the **Galley at Point Arena** restaurant, Port Road, Point Arena (707–882–2189), are photos of the storm as it ripped and roared. The Galley serves chowder, snapper sandwiches, homemade pies, salads, and fresh crab in season. This is a good place to watch whales and crusty old salts. Fishing, crabbing, and whale-watching are good from the pier; tidepooling and abalone hunting, from the rocks.

Walk up to the **Wharf Master's Inn,** on the hill behind the pier. Built in the 1870s for wharf masters who watched over the port until the 1920s, this is the town's most elaborate building, a fantasy of turned posts, scroll brackets, and fancy window moldings. Prefabricated in San Francisco, the house was shipped here as a kit.

Rollerville Junction, 3 miles north of Point Arena, is the westernmost point in the continental United States, the site of many a shipwreck; ten vessels went down on the night of November 20, 1865. The 115-foot **Point Arena Lighthouse** (707–882–2777) was erected here in 1870, then re-erected after the 1906 San Francisco earthquake. The lighthouse is the all-time best location for watching California gray whales; December through April are the prime months. Scramble around in the lighthouse and visit the museum of maritime artifacts below.

Proceed north on the highway to **Elk,** a tiny community perched on cliffs above a spectacular bay. You'll recognize the **Greenwood Pier Inn** complex, 5928 Highway 1 in Elk, by the multitude of blooming flowers and trees. Take your time poking around in the gardens and in the **Country Store and Garden Shop,** 5928 Highway 1, Elk; (707) 877–9997. Owners Kendrick and Isabel Petty are artists, cooks, gardeners, and innkeepers, their works found throughout the store, the cafe, and the inn, which is a redwood castle with fabulous ocean views; fireplaces, decks, and romantic privacy.

LUNCH: Greenwood Pier Cafe, (707) 877–9997. Fresh local seafood, greens and vegetables from the inn gardens, sandwiches, salads, breakfast.

Drive back to the Bay Area by way of Highway 128 through Boonville and the Anderson Valley wine country, or retrace your Highway 1 route.

There's More

Adventure Rents, Gualala Hotel Plaza, Gualala (888) 851–4386, www.adventure rents.com. Rent canoes or kayaks to explore the Gualala River: transport to and from launch sites included. In the spring, wild azaleas are rampant on the riverbanks.

Golf. Bodega Harbour Golf Links, 21301 Heron, off Highway 1 on the south end of Bodega Bay, Bodega Bay; (707) 875–3538. One of the most beautiful courses in the state, with all the characteristics of a traditional links layout, including sand, sea, and breezes. Islands of gorselike scrub and a huge freshwater marsh add challenge and beauty.

Stillwater Cove Regional Park, 16 miles north of Jenner on Highway 1; (707) 847-3245. A favorite surf-fishing spot, with boat access and picnic area. 5 miles of hiking trails in the redwoods, a wheelchair-accessible trail, and a campground.

UC Davis Marine Laboratory, open for free drop-in tours on Friday afternoon; call ahead to tour other days. A half mile of coastline and surrounding marine habitat is protected and studied by the university. Exhibits and working research projects such as aqua farming are fascinating (2099 Westside Road; 707–875–2211).

Special Events

February through May. Gualala Arts Concert Series; (707) 884–1138; www.gualala arts.org. Renowned concert artists, bands, and performers at the Dolphin Gallery.

April. Bodega Bay Fisherman's Festival, Bodega Bay; (707) 875–3704. Thousands come for the blessing of the fleet and boat parade, outdoor fair, food, entertainment, and arts and crafts.

July. Fort Ross Living History Day, Fort Ross State Park; (707) 847–3286. Costumed docents, historic reenactments, demonstrations, and special events.

August. Art in the Redwoods, Gualala; (707) 884–1138; www.gualalaarts.org. Two days of exhibits by more than fifty artists; live music, food, kids' activities, gourmet gala dinner.

September. Bodega Bay Allied Arts Show, Bodega Harbour Yacht Club; (707) 875–2585. Large, annual exhibition of the work of the regional arts community.

Bodega Bay Sandcastle Building Festival, Doran Beach; (707) 875–3540.

December. Heritage Homes of Petaluma annual holiday parlor tour; (707) 762–3456.

Other Recommended Restaurants and Lodgings

Bodega Bay

Bodega Coast Inn, 521 Highway 1; (707) 875–2217. Forty-four simple, contemporary rooms, each with ocean view and balcony, some with fireplaces and spas.

Inn at the Tides, 800 Highway 1; (800) 541–7788; www.innatthetides.com. On a hillside overlooking the town and the harbor, two-story inn buildings on landscaped grounds. Rooms have quite comfortable amenities, like fireplaces, sitting areas, sea views. Completely protected indoor/outdoor pool, spa, sauna. The restaurant here is casual in feel, top-notch in quality—a place to linger when the sun is on the terrace.

Pomo/Miwok Campground, where the Russian River meets the sea at Bridgehaven, ten minutes off Highway 1; (800) 444–7275. Forty walk-in tent sites in a dense redwood forest at the end of the paved road (great for biking).

Sandpiper Restaurant, 1410 Bay Flat Road; (707) 875–2278. Tuck into eggs with home fries, huevos rancheros, or crab omelets for breakfast; enjoy fresh seafood, burgers, clam chowder, and comfort food with the locals; lunch and dinner.

Sonoma Coast Villa Inn and Spa, 16702 Coast Highway 1; (707) 876–9818 or (888) 404–2255; www.scvilla.com. On the way to Bodega Bay, a luxurious boutique hotel with eighteen romantic, antiques-filled suites, each with private patio, whirlpool tub, wood-burning fireplace, and gracious amenities. Swimming pool, gorgeous gardens, expanded continental breakfast, nine-hole putting green.

Seaweed Cafe, 1580 East Shore Drive; (707) 875–2700; www.seaweedcafe.com. New and much heralded for Thursday through Sunday dinners; a casual, artful little place where redheaded chef Jackie Martine concocts creative dishes from local ingredients: urchin fritters, squab salad, crab potpie, and traditional seafood favorites. The Saturday and Sunday brunches, the desserts, and the wine list are legendary.

Gualala

Oceansong, 39350 Highway 1, on the south end of town; (707) 884–1041. With a bank of windows overlooking Gualala Beach and a sheltered dining deck; fresh fish tacos, salmon fish-and-chips, and blackened snapper; breakfast, lunch, and dinner.

Seacliff on the Bluff, P.O. Box 1317, Gualala 95445; (800) 400–5053; www.seacliff motel.com. Simple, nice, reasonably priced rooms with private decks and ocean views, fireplaces, large spa tubs, king beds, binoculars, and refrigerators.

Jenner

River's End, 11048 Highway 1, just south of Jenner; (707) 865–2484; www .ilovesunsets.com. With sunset and sea views for lunch and dinner; Hog Island oysters, lots of fresh seafood, a unique wild salmon tasting menu; exotic, eclectic gourmet fare and an award-winning wine list. Stop in for a cocktail on the deck, or stay overnight in one of the cabins.

Point Arena

Pangaea Cafe, 39165 South Highway 1; (707) 884–9669; www.pangaeacafe.com. Highly praised for years; a warm, art-filled environment for enjoying cassoulet, fresh seafood, pork with peach-mango salsa, grilled lavender duck breast, home-made charcuterie and artisan breads from the wood-fired oven, and more inventive foods; a terrific wine list. Dinner and weekend lunch seasonally.

Wharf Master's Inn, 785 Port Road; (800) 932–4031; www.wharfmasters.com. Garden courtyards surround a fancy landmark Victorian mansion; private decks, fireplaces, spa tubs, ocean or courtyard views, featherbeds; continental breakfast.

For More Information

Sonoma Coast Visitor Center, 850 Coast Highway 1, Bodega Bay 94923; (707) 875–3866; www.bodegabay.com or www.visitsonomacoast.com.

Sonoma County Tourism Program, 520 Mendocino Avenue, Santa Rosa 95401; (800) 576–6662; www.sonomacounty.com.

Redwood Coast Chamber of Commerce, P.O. Box 199, Gualala 95445; (800) 778–5252; www.redwoodcoastchamber.com.

California State Park Campground Reservations; (800) 444–7275; www.parks.ca.gov.

Mendocino and Fort Bragg

Where the Forest Meets the Sea / 3 Nights

- ☐ Hidden coves
- ☐ Redwood groves
- ☐ Art galleries
- ☐ Harbor views
- ☐ Fishing, beachcombing, kayaking
- ☐ Whale-watching
- ☐ Bed-and-breakfasts

Floating like a mirage on high bluffs above a rocky bay, Mendocino seems lost in another century. The entire town is a California Historical Preservation District of early Cape Cod and Victorian homes and steepled clapboard churches. Though thronged with tourists in summer, the town somehow retains the look and feel of a salty fisherman's and lumberman's village.

Old-fashioned gardens soften weather-worn mansions and cottages; picket fences need a coat of paint; dark cypress trees lean into the sea breezes. Boutique and art-gallery shopping is legendary, charming bed-and-breakfast inns abound; in fact, there are more bed-and-breakfasts per capita in and around Mendocino than anywhere else in California.

And, this is a major cultural center with dozens of top art galleries, a large art center, and a busy annual schedule of festivals and exhibitions.

A few miles north of Mendocino, Fort Bragg has been a lumbering and commercial fishing town since 1857. Restaurants and accommodations are more reasonably priced here than in Mendocino, and there are several magnificent coastal and forest state parks, and a picturesque fishing port at the mouth of the Noyo River.

Day 1 / Morning

Head north from the Golden Gate Bridge on U.S. Highway 101 to Santa Rosa, an hour's drive (it's about three and a half hours from the bridge to Mendocino).

Go west on Guerneville Road to Highway 116, heading west toward the coast, then north at the Highway 1 junction at Jenner. On the roller-coaster road from here to Mendocino, make frequent stops to enjoy cliff-hanging views of rocky coves, salt-spray meadows, redwood and pine forests, and a necklace of tiny fishing

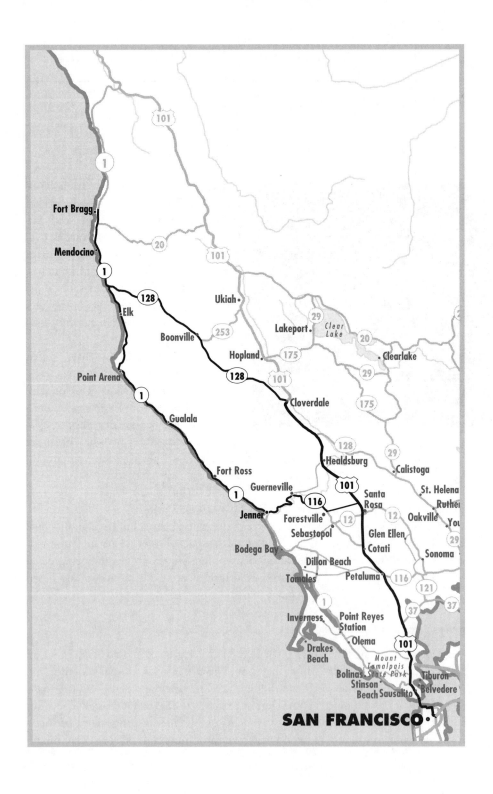

villages and loggers' towns. For a faster, less curvy route, take US 101 north to Highway 128, heading west to Mendocino.

LUNCH: Salt Point Lodge Bar and Grill, 23255 Highway 1, Jenner, just north of Timber Cove; (707) 847–3234; www.saltpointlodge.com. Solarium windows overlooking gardens and Ocean Cove; mesquite-grilled specialties, fresh fish, salad bar, barbecue. Also here, an updated, reasonably priced 1950s-style motel.

Afternoon

After you arrive in Mendocino, revive yourself with a bracing walk along the bluffs, the grassy headlands that surround the town. From the bluffs are views of a deep river valley as it meets the sea at **Big River Beach.** Looking back at the town's skyline, you can imagine when horse-drawn carriages were parked in front of the Mendocino Hotel and ladies with parasols swept along the boardwalk in their long gowns. Restrooms and a picnic area are located on the north end of the park along Heeser Drive.

At the foot of the bluffs on the south side of Mendocino, a brand-new state park, **Big River State Park** combines the gorgeous sandy, driftwoody beach and tidepools at the foot of the cliffs with the river running inland lined with pristine forest and wildlife habitat. The park now connects by old logging roads two adjacent state parks and a state forest (707–937–5804). Harbor seals, river otters, and great blue herons are among the inhabitants. Access the beach by a steep stairway from the headlands trail or from a small parking area off the highway, just south of town.

Kayaking and canoeing are popular on the river (see Catch a Canoe, page 77). You can hike into Jackson Demonstration State Forest and Mendocino Woodlands State Park on the north and to Van Damme State Park to the south.

Good old days in mind, now is the time to visit the **Kelley House Museum** on Albion Street (707–937–5791). A sunny yellow house built in 1852, it's set back from the street next to a huge water tower and a pond surrounded by an old garden. Among the historical photos are those of burly loggers hand-sawing ancient redwoods. Lumber for shipbuilding and for construction of the gold rush city of San Francisco brought Easterners here in the mid-1800s; it took them six months by ship from the East Coast to reach this wilderness of mighty river valleys and seacoast.

On Main Street's headlands is the **Ford House** museum (707–937–5397), built in 1854. A scale model of Mendocino in the 1890s shows the dozens of tall water towers that existed at that time; more than thirty towers, some double- and triple-deckers, are distinctive features of today's skyline. Here you can purchase guidebooks and history books, tide tables, and maps. The picnic tables in the meadow out back are delightful perches from which to watch the whales, which cruise close to the shoreline in the wintertime. During the Whale Festival in March, special exhibits are held here, and guided whale walks are offered.

Step into **Out of This World** at the corner of Main and Kasten to get up-close views of the crashing surf through high-powered telescopes that are trained on the coastline. This unusual store specializes in premium optics, binoculars and scopes, and space and science kits (707–937–3324).

Have a sunset cocktail at the **Mendocino Hotel,** a gloriously overdecorated gathering place since 1878.

DINNER: **MacCallum House Restaurant** and **Grey Whale Bar,** 45020 Albion Street, Mendocino; (707) 937–5763; www.maccallumhousedining.com. Haute cuisine in a rambling Victorian mansion: oysters, gnocchi, sesame-encrusted ahi tuna, duck in blackberry sauce, fresh salmon, and Meyers lemon curd Napoleons. Sophisticated wine list. This long-established and beloved bed-and-breakfast inn has remodeled and refurbished its rooms and suites.

LODGING: **Whitegate Inn,** 499 Howard, Mendocino; (707) 937–4892; www.whitegateinn.com; e-mail: staff@whitegateinn.com. Julia Roberts and Mel Gibson (not together) adored the privacy at this dream of a Victorian mansion right in the heart of town. Behind a pristine white picket fence, a lush English garden and huge old cypress trees hint at the luxury within six inn rooms and a cottage. High-ceilinged and airy in their rococo finery, all rooms have European featherbeds and down comforters, fireplaces, garden or sea views, gorgeous antique beds, and a romantic, but not fussy, aura. A full breakfast is served in the truly spectacular dining room, which looks onto the garden and the coastline 2 blocks away. Think about evening wine parties, a bottomless cookie jar, a concierge to make your local arrangements, sunny afternoons in a lounge chair on the garden terrace, carmel apple French toast, and a long soak in a claw-foot tub.

Day 2 / Morning

BREAKFAST: Whitegate Inn.

Set out from the inn to explore on foot. Browsing the boutiques and galleries in Mendocino village can take an hour or a week, depending on your love of discovery. Many Mendocino artists are renowned not only throughout the state but also internationally, and you will find galleries on every street of the town. At **Creative Hands of Mendocino,** 45170 Main (707–937–2914), look for hand-crafted gifts for children and adults. The **Artists' Co-op,** upstairs at 45270 Main (707–937–2217), is operated by artists who show and sell primarily landscape works in a variety of media.

At Kasten and Ukiah Streets, in a glorious building from the 1870s, is the exceptional **William Zimmer Gallery,** showing fine jewelry, handcrafted furniture, paintings, and more (707–937–5121). Some of the gallery's sculpture collection is displayed at Stevenswood Lodge, just south of Mendocino in a gorgeous forest and garden setting. Look for miraculous wood sculptures of wheeled vehicles. Hub of the artistic community, the **Mendocino Art Center** offers classes, seminars, and special events related to countywide arts all year. **The Gallery** and **The Showcase** here exhibit and sell the fine work of member artists (45200 Little Lake Street between Williams and Kasten Streets; 707–937–5818).

Main Street shops of note include the **Golden Goose** (707–937–4655), two floors of European antiques, country-luxe bed and table linens, and a children's boutique for heirs and heiresses.

Overgrown country gardens will draw you up and down the side streets and alleys; look for the two old cemeteries, not in the least spooky, whose headstones are fascinating relics of the days when European sailors, Russian soldiers, and Chinese workers lived here.

Care for a taste of wine before lunch? Stop in at **Fetzer Vineyards' Mendocino Tasting Room** at 45070 Main, open 10:00 A.M. to 6:00 P.M. (707–937–6190). The organically grown Bonterra wines and the limited-release reserves are grown in the Anderson Valley nearby. The tasting room is a good place to shop for Wine Country souvenirs and gifts, too.

LUNCH: The Moosse Cafe, on the southwest corner of Kasten and Albion Streets, Mendocino; (707) 937–4323. This restaurant in the Blue Heron Inn features Asian-style gourmet fish and seafood dishes as well as pasta, pork, and fancy desserts. Open daily for lunch.

Afternoon

Three miles south of Mendocino on Highway 1, the beach, campground, and hiking trails at **Van Damme State Park** are popular weekend destinations (707–937–4016). This is the home of the uniquely beautiful **Pygmy Forest,** a Registered National Landmark. An easy 0.3-mile trail takes you through a lush fern canyon and spooky woods of dwarf cypress, rhododendrons, and other bonsailike plants and trees. A fifty-year-old cypress, for instance, may be only 8 inches tall and have a trunk less than 1 inch in diameter. To reach the Discovery Trail and other trails, stop at the ranger station or take Little River Airport Road off Highway 1 and go 2.7 miles to the Pygmy Forest parking lot.

There are seventy-four developed campsites at Van Damme and sites for RVs up to 21 feet long. A few hike-in campsites are accessed by a 2-mile scenic trail.

A unique way to explore the coastline here is with **Lost Coast Kayaks,** whose experienced guides conduct sea kayak tours from Van Damme beach (707–937–2434). For both beginners and experienced kayakers, in boats that are easy to maneuver, two-hour tours explore the rocky edges of coves and tidepools, accompanied by shorebirds, seabirds, and harbor seals.

If you crave a little more strenuous outdoor adventure for the afternoon, call **Catch a Canoe and Bicycles, Too!** (707–937–0273) to ask about paddling the **Big River,** which runs into the sea below the high bluffs on the south side of

Mendocino. Along banks lush with fir and redwood groves, wildflowers, and wild rhododendrons, you can paddle a canoe or a kayak from the mouth of the river 7 or 8 miles upstream on an estuary—the longest unchanged and undeveloped estuary in northern California—stopping at a tiny beach or a meadow for a picnic. You will undoubtedly see ospreys, wood ducks, and blue herons, probably harbor seals and deer, too.

Catch a Canoe and Bicycles, Too! is located at the wondrous **Stanford Inn by the Sea** complex on a hillside above the river across from Mendocino. The luxurious, twenty-six-room country inn is surrounded by spectacular gardens. Herds of llamas and horses graze in the meadows. Guests enjoy a spa, a sauna, and an Olympic-size swimming pool enclosed in a greenhouse crowded with tropical plants.

If you stay at the Stanford Inn (Highway 1 and Comptche-Ukiah Road, P.O. Box 487, Mendocino 95460; 800–331–8884; www.stanfordinn.com), you will enjoy a fireplace or wood-burning stove in your sitting area, a down comforter on your four-poster or sleigh bed, a private deck from which to watch the sun set over the sea, complimentary wine, and a bountiful buffet breakfast.

DINNER: Cafe Beaujolais, 961 Ukiah Street, Mendocino; (707) 937–5614; www.cafebeaujolais.com. A 1910 Victorian house is surrounded by lush gardens, so exceptional they are toured at special events. Organically grown local products supply ingredients for the inventive menu of seasonal delights; save room for French bittersweet chocolate and sour cherry cake and passion fruit crème brûlée. The wood-floored dining room is homey and relaxed, with flowery wallpaper and lace curtains; a sunny, glass-enclosed deck floats in the garden; and the wood-fired oven in The Brickery produces take-out breads to dream about. Reserve well ahead.

LODGING: Whitegate Inn.

Day 3 / Morning

BREAKFAST: Whitegate Inn.

On a drive north on Highway 1, on the way to the lumbering and fishing town of Fort Bragg, stop at a beach, forest parks, and a botanical garden.

Two miles north of Mendocino on Highway 1, **Russian Gulch State Park** (707–937–5804) is known for sea caves, a waterfall, and a beach popular for rock fishing, scuba diving, and swimming in chilly waters. From the headlands in the park, you can see the Devil's Punch Bowl, a 200-foot-long tunnel with a blowhole. Inland, the park includes 3 miles of Russian Gulch Creek Canyon, with paved and unpaved trails in dense forest and stream canyons. A hiking trail leads to a 36-foot waterfall and to high ridges where views are breathtaking. A small campground here is particularly lovely, and there is a special equestrian campground with riding trails into **Jackson State Forest.** RVs up to 27 feet are allowed.

One mile north of Russian Gulch State Park, turn west into **Jug Handle State Reserve** (707–937–5804), a 700-acre park notable for an "ecological staircase" marine terrace rising from sea level to 500 feet. Each terrace is 100,000 years older than the one above, a unique opportunity to see geologic evolution. The plants and trees change from terrace to terrace, too, from wildflowers and grasses to wind-strafed spruce, redwood, and pygmy forests of cypress and pine.

Save at least two hours for the **Mendocino Coast Botanical Gardens** (18220 Highway 1, 2 miles south of Fort Bragg; 707–964–4352; www.garden bythesea.org), with forty-seven acres of plantings, forest, and fern canyons on a bluff overlooking the ocean. Easy paths lead through picture-perfect perennial and native-plant gardens, forests, a marsh, and organic vegetable gardens. From late April through early June, hundreds of rhododendrons, azaleas, and spring bulbs are in bloom. From November through January, Japanese maples and winter heathers are aflame. One of the loveliest walks is along a creek in a mossy fern canyon. On the coastal bluff are wildflower meadows above a dramatic, rocky shoreline with waves crashing in the coves below. The garden paths are primarily wheelchair-accessible; two electric carts are available at no charge. You can buy superhealthy plants here at reasonable prices, as well as garden accessories and books. Bring a picnic lunch or snacks and enjoy the garden benches and picnic tables.

LUNCH: The Wharf bar and restaurant at 32260 North Harbor Drive, Fort Bragg (707–964–4283), overlooking the harbor, is a great place for lunch. Try the grilled fresh fish, grilled eggplant salad, mushroom crepe torte, or the apple-wood rotisseried game hen.

Just south of Fort Bragg, at the mouth of the **Noyo River, Noyo Harbor** is headquarters for a large fleet of fishing trawlers and canneries. Barking and posing, sea lions lounge on the wooden piers, waiting for the return of the boats at day's end.

Noyo Harbor is the best place on the coast to take a whale-watching cruise—the boats usually find the whales within fifteen or twenty minutes. Thousands of majestic gray whales parade off the North Coast each winter on their annual 12,000-mile round-trip migration from the Arctic Circle to Baja California. On the 80-mile Mendocino coastline, they are spotted in late November through December, and they head north again in February and March. Some of the best whale-watching sites on the North Coast are MacKerricher State Park, Mendocino Headlands State Park, and Point Cabrillo Light Station. Whale-watching cruise companies include Anchor Charters (707–964–5440), All Aboard Adventures (707–964–1881), *Rumblefish* (707–964–3000), and Telstar Charters (707–964–8770).

DINNER: Old Coast Hotel, 101 North Franklin Street, Fort Bragg; (707) 961–4488. Red-checked tablecloths give no hint of the sophisticated menu and big wine list; oysters, jambalaya, twenty pastas, fresh fish in imaginative sauces, house-smoked ribs. Warm and cozy on a cold night; live jazz on weekends.

LODGING: The Lodge at Noyo River, 500 Casa del Noyo Drive, off North Harbor Drive above Noyo Harbor, Fort Bragg; (707) 964–8045; www.noyo lodge.com. On a forested bluff above Noyo Harbor, The Lodge at Noyo River is a California Craftsman mansion with warmly romantic inn rooms and a new annex with large suites. In 1868 Scandinavian boatbuilders handcrafted this unique home of prime redwood. It is furnished with comfortable antiques, Oriental rugs, and vintage art and photos. Full breakfasts and evening wine are served in the sunny dining room overlooking the harbor or on the outdoor deck. Annex suites are spacious, with private decks, harbor views, fireplaces, huge soaking tubs, and sitting areas. With harbor or garden views, inn rooms vary in size and amenities; some have claw-foot or soaking tubs and sitting areas. If you are a light sleeper, ask for a room away from the barking sea lions.

Day 4 / Morning

BREAKFAST: The Lodge at Noyo River. Stroll the gardens and take the short path to the harbor to watch the fishing fleet head out into the morning mist.

Before heading back to the Bay Area, stop in at **For the Shell of It,** 344 North Main Street in Fort Bragg, to shop for shells and shell jewelry, shell posters, folk art, and all things shellish (707–961–0461). The **Wind and Weather** shop, 147 East Laurel (707–961–4153) is a fascinating place to see and buy weather instruments, vanes, and sundials. At the **Mendocino Chocolate Company** at 542 North Main, pick up handmade truffles, chocolates, and edible seashells. Try these specialties: a dark, Rambo of a truffle—"Mendocino Macho"; "Mendocino Breakers," dark-dipped caramels rolled in almonds; and old-fashioned Convent Fudge (707–964–8800; www.mendocinochocolate.com). Looking for **Papa Birds** in Mendocino? It moved here and is still the same fabulous emporium of bird paraphernalia, from feeders and birdhouses to bird kites, books and toys, and windsocks (131 East Laurel Street; 707–964–5604; www.papabirds.com).

A beautiful three-story, all-redwood home built before the turn of the twentieth century, the **Guest House** is a museum filled with photos and artifacts of local history and antique logging equipment, and it has a lovely garden (343 North Main Street; 707–964–4251). Check out the **U.L. Company Store** at Main and Redwood, an indoor shopping center containing several boutiques. At the Fort Bragg Depot are a clutch of small shops, including **Fuchsiarama,** a gifts and fabulous fuchsias store; the main Fuchsiarama location is 2 miles north, a lush and beautiful five-acre environment for fuchsias and fantasy gifts; you can also picnic here (23201 North Highway 1; 707–964–0429).

To stretch your legs before you head home, head for **Glass Beach** at the foot of Elm Street, where the sand is sprinkled with pebbles of glass and china that have been tumbled and smoothed in the sea. North of town past the first bridge, **Pudding Creek** has a beach play area and tidepools. Eight miles north of Fort

Bragg, **Ten Mile River Beach** is acres of salt marsh and wetlands at the mouth of the Noyo River, inhabited by nesting birds and ducks; a 4.5-mile duney stretch of sand extends south from the river.

Returning to San Francisco, head south on Highway 128 inland, connecting with US 101 South to the Golden Gate Bridge.

There's More

Lost Coast Adventures, 19275 South Harbor Drive, Fort Bragg; (707) 961–1143. Kayak tours, mountain-bike and skin- and scuba-diving rentals, boat charters for fishing, diving, and whale-watching.

MacKerricher State Park, 3 miles north of Fort Bragg off Highway 1; (707) 927–5804; www.parks.ca.gov. Eight miles of beach and dunes, with tidepools at the southern end of the park. Two freshwater lakes are stocked with trout. Horseback-riding, mountain-biking, and hiking trails are found throughout bluffs, headlands, dunes, forests, and wetlands. The headlands at Laguna Point are a prime spot for whale-watching, and harbor seals are seen here. The boardwalk affords wheelchair and stroller access from the southwest corner of the parking lot. Developed camp-sites and RV sites for up to 35-foot vehicles, fire rings, restrooms. Stretching the entire 8-mile length of the park, the paved Haul Road, a former logging road, is a fabulous jogging, biking, and walking route that crosses beautiful sand dunes and has ocean views.

Pacific Star Winery, 12 miles north of Fort Bragg; (707) 964–1155; www.pacific starwinery.com. Sheep and horses share a windy clifftop with a rustic redwood-and-stone winery where barrels stand in the salt air—a practice winery owner Sally Ottoson claims contributes to the character of the wines. Among unusual varieties produced are dark, earthy Charbonos made from a rare grape variety; hearty Zinfandels, Chardonnays, and more. Bring a picnic, and enjoy the crashing waves and the ocean views.

Skunk Train, Laurel Street Depot at Main Street, Fort Bragg; (866) 45–SKUNK; www.skunktrain.com. Hauling logs to sawmills in the 1880s, the California and Western Railroad's historic diesel and steam Skunk Trains carry tourists on half-day trips alongside Pudding Creek and the Noyo River through redwood forests, cross-ing thirty bridges and trestles over river gulches, passing idyllic glades and mead-ows. You can sit inside or wander in and out, standing on open-air cars and enjoying the natural sights and the fresh air. At the halfway point, the train stops to fill up on water, and passengers can stretch their legs, have picnics, and buy souvenirs. On sale are freshly grilled hot dogs, homemade cookies, Pratt's wild organic apple juice, even cappuccino and Mendocino Sunrises—champagne and wild apple juice with fresh mint! Make reservations for summer weekends.

Special Events

January. Crab and Wine Days, Mendocino; (866)–goMendo; www.gomendo.com. Crab cruises and whale-watching trips, cooking demonstrations, wine and crab tasting, carnival, winemaker dinners, crab feed and crab cake cookoff, and more.

March. Fort Bragg Whale Festival; (800) 726–2780. Chowder and microbeer tasting, food and crafts booth, doll show, live music, classic car show.

Mendocino Whale Festival, Mendocino; (800) 726–2780. Chowder and wine tasting, wooden boat displays, food booths, street musicians, horse-drawn carriage rides, and live Saturday night concert.

April through June. Wild rhododendrons erupt into pink, white, and red blossoms April through June at Kruse Rhododendron State Reserve; (707) 847–3286.

July. Mendocino Music Festival, P.O. Box 1808, Mendocino 95460; (707) 937–2044. Classical and jazz.

World's Largest Salmon Barbecue, Fort Bragg; (707) 964–6030.

August. Art in the Gardens, Fort Bragg; (707) 965–4352. Art, music, wine, and food at the Botanical Gardens.

September. Winesong! Buy your tickets early for this annual wine tasting and auction fund-raiser. California wineries and restaurants set up tasting booths throughout the beautiful Mendocino Coast Botanical Gardens in Fort Bragg, and live music is played throughout; (707) 961–4688.

Paul Bunyan Days, Fort Bragg; (707) 964–8687. Parade, arts and crafts, entertainment, games, food, wine, and beer.

November. Wine and Mushroom Festival. Join chefs on forest trails and learn how to spot and prepare edible wild mushrooms. Also mushroom hunts and classes; Brothel, Bar and Boarding House historical walking tours; food fair; wild-mushroom dinners hosted by Mendocino winemakers; (866)–goMendo; www.gomendo.com.

December. Candlelight Tours of Bed-and-Breakfast Inns, Fort Bragg, Little River, Albion, Mendocino; (800) 726–2780.

Other Recommended Restaurants and Lodgings

Albion

Albion River Inn, Highway 1, 6 miles south of Mendocino, P.O. Box 100, Albion 95410; (707) 937–1919. Overlooking the rugged coastline, oceanfront rooms with spectacular views, fireplaces, spas, contemporary decor; full breakfast, private headland path, lush gardens. The clifftop restaurant is one of the best on the coast, serving fresh seafood such as lime and ginger grilled prawns and Cajun oysters. More than one hundred top California labels are on the wine list.

Elk

Zebo at the Elk Cove Inn and Spa, Highway 1; (800) 275–2967; www.elkcove inn.com. Rustic bistro menu with house-made pasta, seafood, inventive dishes using local ingredients; every wine offered by the glass. Dinners Friday through Monday.

Fort Bragg

Beach House Inn, 100 Pudding Creek; (707) 961–1700; www.beachinn.com. Overlooking the water, with spa tubs for two, fireplaces, private balconies; surrounded by lovely wetlands at the mouth of Pudding Creek. You can walk to the beach.

Egghead Omelettes of Oz, 326 North Main Street; (707) 964–5055. Sit in a comfy booth in a Wizard of Oz environment, complete with yellow brick road, and enjoy big, big omelets, burgers, salads, and sandwiches; breakfast and lunch.

Fort Bragg Grille, 356 North Main Street; (707) 964–3663. A casual, fun place with unique specialties: chicken and andouille sausage gumbo, Greek salad sub sandwiches, jambalaya, grilled cod sandwiches, and always burgers and basic dishes for the less adventurous.

Grey Whale Inn, 615 North Main Street; (707) 964–0640 or (800) 382–7244; www.greywhaleinn.com. Built as a hospital in 1915, this three-story landmark has spacious rooms, with high windows looking to the sea or inward through the trees to town. You can walk right out the back door to take a long walk along the waterfront on the Old Coast Road. Rooms have sitting areas with armchairs, deep tubs, some fireplaces, and lots of books. Breakfast is a big buffet in the tiny dining room.

Mendocino Cookie Company, in the Company Store, 301 North Main Street; (707) 964–0282. Fresh double chocolate chip cookies, homemade muffins, scones, pastries; ice-cream cones and shakes.

North Coast Brewing Company, 455 North Main Street; (707) 964–BREW. Exotic beers, ales, stouts, local fresh fish, ribs, Mendocino mud cake. If your innards are in good shape, try the Old Rasputin Russian Imperial Stout, the Route 66 chili, and the Cajun black beans and rice.

Little River

Heritage House, 5200 North Highway 1; (707) 937–5885. Rooms and cottages on a bluff above a cove with sea views. Part of the lodge was built in the late 1800s, and the entire complex looks like New England. This is one of the most desired lodgings in the area, making it necessary to book weeks, perhaps months, ahead. Rooms include full breakfast and dinner in a sedate and elegant atmosphere in three lovely dining rooms; almost every table has a view of the sea. Fresh local fish, Sonoma County poultry, lamb, and cheeses are put together for some of the best food you'll find in the region. Decor varies from old-fashioned comfortable to luxurious. Most rooms have fireplaces or wood-burning stoves; some have Jacuzzi tubs and ocean-view decks. Among the vast natural and introduced plantings, you will find Mediterranean, English country, and woodland gardens.

Little River Inn, 7751 Highway 1; (707) 937–5942 or (888) 466–5683; www.little riverinn.com. In the same family since it was built in the 1850s, a white wedding cake of a house that's expanded to become a sizable resort with one of the best restaurants in the area, a nine-hole golf course in the redwoods, and tennis. The bar is a favorite locals' meeting place. Rooms behind the inn have porches overlooking a beautiful beach and bay. On the menu may be rack of lamb marinated in Cabernet, polenta with porcini mushroom sauce, and warm ollalieberry cobbler. The golf course has been improved, with paved cart paths, a bigger putting green, and much-needed drainage work. Look for the sea otter in the pond on the fourth tee. Ask about golf/room packages. A new day spa is open, offering complete salon, beauty, and body treatments.

Mallory House; 7751 North Highway 1; (888) 466–5683; www.littleriverinn.com. Newly opened, owned by the Little River Inn, on a bluff with sea views framed by coastal pines. Three suites in an 1890 farmhouse, and an adjacent Cape Cod-style cottage, among the largest, most private, and most commodious accommodations on the coast. Seals cavort in Buckhorn Cove, below. Hot tubs, Jacuzzis, fireplaces. For breakfast, crab cakes Benedict, huckleberry scones, ollalieberry cobbler.

Mendocino

Agate Cove Inn Bed and Breakfast, 11201 Lansing Street; (800) 527–3111. Right in town, garden cottages with fireplaces and private decks, ocean views. Breakfast by the fireplace in the dining room with a wonderful sea view.

Brewery Gulch Inn, 9401 Coast Highway 1 North; (800) 578–4454; www.brewery gulchinn.com. This newest inn on the coast is a grand lodge constructed with salvaged redwood. Grounds feature a heritage apple orchard, olive grove, trout pond, and mushroom forest. A pleasant trail winds through the property.

Dennen's Victorian Farmhouse, off Highway 1, 2 miles south of town; (800) 264–4723; www.victorianfarmhouse.com. The inspiration for Thomas Kinkade's painting *Home Is Where the Heart Is II,* a charming garden inn with eleven rooms and suites and a cottage; featherbeds, period antiques, spa tubs, fireplaces; full breakfast, concierge service.

Glendeven Inn and Gallery, 1.5 miles south of Mendocino on Highway 1, P.O. Box 282, Mendocino 95460; (800) 822–4536. Antiques and eclectic art decorate rooms and suites in a gray-and-white farmhouse; big breakfasts. Walking path to the sea, gardens. Next door is a gallery of contemporary handcrafted furniture, art, jewelry.

Joshua Grindle Inn, 44800 Little Lake Road; (707) 937–4143 or (800) 474–6353; www.joshgrin.com. One of the oldest homes in town, a circa 1880 beauty overlooking the town. Spacious New England–style rooms in the main house and very private accommodations in the water tower and the "chicken coop." Breakfast at the old harvest table may be baked pears, quiche, frittata, and fresh apple juice.

Mendocino Hotel, 45080 Main Street; (707) 937–0511 or (800) 548–0513; www .mendocinohotel.com. This classic Victorian hotel built in 1878 is chock-full of period antiques, artifacts, and atmosphere. The smallish rooms in the hotel are charming, with ocean or town views. Some with fireplaces and four-posters, the luxurious cottage suites float in glorious gardens; all have down comforters and pampering amenities. The dinner restaurant serves top-notch California cuisine and American comfort food; think about grilled game hen, double-baked Brie with roasted garlic, and the hotel's signature French onion soup. The blooming Garden Room, brightened by skylights and ocean-view windows, is open for brunch and lunch at marble-topped tables, with a cafe bar menu in late afternoon. Notice the stunning stained-glass ceiling and the 200-year-old Dutch fireplace.

955 Ukiah Street Restaurant, 955 Ukiah Street; (707) 937–1955. In a rescued water tower, this is one of the best restaurants in town. Think about duck cannelloni, pork loin with port sauce, blackberry toasted-hazelnut ice cream, and strawberry-rhubarb pie. The upper dining area has an ocean view.

The Ravens, Stanford Inn by the Sea, Highway 1/Comptche-Ukiah Road; (707) 937–5615; www.stanfordinn.com. The only fine-dining restaurant on the coast serving totally vegetarian food. Even carnivores like the creative specialties, such as Caribbean jerk-rubbed tempeh with plantains and pistachio-crusted tofu with grilled veggies. Breakfast and dinner in a pretty setting just over the bridge from Mendocino.

Sea Rock Inn, 11101 Lansing Street; (800) 906–0926; www.searock.com. One-half mile south of Mendocino in a wild garden, country cottages with kitchens; expanded continental breakfast.

Stevenswood Lodge, 8211 Highway 1, 2 miles south of Mendocino; (707) 937–1237 or (800) 421–2810; www.stevenswood.com. Surrounded by Van Damme State Park in a lovely forest setting with a sculpture garden and a dazzling collection of contemporary art. Suites are very nice, with handcrafted furniture and some ocean views. Gourmet restaurant serves breakfast/brunch and dinner.

For More Information

Coastal Visitors Center, 990 Main Street, Mendocino 95460; (707) 937–1938.

Fort Bragg–Mendocino Coast Chamber of Commerce, 332 North Main Street, Fort Bragg 95437; (707) 961–6300 or (800) 726–2780; www.mendocino coast.com.

Mendocino Area State Parks; (707) 937–5804; www.mcn.org/1/mendoparks/ mendo. Information about camping, day use, and interpretive programs. For camp- site reservations call (800) 444–PARK.

Mendocino Coast Reservations, 1000 Main Street, Mendocino 95460; (707) 937–5033; www.mendocinovacations.com. In the Mendocino/Fort Bragg area, rental cottages and homes, some family- and pet-friendly, some with hot tubs and ocean views.

Advice: Driving can be hazardous on the twists and turns of Highway 1, and it's not recommended that you attempt it after dark or during storms. Farm animals and deer in the road can be a scary, and maybe deadly, surprise as you're coming around a blind curve.

Marin Waterfront

Sausalito and Tiburon / 1 Night

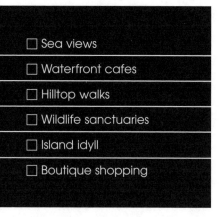

☐ Sea views

☐ Waterfront cafes

☐ Hilltop walks

☐ Wildlife sanctuaries

☐ Island idyll

☐ Boutique shopping

On the north side of the Golden Gate, Marin County is a "banana belt," sunny and warm all summer when San Francisco is socked in with fog. It's nice to get away for a couple of quiet days in Marin's small, seaside towns.

Sausalito tumbles down steep, forested hillsides to the edge of the bay. Sophisticated shops, sea-view restaurants, and marinas lined with yachts and funky houseboats share postcard views of the San Francisco skyline.

A residential community of vintage mansions and luxury condos, Tiburon occupies a spectacular peninsula surrounded by the quiet waters of Richardson Bay, where kayakers paddle and sailboarders fly about. Raccoon Straits, a narrow, windswept channel carefully navigated by sailboats and ferries, runs between Tiburon and Angel Island, which is a state park.

Shopping, walks in the salty air, and fine dining are primary activities on this trip, with a Mount Tamalpais side trip on the way home.

Day 1 / Morning

Take a ferry to Sausalito. Or, in your car, immediately to the north of the Golden Gate Bridge, take the Alexander Avenue exit, descending down into Sausalito. Alexander becomes Bridgeway, the main street.

BREAKFAST: Seven Seas, 682 Bridgeway, Sausalito; (415) 332–1304. From 8:00 A.M. every breakfast specialty you can think of is served, indoors or on the patio. Best breakfast in town.

Downtown Sausalito is a National Historic Landmark District and a long-established haven for artists, writers, and craftspeople. The annual **Sausalito Art Festival** attracts 50,000 people over Labor Day weekend.

In midtown, where a hundred or so shops and restaurants are concentrated, is a small city park with palm trees and huge stone elephants with streetlights on their heads, leftovers from San Francisco's 1915 Exposition. Behind the park, ferries come and go to San Francisco and Tiburon.

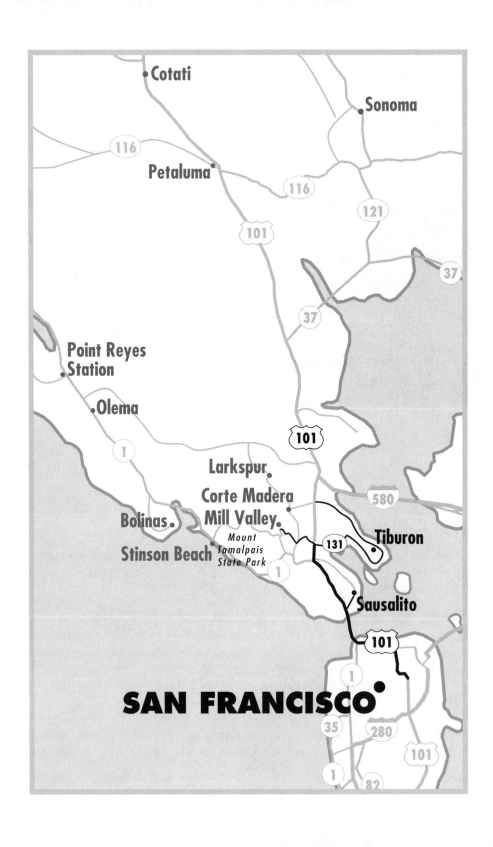

Now, hit the Bridgeway shops and galleries! **Petri's** beautiful, big store holds a museum-like collection of art glass, the largest and most spectacular array I've ever seen (675 Bridgeway; 415–332–2225); look for the jellyfish. More art glass and crystals are on display at **Collector's Gallery** at 745 Bridgeway. A two-story tasting room and art gallery, **Bacchus and Venus Wine Tasting and Art Gallery** is a multifaceted destination (769 Bridgeway; 415–331–2001). Try the daily "flights" of premium California wines, and buy bottles to take away. Browse the array of Wine Country art and Sausalito seascapes; wine-related art and giftware. Aloha-shirt collectors head for **Odyssey** at 673 Bridgeway (415–331–8677). A phenomenon in the art world in the last few years, sleek Zimbabwean Shona stone sculpture is featured at **Spirits in Stone** (585 Bridgeway; 415–332–2388).

Off Bridgeway, the **Armchair Sailor,** at 42 Caledonia (415–332–7505), has books, charts, games, and art for the nautically inspired. Just north of midtown, the **Heathware Ceramics Outlet,** 400 Gate 5 Road off Bridgeway (415–332–3732), is worth a stop for seconds from a major producer of stoneware. If you are interested in sports, entertainment, and historic figures, stop in at the **Mark Reuben Gallery** to see black-and-white photos of legendary stars and athletes (34 Princess Street, off Bridgeway; 415–332–8815). Explore the **Tapia Art Gallery** at 52 Princess Street (415–332–6177). Bob Tapia's local landscapes are luminescent, stormy skies and sunsets at the beach.

Heading north on Bridgeway, watch for the sign for **Bay Model,** 2100 Bridgeway at Spring Street (415–332–3871), a one-and-a-half-acre, hydraulic working scale model of the San Francisco Bay Delta, a fascinating research tool used by the U.S. Army Corps of Engineers. The natural and cultural history of the bay are traced in exhibits—wetlands, wildlife, shipwrecks, antique equipment.

From the Bay Model, a 3.8-mile flat, paved path between Sausalito and Mill Valley, called the **Sausalito Bikeway,** makes a nice bike ride or walk (from Bridgeway and Wateree Street in Sausalito to Tennessee Avenue and Shoreline Highway in Mill Valley). You will pass the edge of Richardson Bay and Bothin Marsh Open Space Preserve, where shorebirds reside; a heliport; the famous Sausalito houseboats; and an old shipyard.

Nearby at **Open Water Rowing,** off Bridgeway at 85 Liberty Ship Way (415–332–1091), take a kayaking lesson on Richardson Bay. All ages find it easy to learn, and it's a great way to get a gull's-eye view of wildlife on the bay. Along the Sausalito shoreline in this area is a series of yacht harbors, marinas, and houseboat moorings. **Sausalito Waterfront Activities** offers bike and kayak rentals, tours, sunset cruises, and more outdoor recreation (803 Bridgeway; 415–331–4448).

At the end of Liberty Ship Way near the marina, **Schoonmaker Beach** is a little patch of palm-fringed sand; the Waterfront Cafe here is popular with locals.

Stop in at the **Arques School of Wooden Boatbuilding** off Harbor Drive between noon and 1:00 P.M. most days to see custom boats and the woodworking, casting, and bronzing going on (415–331–7134; www.arqueschl.org).

Drive south out of town to U.S. Highway 101 to the Tiburon exit, taking Tiburon Boulevard south along Richardson's Bay to **Tiburon.**

LUNCH: Sam's Anchor Cafe, 27 Main Street, Tiburon; (415) 435–4527. One of several harborfront restaurants with views of the San Francisco skyline. Ferries, yachts, and seagulls slide by; time slides by, too, as you sip a beer on the sunny deck and tuck into clam chowder, fresh crab, and fish of all kinds. Casual, with a frisky bar crowd. Weekend brunches are a reason to spend the day at Sam's.

If you plan to be here on the opening day of yacht season in April, arrive early for a good seat at Sam's or grab enough space for a picnic blanket on the lawns beside the bay. Decorated to the max, hundreds of pleasure craft are blessed; then they sail or motor back and forth while landlubbers engage in vernal behavior, like kite flying and boom-box playing.

Afternoon

Prior to the 1920s, Tiburon was a lagoon lined with houseboats, called arks. When the lagoon was filled in 1940, the arks were placed on pilings. Today, curvy, tree-lined **Ark Row,** at the west end of Main, is a charming shopping street.

Windsor Vineyards, 72 Main (415–435–3113), will ship gift boxes of wine with your name on the bottles. **Westerley's Tea and Spice House,** 46 Main (415–435–4233), has old-fashioned penny candy, bubble gum cigars, chocolate sardines, and licorice pipes.

On Ark Row at 90 Main, **Baobab Gallery** is a showplace of imports from Zimbabwe: Shona sculpture, pottery and textiles, jewelry, baskets, and unique handcrafts (415–435–4471; www.baobab.org). Bandit, a silky Papillon, is the official "paw-priotor" of **Tails of Tiburon** at 34 Main, where pets are pampered with brocade jackets, faux fur collars, fluffy bedding, the latest in toys and accessories, and myriad healthy treats (415–789–1301). **The Attic** is a collector's dream of vintage video games, comic books, baseball cards, and other finds (96 Main Street; 415–435–0351).

On the west side of Ark Row, at 52 Beach Road on an inlet of the bay, **China Cabin** is a delightful fragment from a sidewheel steamer that plied the trade routes between San Francisco and the Orient in the late 1800s. The saloon was salvaged when the ship burned, and it served as a home for decades before becoming a maritime museum furnished with period antiques and elaborate gold-leaf ornamentation. Call for a seasonal schedule (415–435–5633).

There are a number of historic buildings in Tiburon. You can get a walking-tour brochure from the Tiburon Peninsula Chamber of Commerce (415–435–5633).

From Main walk north on Tiburon Boulevard 3 blocks to the **Boardwalk** shopping center, where tucked into an alleyway are small shops, including **Shorebirds** and **Shorebirds Kids,** 1550 Tiburon Boulevard (415–435–0888), worth searching out for one-of-a-kind jewelry pieces, locally crafted ceramics and woodware, European toys, paintings, and nautical gifts.

From downtown Tiburon to the north end of Richardson Bay is a beautiful waterfront walk, 2 miles long, on a flat, paved path; there are benches along the way and a huge lawn for Frisbee tossing and sunbathing. The path is popular with joggers, in-line skaters, bikers, and tykes on trikes. At the north end of the path is the **Richardson Bay Audubon Center and Wildlife Sanctuary,** (376 Greenwood Beach Road; 415–388–2524; www.egret.org), where thousands of sea- and shorebirds, accompanied by harbor seals in wintertime, inhabit a 900-acre preserve. A self-guided nature trail and a bookstore are adjacent to **Lyford House,** a lemonyellow landmark Victorian open to the public.

Reachable by a short ferry ride from Main Street (Red and White Fleet; 415–435–2131), **Angel Island State Park** (415–435–3522; www.angelisland .com) is just offshore. Popular activities here are walking and biking the breezy island paths and roads to get a gull's-eye view of three bridges and the bay. Once a Miwok hunting ground, then a cattle ranch, a U.S. Army base, and a prisoner of war camp, Angel Island has a unique past, and you will see several historical sites. Take a narrated tour in an open-air tram.

Thirteen miles of hiking trails and 8 miles of mountain-biking roads crisscross the island. Mountain bikes are available to rent, or you can take sea kayaking tours—even moonlight paddle trips—that are conducted around the perimeter of the island with historical and ecological interpretation (415–332–4465). Less energetic visitors will enjoy sitting on the deck of the cafe with an espresso and a light lunch, watching sailboats and freighters glide by. A few environmental campsites are available (800–444–7275). No dogs, skateboards, or in-line skates are allowed on Angel Island.

The Angel Island–Tiburon Ferry offers a Sunset Cruise on weekends where you bring your own picnic dinner and enjoy cruising the bay in the early evening (415–388–6770). A popular new five-hour tour, called the **Island Hop,** combines visits to Angel Island State Park and Alcatraz. Included are ferries, admission fee of about $30, audio tour of Alcatraz, and the motorized, narrated open-air tram tour of Angel Island (Pier 41 at Fisherman's Wharf, San Francisco; 415–705–5555).

DINNER: Guaymas, 5 Main, Tiburon; (415) 435–6300. Spectacular waterfront location; nouvelle Southwest/Mexican food; lively bar and outdoor terrace.

LODGING: Casa Madrona Hotel and Spa, 801 Bridgeway; (415) 332–0502; www.casamadrona.com. A circa 1880 landmark inn on a hillside above the bay, with luxurious rooms, suites, and cottages; some with fireplaces and private balconies; all with European antiques or stunning contemporary decor, garden or harbor views, outdoor Jacuzzi—some of the most romantic and sumptuous accommodations in the Bay Area. On-site full-service spa, in-room dining, and massage available. Complimentary breakfast and evening refreshments. Ask about a room/dinner package at the on-site trattoria, Poggio.

A forest of masts at the Tiburon marina.

Day 2 / Morning

BREAKFAST: Sweden House, 35 Main, Tiburon; (415) 435–9767. On a bay-side deck with the denizens of Tiburon; pastries, Swedish pancakes topped with fresh berries, egg dishes; breakfast and lunch.

From the east end of Main Street, take Paradise Drive around the west side of the Tiburon Peninsula, a narrow, winding road through forestlands on the edge of the bay. After 1 mile, before Westward Drive, watch for the **Nature Conservancy Uplands Nature Preserve,** also known as the **Ring Mountain Preserve,** 3152 Paradise Drive (415–435–6465), a 377-acre piece of ridgetop wilderness with walking trails and wonderful views. It's less than 1 mile's walk to the summit on a trail edged with knee-high native grasses dotted with wildflowers in spring. On the hilltop you'll have a 360-degree view of San Francisco Bay, Mount Tam, Marin County, and the East Bay hills.

LUNCH: Buckeye Roadhouse, 15 Shoreline Highway, adjacent to US 101 on the south end of Mill Valley; (415) 331–2600. A winding garden path lures you into a historic Bavarian-style lodge right off the freeway, warm and inviting with a fire-place, cushy booths, and Big Band–era music. The food is anything but Bavarian:

California cuisine and American comfort food, light-hearted ethnic specialties. Open from lunch straight through the evening.

Afternoon

From the Buckeye take the Panoramic Highway north, winding several miles up on the east side of **Mount Tamalpais State Park** (415–388–2070). You can't miss Mount Tam—it's the 2,500-foot mountain peak that you can see from everywhere in Marin. Park at the Pan Toll Ranger Station and Visitor Center, get a trail map, and walk a bit on one of several hiking trails that start here; the shortest one is the **Twenty-Minute Verna Dunshea Trail,** which circles the peak. Views are beyond description, and it's often sunny up here when it's foggy everywhere below. Mount Tam's natural wonders are legion—canyons, forests, streams and meadows, waterfalls, and wildflowers—and offer opportunities for wild-and-woolly mountain biking or easy downhill walking.

Perhaps you'll want to stop for a sunset cocktail on the deck at **Mountain Home Inn,** 810 Panoramic Highway (415–381–9000), if you have a designated driver for the trip back to San Francisco. Or stay overnight here. Eleven cozy rooms have French doors or big windows; some have fireplaces and Jacuzzi tubs (415–381–3615; www.mtnhomeinn.com).

There's More

Boating and Bay tours. Captain Case Powerboat and Waterbike Rental, Schoonmaker Point Marina off Bridgeway, Sausalito; (415) 331–0444. Boston whalers, tours on the bay, sunset cruises, water taxis, high-tech water bikes to play with on calm Richardson Bay.

Commodore Seaplanes, from the north end of Sausalito; (800) 973–2752; www.sea plane.com. San Francisco Bay tours, sunset champagne flights.

Hawaiian Chieftain; (415) 331–3214; www.hawaiianchieftain.com. One-hundred-three-foot replica of a 1790 square-rigged topsail ketch, romantic sunset sails, Sunday brunch, sail up the northern coast.

Sea Trek, Schoonmaker Point, Sausalito; (415) 488–1000; www.seatrekkayak.com. Guided kayak tours of the bay, classes, sunset and full-moon paddles.

China Camp State Park, San Rafael; (415) 456–0766. North of San Rafael, take the Civic Center exit off US 101 to North San Pedro Road, heading east. A 1,640-acre waterfront park on San Pablo Bay, with beach, hiking trails, a small museum, and primitive camping. Sailboarding is a big deal from May through October.

Ferries. Tiburon, Sausalito, and Larkspur are accessible by oceangoing ferry: Angel Island Ferry (415–435–2131; www.angelislandferry.com); Blue and Gold Fleet

(415–705–5555; www.blueandgoldfleet.com); Red and White Ferries (800–229–2784; www.redandwhite.com).

Marin Headlands, accessible from Bunker and Conzelman Roads west of US 101, just north of the Golden Gate Bridge. Twelve thousand acres of wilderness with famous views of San Francisco, the bay, and the Pacific. Scattered throughout the headlands are old military tunnels and bunkers that guarded the Gate from the Spanish-American War through the Cold War. Get a map of trails and historic and natural sites by calling (415) 331–1540 or visiting www.nps.gov/goga.

Marine Mammal Center in the Marin Headlands; (415) 289–7325. A rare opportunity to see rescued marine mammals at this hospital for orphaned, sick, and injured seals, sea lions, dolphins, otters, and whales from California's 900-mile coast, from ten-pound newborn harbor seals to 600-pound sea lions. During some months, there are few animals on view; call ahead.

Muir Woods National Monument, 3 miles north of Highway 1 on Muir Woods Road; (415) 388–7059; www.nps.gov/muwo. The only remaining old-growth redwood forest in the Bay Area. It's a popular tourist destination frequented by tour buses, so arrive early in the day (opens at sunrise). Beside walking paths beneath towering redwoods are beautiful wildflowers and ferns. There is a visitor center, a gift shop featuring the works of more than 150 local artisans, and a snack bar.

The Point Bonita Lighthouse in the Marin Headlands is perched on a bit of rock at the entrance to the Golden Gate, with incredible views and a (slightly) swaying footbridge over crashing waves. Walk down and back on your own, and get the history from the ranger in the tiny visitor center, or take the guided walk, which takes (it seems) forever. Precipitous clifftop trails near here are not for little kids.

Stinson Beach Park, Highway 1 and Panoramic Highway; (415) 868–0942. Many Marin beaches are unsafe for swimming and surfing due to undertows and currents; 3-mile-long Stinson is an exception. There are picnic tables, barbecues, restrooms; a snack bar and lifeguards in summer; no pets allowed. Have breakfast, lunch, or dinner at the Stinson Beach Grill (3465 Shoreline Highway, Stinson Beach; 415–868–2002). Fresh seafood, barbecued oysters, pasta, Southwest cuisine, and fifty varieties of beer.

Special Events

April. Opening Day of Yacht Season, Tiburon and Sausalito waterfront; (415) 435–5633. Pleasure craft decorated and blessed; a beautiful and exceedingly high-spirited day on the bay.

May. Tiburon Wine Festival, Tiburon; (415) 435–5623.

June. Floating Homes Tour, Sausalito; (415) 332–1916. A chance to see surprising sophistication and inventive decor in Sausalito's famous houseboats.

Marin Open Studios (415–499–8350; www.marinarts.org); more than 300 artists throughout the county show their works in their studios.

September. Sausalito Art Festival (415–332–3555), a gigantic event attracting top-notch artists and thousands of visitors, plus food and music.

December. Lighted Yacht Parade, Sausalito; (415) 331–7262.

Other Recommended Restaurants and Lodgings

Corte Madera

Corte Madera Inn, 1815 Redwood Highway; (800) 777–9670; www.best western.com. Nice motel overlooking gardens and lawns, with swimming and wading pools, a laundry, playground, and a good coffee shop. Continental breakfast is free, and so is the shuttle to the San Francisco ferry. Can't beat this combo anywhere in Marin.

Larkspur

The Lark Creek Inn, 234 Magnolia Avenue; (415) 924–7767. Internationally famous chef Bradley Ogden, American heartland and nouvelle cuisine, garden patio, vintage architecture.

Sausalito

Cafe Trieste, 1000 Bridgeway Boulevard; (415) 332–7660; www.cafetrieste.com. An annex of the first, and some say best, coffeehouse in San Francisco. Italian pastries, muffins, bagels, sandwiches, salads, light fare, wood-fired pizza and focaccia. Breakfast, lunch, and dinner.

Caruso's Fish Market & Cafe, off Bridgeway Boulevard, at the foot of Harbor Drive; (415) 332–1015. Since 1957 Caruso's has been the place to come for Dungeness crab. Their soups, salads, and fish specials highlight the bounty of the deep blue sea. If they have the swordfish sandwich on the chalkboard, you won't need to read further. The grill closes at 3:00 P.M.

Hotel Sausalito, 16 El Portal; (415) 332–0700; www.hotelsausalito.com. As if on the French Riviera, this small, charming boutique hotel is across from the waterfront park. Lovely pastel colors in rooms that vary in size and price, with armoires, wrought-iron beds, a small patio; some streetside rooms are noisy.

The Inn Above Tide, 30 El Portal; (800) 893–8433; www.innabovetide.com. Next to the ferry dock, luxurious suites with wide water views, fireplaces, private decks; breakfast and wine hour.

Kitti's Place, 3001 Bridgeway; (415) 331–0390. In a homey atmosphere, comfort food extraordinaire, from homemade soup to Asian-inspired salads and entrees; great sandwiches (try the portobello). Breakfast, lunch, and early dinner.

Ondine, 558 Bridgeway; (415) 331–1133. In a spectacular waterfront location with smashing views of the San Francisco skyline, Ondine has sleek, contemporary modern Japanese decor; a memorable wine list; and wonderful California cuisine with an Asian touch. Dinner and Sunday brunch.

Poggio, 777 Bridgeway; (415) 332–7771, www.poggiotrattoria.com. Flooded with rave reviews since its 2003 opening, a warm, rich and inviting Northern Italian trattoria open for breakfast, lunch, and dinner. Homemade, rustic pasta, from fettuccine with squab Bolognese to spinach ricotta gnocchi and cannelloni; spit-roasted meats and poultry; crostata with various fillings, wood-fired pizza, grilled fresh seafood, and more classic dishes.

Scoma's, 588 Bridgeway; (415) 332–9551. On the water at the south end of town, in a baby-blue clapboard building. Dependably good seafood.

Tiburon

Waters Edge, 25 Main Street; (415) 789–5999; www.marinhotels.com. In a town with almost no accommodations, simple, very nice contemporary rooms next to the ferry dock, with skylights, private balconies, fireplaces, featherbeds. Complimentary continental breakfast.

For More Information

Marin County Convention and Visitors Bureau, 1013 Larkspur Landing Circle, Larkspur 94939; (415) 925–2060; www.marincvb.com.

Sausalito Chamber of Commerce Visitor Center, 10 Liberty Ship Way, Sausalito 94965; (415) 332–0505; www.Sausalito.org. Open weekdays 9:00 A.M. to 5:00 P.M.

Tiburon Peninsula Chamber of Commerce, 96 Main Street, Tiburon 94920; (415) 435–5633; www.tiburonchamber.org.

Point Reyes and Inverness

The National Seashore / 2 Nights

☐ Natural seashore

☐ Beachcombing

☐ Bird-watching

☐ Wildflower walks

☐ Oyster farms

☐ Inns by the sea

More than a few weekends are needed to discover the many joys of the Point Reyes National Seashore, comprising 71,000 miraculous acres on the edge of the continent: two fingerlike peninsulas pointing jaggedly into the Pacific; the long, shallow biodiversity of Tomales Bay; the big curve of Drakes Bay, where the English explorer Sir Francis Drake set foot in 1579; and oyster farms, clamming beaches, tidepools, and wildlife sanctuaries.

Separated from the mainland by the San Andreas Fault, the unique location of the peninsula gives rise to several distinct habitats. More than 45 percent of the bird species in North America have been sighted here.

From February through early summer, the meadows and marine terraces of Point Reyes are blanketed with California poppies, dark blue lupine, pale baby blue eyes, Indian paintbrush, and a few varieties of wildflowers existing only here. Dominating the landscape is the green-black Douglas fir forest of Inverness Ridge, running northwest to southeast alongside the San Andreas earthquake fault. The summit of Mount Wittenberg, at 1,407 feet, is reachable in an afternoon's climb.

Subject to summer fogs and winter drizzles, Point Reyes is a favorite destination not only for those who love a sunny day at the beach but also for intrepid outdoor types who follow cool-weather nature hikes with cozy evenings by a fireplace in a vintage bed-and-breakfast inn.

Day 1 / Morning

Take U.S. Highway 101 north to the Tamalpais-Paradise Drive exit, fifteen minutes north of the Golden Gate Bridge. Exit right and take the overpass to your left over the freeway. Turn left on Redwood Avenue then right on Corte Madera Boulevard, which becomes Magnolia Avenue.

BREAKFAST: Pull up to a pasticceria straight from San Marco Square with Italian mahogany, marble inlay, and a hand-painted mural. **Emporio Rulli** (464 Magnolia Avenue, Larkspur; 415–888–88RULLI; www.rulli.com) has traditional

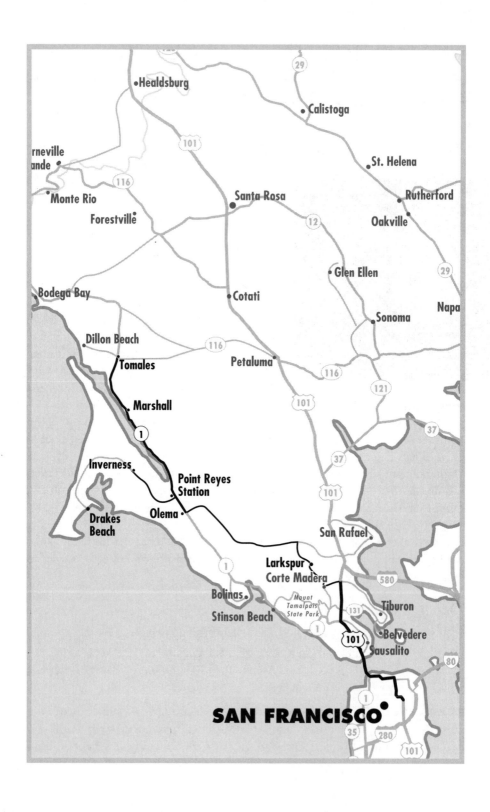

breads, pastries, hand-dipped chocolates, and more than nine house-roasted coffee blends. You can assemble an excellent picnic by choosing from the daily selection of panini (Italian sandwiches).

Continue driving north on Magnolia Avenue, then turn left onto Sir Francis Drake Boulevard. Proceed west forty-five minutes on winding, two-lane Sir Francis Drake Boulevard to the **Point Reyes National Seashore Visitor Center** at **Olema** (415–663–1092; www.nps.gov/pore).

Exhibits, guidebooks, and trail maps at the Point Reyes Visitor Center will help orient you to the many destinations within the National Seashore. According to the day's weather, you may choose beachcombing and sunbathing (or fogbathing), backpacking to overnight sites, or easy walks or bike rides on meadowland paths, or challenging hikes. The American Hiking Society has named Point Reyes one of the top-10 most family-friendly hiking areas in the country. One of the most popular of the more than 150 miles of hiking, biking, and horseback riding trails is the **Bear Valley Trail** through forest tunnels, along creeks, and through meadows, ending on a bluff 50 feet above the sea. This easy hike is about 8 miles round-trip; restrooms are located halfway.

At the end of Limantour Road, **Limantour Beach** is a long stretch of windswept sand that is good for surf fishing and sunbathing. Look for the Muddy Hollow Trail for an easy 1-mile bird-watching and wildflower walk.

Bird-watching is excellent in the 500-acre **Limantour Estero Reserve,** west of Limantour Beach. You get to **Drakes Estero,** a much larger saltwater lagoon, from Sir Francis Drake Boulevard on the west side. This rocky intertidal area is a giant tidepool and bird sanctuary, rich with such wildlife as anemones, sea stars, crabs, and even rays and leopard sharks.

LUNCH: Picnic on the beach or in a trailside meadow.

Afternoon

Energetic hikers can make the steep but short ascent on Sky Trail to the summit of Mount Wittenberg; beach bums will choose from many coastal access trails. The long sandy stretch of Point Reyes Beach is accessible in two places by car.

Short, easy walks near the visitor center include **Kule Loklo,** the Miwok Village, where an ancient Indian site has been re-created, and the **Woodpecker Trail,** a self-guided nature walk leading to the park rangers' Morgan horse ranch and a Morgan horse museum. Horses are bred and trained here on a hundred beautiful acres for the use of the National Park rangers in this park and in Zion and Hawaii Volcanoes National Parks.

The **Earthquake Trail,** less than a mile in length, is where you'll see photos of the effects of the 1906 earthquake and signs explaining earth movement.

DINNER: Station House Cafe, Main Street, Point Reyes Station; (415) 663–1515. In a historic red building on Main Street for nearly three decades; good food and fun; breakfast, lunch, and dinner in the casual dining room or on the garden patio, with live weekend entertainment and weekday free happy hour hors d'eouvres. Homemade breads, free-range poultry and meats; the harvest from an on-site organic garden and a plethora of local products go into a contemporary comfort food menu, from pot roast and duck breast with cherry sauce to lots of fresh seafood; don't miss the pecan pie.

Kick up your heels to country music at the **Western Saloon** on Main Street (415–663–1661).

LODGING: Point Reyes Seashore Lodge, 10021 Highway 1, Olema; (415) 663–9000 or (800) 404–LODGE; www.ptreyesseashorelodge.com. Just south of Point Reyes. Reminiscent of national park lodges from a century ago, a castlelike re-creation of a large Victorian inn on the exterior, modern California Craftsman–style inside, sweeping lawns above a creek and woods. Twenty-two rooms and suites with featherbeds, down comforters, bay windows, fireplaces, and Jacuzzi tubs. Breakfast is generous, with bowls of fresh fruit, yogurt, granola, pastries, and breads. A large library of guidebooks and restaurant menus is a big help. The staff will arrange bike, kayak, and horse rentals for you.

Day 2 / Morning

BREAKFAST: At the Point Reyes Seashore Lodge.

Give your hiking legs a break and spend the morning shopping and cafe lounging in the town of **Point Reyes Station.** Many one-hundred-year-old buildings remain on the main street of this narrow-gauge railroad town founded in the 1800s. The train depot is now the post office, the Fire Engine House a community center. Dairy ranches and commercial oyster companies fuel the rural economy.

Black Mountain Weavers, on Main Street (415–663–9130), is a co-op gallery of fine woven rugs, sweaters, and tapestries, plus jewelry and art. At **Susan Hayes Handwovens,** slip into luscious silk and chenille jackets and vests (80 Fourth Street; 415–663–8057). Equestrians will go into **Cabaline Saddle Shop,** on Main Street (415–663–8303), for English and western saddlery and clothing. Also on Main is **Toby's Feed Barn** (415–663–1223)—fresh flowers, plants, produce, T-shirts, body and bath items, souvenirs, and hay for your horse. In front of Toby's every Saturday, June through October, a farmers' market takes place. Vendors sell local produce and flowers, wool, poultry and meats, olive oil, preserves, and more.

Shakers Shops West is a unique resource for authentic Shaker-design furniture and furniture kits, tinware, baskets, and rag rugs (415–669–7256; www.shakershops.com). This and several other specialty stores are in the Livery Stable at Fourth and B Streets, next door to **Tomales Bay Foods,** which is owned by a graduate of the restaurant Chez Panisse, the birthplace of California cuisine. An airy emporium of luscious hot and cold take-out foods, organic produce, flowers, and homemade ice cream, the place features products from local farms, ranches, and wineries (415–663–9335). On weekends there are often wine, cheese, and seafood tastings and cooking demonstrations.

Marin County's only kite store is a great one, at Third and B Streets, **Into the Blue.** You will find dual-line, stunt, and acrobatic kites, as well as parafoils, boomerangs, and Frisbees (415–663–1147).

LUNCH: From Point Reyes drive north on Highway 1 along the shoreline of Tomales Bay 10 miles to Marshall to **Hog Island Oyster Company,** where you can bring a picnic, purchase oysters plucked fresh from their nearby beds, and eat them raw or grill them on the barbecue (20215 Highway 1; 415–663–9218). In Marshall, at a historic waterfront location, watch for the opening of a new complex of restored cottages and a restaurant at **Nick's Cove.**

Afternoon

Five miles farther north, the minitown of **Tomales** is a 2-block-long headquarters for crabbing, clamming, and surf fishing. At low tide in winter, catch a clammer's barge from here out to the flatlands around Hog Island in the bay. Hog Island and nearby Duck Island are private wildlife sanctuaries frequented by harbor seals.

Bicyclists and picnickers love to stop at the **Tomales Bakery,** Thursday through Sunday, for European-style breads and pastries, pies, amazing calzones, focaccia with exotic toppings, and croissants, all made with local ingredients by a noted chef (27000 Highway 1; 415–878–2429).

On your way back from Tomales to Point Reyes, then around to Inverness, take a walk or swim in the quiet waters of **Heart's Desire Beach** in **Tomales Bay State Park** off Sir Francis Drake Boulevard on Pierce Point Road; (415) 669–1140. Backed by a dramatic stand of first-growth Bishop pine, the wind-protected, easily accessible beach on the bay is the mildest environment in the area for swimming, sailboarding, kayaking, and clam digging. There are picnic tables, 6 miles of easy to moderate trails, and a few hike-in or bike-in campsites.

A resort village since 1889, **Inverness,** population 1,000, is a day-tripper's rest stop and a community of country cottages on steep wooded slopes at the northern end of **Inverness Ridge,** overlooking Tomales Bay. There are seafood cafes, bed-and-breakfast inns, a small marina, and not much else but eye-popping scenery.

Discovered by Spanish explorers in the 1600s, **Tomales Bay** is 13 miles long, 1 mile wide, and very shallow, with acres of mudflats and salt- and freshwater marshes. Commercial oyster farms line the western shore. More than one hundred species of resident and migrating waterbirds are the reason you'll see anorak-clad, binocular-braced bird-watchers at every pullout on Highway 1. Perch, flounder, sand dabs, and crabs are catchable by small boat.

Rent a kayak and paddle around the bay, where you will likely see bat rays, jellyfish, and ospreys and seal, among other wildlife. Rent kayaks and wet suits and get instructions at **Blue Waters Kayaking** (12938 Sir Francis Drake Boulevard, Inverness; 415–669–2600; www.bwkayak.com).

DINNER: Manka's Inverness Restaurant, 30 Calendar Way, Inverness; (415) 669–1034. A 1917 fishing lodge nestled under the pines; game and fresh fish grilled in an open fireplace, house-cured meat and poultry, homegrown produce; comfortably cozy, candlelit atmosphere; notable chefs; reservations essential. Accommodations here are in a country-luxe lodge in Adirondack style with log beds, Arts and Crafts furnishings, fireplaces, and Ralph Lauren linens; plus a rose-covered cottage.

LODGING: Ten Inverness Way, 10 Inverness Way, Inverness; (415) 669–1648; www.teninvernessway.com. Country-style inn with five rooms filled with quilts, lace curtains, comfort, and light. Common room with big stone fireplace; lovely gardens, hot tub, full breakfast; walk to hiking trails.

Day 3 / Morning

BREAKFAST: At Ten Inverness Way.

Drive north on Sir Francis Drake Boulevard to the Pierce Point Road; take a right and park in the upper parking lot at **McClure Beach.** It's a 9-mile round-trip around **Tomales Point** and along the coastline. Spring wildflowers float in the meadows; whales spout December through February. A herd of elk live in the grassy fields of **Pierce Ranch** on the tip of the peninsula. These windswept moors remind some visitors of Scotland.

McClure Beach is wide, sandy, backed by high cliffs, and dotted with rocks and great tidepools. Bluffs framed by groves of Bishop pine look like Japanese woodcut prints; these pines are found only in a few isolated locations on the California coast.

Point Reyes Lighthouse, at the end of Sir Francis Drake Boulevard, 15 miles south of Inverness, is reachable by 400 steps leading downhill from a high bluff. Many shipwrecks occurred off the **Point Reyes Headlands** until the lighthouse was built in 1870. Below the dramatic cliffs are miles of beaches accessible from Sir Francis Drake Boulevard. Exposed to the full force of storms and pounding surf, these beaches are unsafe for swimming or surfing. The headlands, tidepools, sea stacks, lagoons, wave-carved caves, and rocky promontories are alive with birds— endangered brown pelicans, cormorants, surf skooters, sandpipers, grebes, terns— and sea life such as giant anemones and sea palms, urchins, fish, and even the occasional great white shark offshore of Tomales Point.

From Sir Francis Drake Boulevard near the lighthouse, take the turnoff to Chimney Rock to the most spectacular wildflower walk in the park, an easy, 1.5-mile route.

At the 7-mile-long crescent of **Drakes Beach** are a visitor center and picnic tables. During whale-watching season, December through spring, a shuttle bus may be operating between the lighthouse and the beach. Some 20,000 California gray whales travel the Pacific coastline going south to breed in Mexican waters and then return with their calves to the Arctic.

LUNCH: Barnaby's by the Bay, 12938 Sir Francis Drake Boulevard, 1 mile north of Inverness at the Golden Hind Inn; (415) 669–1114. Two decks overlooking a marina; fresh fish, salads, barbecued oysters and chicken, and ribs from the applewood smoker; jazz on weekends; you'll be tempted to stay here for the rest of the day.

Head back to the Bay Area.

There's More

Bolinas. Just north of Stinson Beach off Highway 1, Olema–Bolinas Road; (415) 499–6387. A rustic nineteenth-century village near beautiful **Bolinas Lagoon,** where salt marsh, mudflats, and calm sea waters harbor thousands of birds and ducks, and a mile of shallow tidepools (415–868–9244; www.egret.org). Agate Beach is a small county park. Four miles northwest of Bolinas on Mesa Road, a short nature trail leads to the **Point Reyes Bird Observatory,** where you can observe bird banding (415–868–1221). This is the Palomarin Trailhead which leads to four freshwater lakes and to Double Point Bay; 3 miles from the trailhead, watch for Bass Lake, a secret swimming spot. Have breakfast, lunch, and yummy snacks at the **Bolinas Bay Bakery and Cafe,** 20 Wharf Road, Bolinas (415–868–0211); organic-ingredient pastries, breads and pies, pizza, soups, sandwiches. Stop in at the tiny **Bolinas Museum** (48–50 Wharf Road; 415–868–0330) and prowl the interesting old cemetery off Olema-Bolinas Road.

Five Brooks Ranch, 3 miles south of Olema; (415) 663–1570; www.fivebrooks .com. Guided horseback rides, from a one-hour slow trail ride to longer treks up the Inverness ridge, and incredible beach rides.

Wildlife Watching. Jutting 10 miles into the Pacific, the Point Reyes Peninsula makes for prime whale-watching, December through April, when more than 30,000 gray whales pass by. Best viewing spots: around Chimney Rock and the lighthouse. In winter you can see some of 1,000 elephant seals—9 to 16 feet long and up to 5,000 pounds—and their new pups from the lighthouse parking lot, by the lifeboat station, and at a viewing area a quarter-mile walk from the Chimney Rock parking lot.

Special Events

July. Coastal Native American Summer Big Time, Point Reyes National Seashore; (415) 663–1092. Demonstrations of crafts, skills, music, dancing.

Other Recommended Restaurants and Lodgings

Inverness

Blackthorne Inn, 266 Vallejo; (415) 663–8621. Five charming rooms in a wooded canyon, a treehouse with decks, hot tub, fireman's pole, spiral staircase, and glass-sided "eagle's nest." Includes buffet breakfast.

Dancing Coyote Beach bed-and-breakfast, P.O. Box 98, Inverness 94937; (415) 669–7200. Four Southwest-style cottages with decks, views, fireplaces, kitchens.

Golden Hind Inn, 12938 Sir Francis Drake Boulevard; (415) 669–1389. A fresh-looking, white-painted, unassuming motel on Tomales Bay, with a small pool and fishing pier. Two-room suites have queen beds and sofabeds, microwaves, refrigerators, and fireplaces. Suite 5 has a king bed, sofabed, kitchen, and dining area. Next to Barnaby's by the Bay and Blue Waters Kayaking.

Sandy Cove Inn, 12990 Sir Francis Drake Boulevard; (415) 669–2683. Three suites with fireplaces, sitting areas with garden views, hammocks, path to a cove on Tomales Bay, full breakfast.

Olema

Olema Farm House Restaurant. 10005 Highway 1; (415) 663–1264. Once an 1845 stagecoach stop, a farmhouse decked out with antique bottles, Elvis memorabilia, and fun collectibles. The heated garden patio is the place to be. Fish-and-chips, clam chowder, meat loaf, prime rib, roast chicken, oyster stew, Philly cheese steak; lunch and dinner, with breakfast on weekends.

Olema Ranch Campground, 0.25 mile north of Highway 1 and Sir Francis Drake Boulevard, 10155 Highway 1; (415) 663–8001 or (800) 655–2267; www.camp grounds.com/olemaranch. RV facilities, tent sites, forest and meadow setting, gas, store. Campfires allowed.

Point Reyes Station

Bovine Bakery, Highway 1; (415) 663–9420. Lines may be out the door for fresh artisan breads, pastries, muffins, and scones.

Holly Tree Inn and Cottages, 3 Silverhills Road; (415) 663–1554. On nineteen acres of lawns, gardens, and wooded hillsides; French provincial decor, antiques, fireplaces; French doors open to the meadows. Four guest rooms. Cottages have hot tubs and fireplaces.

Taqueria La Quinta, Third Street and Highway 1; (415) 663–8868. In a very casual setting, fresh Mexican food (made without lard), homemade tortillas, fruit smoothies.

Thirty-nine Cypress, 39 Cypress Road; (415) 663–1709. With wonderful views of the Point Reyes Peninsula, a redwood country inn with four guest rooms. Private patio, hot tub, antiques, fireplace; breakfast with stay.

For More Information

Coastal Traveler; www.coastaltraveler.com. Information and Web pages for artisans, lodgings and restaurants, events and town histories.

Inns of Point Reyes, P.O. Box 145, Iverness 94956; (415) 485–2649. Referral service for several inns.

Point Reyes Lodging Association, P.O. Box 878, Point Reyes 94956; (415) 663–1872 or (800) 539–1872; www.ptreyes.com. Inns, small hotels, cottages.

West Marin Chamber of Commerce, P.O. Box 1045, Point Reyes Station 94956; (415) 663–9232; www.pointreyes.org.

SOUTHBOUND
ESCAPES

SOUTHBOUND ESCAPE ONE

Santa Cruz

A California Beach Town / 1 Night

The resort town of Santa Cruz is famous for more than 20 miles of wide, sandy, warm-water beaches and an old-fashioned waterfront boardwalk with rides and concessions. Here at the top end of Monterey Bay, the climate is mild, surf's up every month of the year, and the attitude is young and healthy, due to a large population of university students and residents who love outdoor recreation.

☐ Beaches

☐ Bikes

☐ Butterflies

☐ The Boardwalk

☐ Wineries

☐ Redwoods

☐ Shopping

The town has many fanciful homes in a variety of architectural styles, such as Queen Anne, Gothic Revival, Mission Revival, and California bungalow. Pacific Avenue, the main street, is a tree-shaded boulevard with outdoor cafes and dozens of shops. The University of California at Santa Cruz and Cabrillo College are located here, and the community is culturally oriented, with a large contingent of artists and musicians in residence and a lively annual schedule of arts events and music festivals.

Even if you are not a beach person, there is much in the way of outdoor recreation and sightseeing to enjoy, and not just in summer. Near the city of Santa Cruz and in the **Santa Cruz Mountains** are country roads that meander through ancient redwood groves and along the banks of the San Lorenzo and Santa Cruz Rivers. Walking and biking trails and campgrounds are liberally scattered throughout the region.

Day 1 / Morning

Drive south from San Francisco on Interstate 280, south on Highway 85 to Highway 17 to **Santa Cruz,** about a ninety-minute drive, unless it's late Friday afternoon, when it will be a longer trip. As an alternative to the Bay Area's congested highways, the coast route, Highway 1, is longer but far more scenic.

Get right to the ocean views on West Cliff Drive at **Mark Abbott Memorial Lighthouse,** at Lighthouse Point Park overlooking Monterey Bay and the city. Walkers, bikers, joggers, and passengers in baby strollers love the city, sea, and sea-lion views. Go into the lighthouse to see a small surfing museum (831–420–6289); it's free.

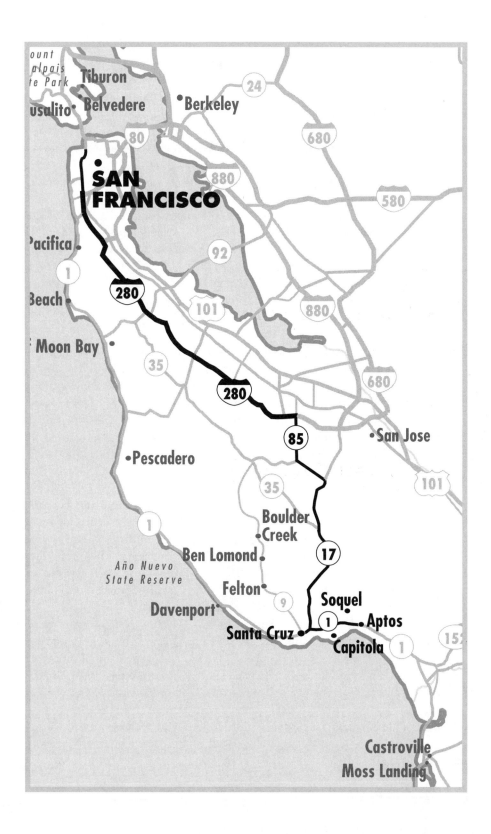

Almost every day there are surfers in "Steamers Lane" below. In May the **Longboard Invitational** is held here, and hundreds of surfers from all over the world compete (831–684–1551). The major surf competition, the **O'Neill Coldwater Classic,** is held in the fall (831–479–5648). **Club Ed** at **Cowell Beach** is the place for lessons and board rentals (831–464–0177). **Richard Schmidt School of Surfing,** at 849 Almar Avenue, is also well regarded (831–423–0928; www.richardschmidt.com).

Twin Lakes State Beach below East Cliff Drive is where the sailboarders go. There are fire rings here, outdoor showers, and, nearby, wild-bird sanctuaries at **Schwan Lake** (831–429–2850). Prowl around (watching out for poison oak) to see Virginia rail, chickadees, swallows, and belted kingfishers, among dozens more species of birds and waterfowl. You can kayak and canoe on the lake.

The main Santa Cruz beach at the boardwalk and the pier, **Cowell Beach** (831–420–6014) is the most popular piece of sand on the central coastline for sunning, swimming, and volleyball. The relatively tame waves here are perfect for beginning surfers.

Proceed on West Cliff Drive to Pacific Avenue and downtown Santa Cruz with 2 blocks of boutiques, sidewalk cafes, coffeehouses, and galleries—more than 200 stores in all. In this artists' town, notice the many sidewalk sculptures, and watch for building-size murals on side streets. The tree-lined, flower-bedecked boulevard is loved by the browser. Book lovers make a beeline to the restored St. George Hotel building at Pacific and Front to **Bookshop Santa Cruz** (831–423–0900), one of the largest independent bookstores in northern California. Scattered throughout are benches, stools, and armchairs, comfortable spots to peruse the books and the huge variety of international magazines and newspapers. There is a cafe in the store, and they serve fresh organic salads, sandwiches, pastas, and chocolate (831–427–9900).

At the corner of Pacific and Cooper, **Pacific Wave** is headquarters for surfboards, skateboards, and all the cool accessories and clothing to go with them (831–458–9283). At **Pacific Edge Indoor Climbing Facility,** try the newest California craze. With the use of safety harnesses, the climbing wall is safe and fun, and you can cool off at the juice bar (104 Bronson; 831–454–9254). River and sea kayaking for all ability levels are also offered by **Adventure Sports** (303 Potrero #15, in the Old Sash Mill; 831–458–3648; www.asudoit.com).

Shen's Gallery (2404 Mission Street; 831–457–4422) is seductive with exotic scents, flute sounds, and Asian antiques and art. It has a large collection of one-of-a-kind tiny ceramic teapots from mainland China, "shard" boxes, and beautiful tea chests. Look for fine, locally produced crafts and art at **Annieglass** (110 Cooper Street; 831–427–4260)—one of the largest showplaces of blown glass and art glass in the state.

In the oldest building downtown, circa 1850, **LuLu Carpenter's Cafe** has divine pies, salads and sandwiches, home-baked muffins and scones; Wi-Fi; and a nice courtyard (1545 Pacific; 831–429–9804).

Historic buildings line the Pacific Garden Mall shopping district of Santa Cruz.

The **Santa Cruz Art League,** nearby at 526 Broadway (831–426–5787), has three galleries and a shop selling fine arts and crafts.

The **Museum of Art and History at the McPherson Center** is a cultural ghetto, encompassing the Art Museum and the History Museum of Santa Cruz County and shops (705 Front Street; 831–429–1964).

LUNCH: **Gabriella's** is a romantic, cozy, much-heralded bistro for lunch and dinner (910 Cedar Street, parallels Pacific on the west side; 831–457–1677; www .gabriellacafe.com). In the mood for something spicy? Popular for two decades, **El Palomar** serves fabulous Mexican food and top-notch margaritas in a stunning dining environment—ask for a booth (1336 Pacific; 831–425–7575).

Afternoon

Proceed to the foot of Beach Street for a beach ramble, or go to the **Santa Cruz Beach Boardwalk,** the only beachside amusement park on the West Coast, to indulge in some of the twenty-five rides, the old-time arcade, the shops, and restaurants (831–423–5590; www.beachboardwalk.com). The classic 1911 carousel and the Giant Dipper roller coaster are National Historic Landmarks. At Neptune's Kingdom, an indoor miniature golf course, volcanos erupt, pirates threaten, cannons fire. If you hear screaming, it's probably coming from the roller coaster, the Hurricane, guaranteed to make you forget your name. Five rides are located at a new area called Riverwalk: the Cave Train, a spooky prehistoric journey; the Pepsi Convoy, Tornado thrill ride, the Sea Serpent family roller coaster, and Space Race bumper cars. Get rid of your spare cash in the Casino Arcade, or just sit on the boardwalk and watch the bikinis and the sailboats glide by. Don't miss **Marini's Candies,** since 1915 on the wharf, for salt water taffy, fresh caramel corn, candy apples, and handmade chocolates and fudge (866–MARINIS; www.mariniscandies .com); two stores on the boardwalk, one on the wharf, and one downtown in the Pacific Mall.

Within sight of the boardwalk, **Santa Cruz Municipal Wharf** (831–420–6025) is all about fishing off the pier, shopping in tourist traps, browsing the fresh-fish markets, eating chowder and shrimp cocktail in waterside cafes, and watching the sea lions, the pelicans, and the passing boats. Deep-sea fishing trips and bay cruises depart from the harbor.

On the south side of Santa Cruz, **Santa Cruz Yacht Harbor** (831–475–6161) and its beach are where the locals go to escape the tourists. You can kayak and sail and have a sandwich or a seafood plate at the **Crow's Nest** (2218 East Cliff Drive; 831–476–4560; www.crowsnest-santacruz.com). The casual, multilevel restaurant has a heated, glassed-in deck overlooking the busy harbor; locals crowd the bar at night.

Drive south 4 miles from the Santa Cruz Wharf on East Cliff Drive to **Capitola Village** (or take the quicker, less-winding route, Highway 1). An oceanside resort since 1861, Capitola remains a quaint artists' colony. Swimmers, waders, and sunbathers flock to **Capitola Beach,** sheltered by two high cliffs. A riparian shelter for birds and ducks, Soquel Creek meanders right through town into the sea. Restaurants with outdoor patios are lined up at beachfront on the Esplanade, and there are a few blocks of boutiques, art galleries, and beachwear shops. Check out the charming **Capitola Museum** in a little red house (831–464–0322). Rent a kayak for a paddle around the quiet cove (831–462–2208), amble along the river trail, or take a blufftop walk on Grand Avenue at sunset.

DINNER: **Shadowbrook Restaurant,** 1750 Wharf Road, Capitola; (831) 475–1511; www.shadowbrook-capitola.com. Since 1947, likely the most famous and prettiest restaurant in the area. On the banks of Soquel Creek, Shadowbrook is reached by a self-operated cable car down a flower-bedecked hillside or by a winding pathway. In a warren of cozy dining nooks and rooms, most with garden views; signature dishes such as artichoke soup, Dungeness crab–stuffed portobello mushrooms, grilled salmon, slow-roasted prime rib, and lots of fresh seafood; five-course tasting menu, kids' menu, nice bar. Ask about Winemaker Wednesday; Sunday brunch, too.

LODGING: Inn at Depot Hill, 250 Monterey Avenue, Capitola; (831) 462–3376; www.innatdepothill.com. Eight suits with fireplaces, featherbeds, marble bathrooms, private garden patios, hot tubs, European traditional furnishings, and antiques. Award-winning luxury and service. Wonderful breakfasts; walking distance to Capitola Beach.

Day 2 / Morning

BREAKFAST: Zelda's, #203 on the Esplanade at the beach Capitola; (831) 475–4900. Sit by the window or on the deck while the early morning sea turns from rosy to silver-blue as it laps Capitola's scruffy old fishing pier. Home-fry scramble, blackened snapper with eggs. Zelda's is a fun hangout any time of day. Live jazz on the weekends.

Capitola Beach and most public beaches in the area are cleaned nightly; even in summer they start out trash-free and pearly white every day.

The shops and galleries near the beach are touristy but fun. **Dragginwood** (216 Capitola Avenue; 831–475–0915) sells crystals and magical chotchkes. **Capitola Dreams** (118 Stockton Avenue; 831–476–5379) has an eye-popping collection of bikinis and wild beachwear. Painted wood gewgaws and jewelry from Thailand are featured at **Oceania** (204 Capitola Avenue; 831–476–6644). For a hundred stores in an indoor mall, go up the hill to the **Capitola Mall** on Forty-first Avenue (831–476–9749).

Dead on your feet? Retreat to **Country Court Tea Room**, where for nearly three decades, tea and light meals and snacks have been served in a 150-year-old carriage house. The feminine, airy garden setting is as sweet as can be. Prix fixe dinners are now available on Friday and high tea on the last Sunday of each month (911 Capitola Avenue; 831–462–2498).

Newly reopened after a grand renovation, **Margaritaville** in the Esplanade is a lively locals gathering place for drinks, good Mexican food, and live weekend entertainment (831–476–2263). Look for the mermaid over the door, and sit on the heated patio above the bay.

On the south end of town, at **New Brighton Beach** (831–464–6330) there is a nice campground, where cypress and pines provide a sense of privacy between campsites.

The next beach south of New Brighton, **Seacliff State Beach** at **Del Mar** has almost 2 miles of shoreline backed by steep sandstone cliffs. A 500-foot wooden pier and the wreck of a concrete ship are roosting spots for birds, and you can fish off the pier. There is a campground and a small visitor center where you can sign up for walking tours to see the fossilized remains of multimillion-year-old sea creatures lodged in the cliffsides (831–685–6442). The paved path here is popular for strollers, wheelchairs, and in-line skates.

Just south of Capitola at **Aptos, Rio Del Mar Beach** is a wide stretch of sand with a jetty and lifeguards. Shopping and restaurants are within walking distance (831–685–6500).

On the north side of Highway 1, just south of Capitola, the village of Aptos is where you'll find **Village Fair Antiques,** behind the Bay View Hotel on Soquel Road (831–688–9883). This is a big antiques collection in a huge old barn, a place for losing track of time. The next village north, **Soquel** is a one-horse town with more than twenty antiques shops on Soquel Drive.

LUNCH: **Cafe Sparrow,** 8040 Soquel Drive, Aptos; (831) 688–6238; www.cafe sparrow.com. Across the street from the Bay View Hotel is this charming dining room serving chicken and fresh fish entrees plus seasonal specialties.

Afternoon

A cool, green place to take a walk in the highlands near Santa Cruz is the **Forest of Nisene Marks State Park,** a densely forested 10,000-acre wilderness on Aptos Creek (831–763–7063). Popular with runners, bikers, horseback riders, hikers, and picnickers, the park ranges in elevation from 100 to 2,600 feet. Unpaved roads and trails lead to evergreen woods and creekside willows and ferns. Walk-in camping is permitted, as are horseback riding and steelhead fishing in certain areas.

Near the entrance to the park, **Mangels House** bed-and-breakfast is in a wedding cake–white, circa 1880 mansion, with six rooms (831–688–7982).

A beautiful beach that makes a nice stop on the way home from Santa Cruz is **Natural Bridges State Beach,** whose entrance is at 2531 West Cliff Drive at the intersection of West Cliff Drive and Swanton Boulevard (831–423–4609). Named for dramatic sandstone arches, Natural Bridges has tidepools rich with sea life; guided tidepool tours are often conducted. A short boardwalk from the beach parking lot leads through a eucalyptus forest to the **California Monarch Butterfly Preserve.** Depending on the time of year—early October through February—you'll see hundreds of thousands of butterflies hanging in the trees and moving about in great golden clouds. A 0.75-mile self-guided nature walk begins at the Monarch Trail and heads for Secret Lagoon, where blue herons, mallard ducks, and more freshwater and seagoing birds live.

Seymour Marine Discovery Center, at Long Marine Lab, a University of Santa Cruz research facility near Natural Bridges, is at 100 Shafer Road (831–459–3800). On a bluff with spectacular ocean views, the facility focuses on marine research and shows how scientists study, care for, and explore ocean life. Features include interactive exhibits, aquariums, touch tanks, an 85-foot blue whale skeleton, and more, plus a gift shop and bookstore.

If you have time to spare on your way back to San Francisco, dawdle in the Santa Cruz Mountains among ancient redwood groves, on sunny riverbanks, and in quiet little resort towns affording peaceful getaway days. Discover rustic boutique wineries, known for their dark Pinots and German varietals. Take a ride on a rollicking steam train, chugging up into redwood country or all the way down to the beach (more on the mountains follows).

Retrace your route back to San Francisco.

There's More

Big Basin Redwoods State Park, off Highway 236 near Boulder Creek in the Santa Cruz Mountains; (831) 338–8860. Thousand-year-old redwoods, fern canyons, waterfalls, 80 miles of skyline-to-sea trails. The Sea Trail drops from mountain ridges to Waddell State Beach through dense woodlands, along Waddell and Berry Creeks; 11 miles one-way. Bike, horse rentals; campground, store.

Boating. Chardonnay Sailing Charters, at the harbor, Santa Cruz; (831) 423–1213; www.chardonnay.com. Whale-watching, ecology, and brunch cruises; and sunset sails.

Pacific Yachting, 790 Mariner Park Way, Santa Cruz; (831) 423–7245. Day tours.

Felton Covered Bridge, on Highway 9 near Highway 236. Built in 1892, this is the tallest bridge of its kind in the country and one of the few left in the state.

Golf. Aptos Seascape Golf Course, 610 Clubhouse Drive, Aptos; (831) 688–3213. Eighteen holes by the sea.

Boulder Creek Golf and Country Club, 16901 Big Basin Highway, Boulder Creek; (831) 338–2111. Eighteen beautiful holes in the redwoods; restaurant, tennis.

DeLaveaga Golf Course, 401 Upper Park Road at DeLaveaga Drive, Santa Cruz; (831) 423–7212. Eighteen holes.

Pasatiempo Golf Club, 20 Clubhouse Road, off Highway 17 near Santa Cruz; (831) 459–9169; www.pasatiempo.com. One of the top one hundred courses in the United States. Top-notch restaurant. Adjacent to the course, the Inn at Pasatiempo has very nice rooms (800–834–2546; www.innatpasatiempo.com).

Henry Cowell Redwoods State Park, 101 North Big Trees Park Road, Felton; (831) 335–4598. Eighteen hundred acres of stream canyons, meadows, forests, and chaparral-covered ridges along the meandering San Lorenzo River and Eagle Creek. Short, easy trails, such as **Redwood Grove Nature Trail** to the **Big Trees Grove,** offer a rare opportunity to see first-growth redwoods. The redwood-dotted campground in the park has more than a hundred tent and RV sites, for vehicles up to 24 feet, with no hookups (800–444–7275).

Quail Hollow Ranch County Park, near Ben Lomond off Graham Hill Road; take East Zayante Road 1.9 miles; (831) 454–7900. A meadowy historic site where easy trails lead to the original ranch house, a pond inhabited by bass and bluegill, a shady picnic area, and a dwarf redwood forest.

Roaring Camp and Big Trees, just south of Felton on Graham Hill Road in the Santa Cruz Mountains; (831) 335–4484; www.roaringcamp.com. A re-creation of an 1880s logging town, complete with covered bridge, general store, and a wonderful narrow-gauge steam train that you can ride up through forests of giant redwoods to the summit of Bear Mountain on the steepest railroad grade in North America. A second route runs along the San Lorenzo River down to Santa Cruz Beach. A chuck-wagon barbecue serves charcoal-broiled steak and chicken burgers in a forest glade.

Wilder Ranch State Park, 1401 Coast Road, 2 miles north of Santa Cruz; (831) 426–0505. A 6,000-acre dairy ranch since the 1800s is now a leafy park. Picnic in the apple orchard; see historic displays in the Victorian home and take a guided walk on weekends; or hike, horseback ride, or bike on your own on miles of trails. From here you can connect to the newly donated Gray Whale Ranch. Just north of the ranch, Four Mile Beach is reachable by a hike down a bluff—a nice spot to lie on the sand.

Wineries in the Santa Cruz Mountains. Bonny Doon Vineyard, 10 Pine Flat Road, 3 miles northeast of Highway 1 and Davenport via Bonny Doon Road; (831) 425–4518. The winemaker has made his wines famous with crazy labels like Clos de Gilroy, Le Cigare Volant, Big House Red, and Old Telegram. Hang out in the redwood grove on Soquel Creek and try his European "ice wines," produced in just a handful of American wineries.

Byington Winery and Vineyard is on Bear Creek Road, with dizzying views of Monterey Bay from the picnic grounds (408–354–1111).

David Bruce Winery, Bear Creek Road east of Boulder Creek; (408) 354–4214. A gold-medal maker of Pinot Noir and Chardonnay. Open for tasting on the weekends, by appointment during the week.

Hallcrest Vineyards, 379 Felton-Empire Road; (831) 335–4441. Specializing in organic Gewürztraminers, Rieslings, and grape juices. From the sunny garden deck behind the old cottage, look out over old vines while tasting a lush Pinot Noir.

Special Events

February. Migration Festival, Natural Bridges State Beach, Santa Cruz; (831) 423–4609. The monarchs are celebrated at the largest butterfly colony in the west.

March. Jazz on the Wharf, Municipal Wharf, Santa Cruz; (831) 420–5273; www.santacruzwharf.com.

Kayak Surf Festival, Steamer Lane, Santa Cruz; (831) 458–3648; www.asudoit.com. Hundreds of kayak surfers from all over the world compete at the national championships; free kayak clinics.

April. Wineries Passport Program, Santa Cruz County; (831) 479–9463. Open house at wineries, meet winemakers, tours, special tastings, music, food.

May. Art and Wine Festival, Boulder Creek; (831) 338–7099.

Civil War Battles and Encampment, Roaring Camp; (831) 335–4484. Reenactment of Civil War battles and camp life; the largest encampment in the United States.

Longboard Invitational, Steamers Lane, Santa Cruz; (831) 684–1551. Hundreds of surfers compete. Watch from Cliff Drive.

June. Art on the Wharf, Santa Cruz Municipal Wharf; (831) 420–5273. Art show and live jazz.

July. Summertime Free Concerts, Santa Cruz Boardwalk; (831) 423–5590. Free Friday night concerts, hits of the '60s, '70s, and '80s.

August. Cabrillo Music Festival, held at various locations on the Cabrillo College campus; (831) 426–6966. An internationally acclaimed two-week musical extravaganza.

September. National Begonia Festival, Capitola; (831–476–3566). Residents vie for awards for their spectacular waterborne floats that are maneuvered perilously down Soquel Creek into town; you've never seen a watery parade like this one.

December. Lighted Boat Parade, Santa Cruz Yacht Harbor; (831) 457–6161.

Other Recommended Restaurants and Lodgings

Aptos

Seascape Resort, 1 Seascape Resort Drive off San Andreas, south of Santa Cruz; (800) 929–7727; www.seascaperesort.com. On a bluff overlooking miles of beach, upscale, comfortable studio, and condos for up to eight people, with balconies or patios, sofa sleepers, fully equipped kitchens, fireplaces, ocean views. This is a full-service resort with a nice sea-view restaurant, supervised activities for kids, golf packages, and extras like in-suite massage, "Beach Fires to Go"—you are driven down to the beach, where a fire is built for you, "s'mores" are provided, and you are picked up later, after a romantic evening on the beach. The resort offers access to an adjacent golf course and sports club with lighted tennis courts, an Olympic-size pool, and fitness center.

Capitola

Capitola Venetian Hotel, 1500 Wharf Road; (800) 332–2780; www.capitolavenetian .com. On the beach, a 1920s Mediterranean pink stucco motel, unassuming eclectic/eccentric decor, kitchens. Reasonable rates for families and groups.

Gayle's Bakery and Rosticceria, 504 Bay Avenue, on the corner of Bay and Capitola Avenues; (831) 462–1127. Homemade pasta, salad, pizza, sandwiches, spit-roasted meats. The bakery is famous for pies, cheesecake, breads, and pastries.

Monarch Cove Inn, 620 El Salto Drive; (831) 464–1295. In a luxurious garden overlooking Monterey Bay, beautifully furnished Victorian guest rooms, cottages, and apartments. Continental breakfast.

Paradise Beach Grille, 215 Esplanade; (831) 476–4900. A casual cafe with a juke-box and charcoal grill. The menu, printed every day, includes a huge variety of fresh seafood.

Santa Cruz

Babbling Brook Inn, 1025 Laurel Street; (831) 458–9166. Country French bed-and-breakfast inn, lovely gardens, full breakfast. Ask for a room near the creek.

Beach Street Cafe, on the corner of Beach and Cliff Streets across from the board-walk; (831) 476–0636. The walls are literally covered with prints by Maxwell Parrish, a famous pre–Art Deco artist. Bistro food, espresso.

Casablanca, 101 Main Street; (831) 426–9063. Overlooking beach and boardwalk, elegant, candlelit, fresh seafood, notable wine list, wine-tasting dinners. Some of the very nice thirty-three ocean-view rooms here have fireplaces, kitchens, balconies, or terraces.

Chaminade at Santa Cruz, 1 Chaminade Lane; (800) 283–6569; www.chaminade .com. An executive retreat, resort, and a restaurant in a eucalyptus forest on a hill overlooking Monterey Bay on the south side of Santa Cruz. Fitness center, new full-service spa, lighted tennis courts, pool. Suites are often available, and this is a good place for families to stay. Sunday brunch here is legendary.

Soif, 105 Walnut Avenue; (831) 423–2020, www.soifwine.com. A trendy new wine and tapas bar and wine merchant, with wine flights each evening and fifty wines by the glass. Small plates of sophisticated, contemporary, and traditional Spanish-, Italian-, and Asian-inspired appetizers for snacks or light meals. Special weekend tastings and live music. Open late on weekends.

Villa Vista, 2-2800 East Cliff Drive; (408) 866–2626; www.villavista.com. Two per-fectly wonderful condo units with living rooms, each with three master bedrooms with baths, gourmet kitchen, sea-view patio, home entertainment center, and laun-dry facilities. Great for several couples or a large family.

Zachary's, 849 Pacific Avenue; (831) 427–0646. Voted "Best Breakfast in Santa Cruz"; sourdough pancakes, scones, corn bread, and more. Breakfast, lunch, brunch.

For More Information

Santa Cruz Mountains Winegrowers, 7605 Old Dominion Court, Suite A, Santa Cruz 95063; (831) 479–WINE. Free brochure and map describing nineteen wineries.

Santa Cruz Visitor Information Center, 3 blocks from Highways 1 and 17; 1211 Ocean Street, Santa Cruz 95060; (831) 425–1234 or (800) 833–3494; www.santa cruzca.org.

SOUTHBOUND ESCAPE TWO

Half Moon Bay

Harbor Lights, Tidepool Treasure / 2 Nights

The small Victorian town of Half Moon Bay and the beaches and harbors nearby hold several days' worth of discoveries. Accessibility to the San Francisco Bay Area, good weather, sea air, and the outdoor fun to be had here are what create bumper-to-bumper traffic at times on summer weekends. Weekdays and off-season are the times to come, although you can get pleasantly lost and alone in the redwoods or on the beach any day of the year.

☐ Beaches, bikes, hikes, fishing

☐ Wellness retreat

☐ Art and antiques

☐ Flower marts, veggie farms

Besides commercial ocean fishing, the important endeavor in Half Moon Bay is flower and vegetable growing. The annual Pumpkin and Art Festival and Great Pumpkin Parade in October draw hundreds of thousands of revelers and their children.

Within huge greenhouses and in the fields around them, flowers are grown for shipment all over the world, and you can buy plants and flowers—and Christmas trees—at several places along the highways.

A stroll through the town of Half Moon Bay turns up Western saloons, country stores, fancy boutiques, galleries, and hundred-year-old hotels and homes, many on the National Register of Historic Places.

At the north end of the big curve of the bay, Pillar Point Harbor is a good place to escape the tourist mania. You can watch fishing boats and yachts go in and out of the marina, fish for flounder and rockfish from the wharf, or go shelling on the little beach west of the jetty. South along the coast, within an hour of Half Moon Bay, beaches, nature preserves, and two tiny old villages await the visitor.

Day 1 / Morning

Drive south from San Francisco on Highway 1, along the Pacific Coast through Pacifica to **Moss Beach,** an hour's drive. This estimated time does not account for heavy weekend and holiday traffic.

The **Fitzgerald Marine Reserve** in Moss Beach (650–728–3584) is a good place to stretch your legs. A walking trail loops through meadows and along a bluff above some of the richest tidepools on the Pacific Coast. At low tide, a kaleidoscope of sponges, sea anemones, starfish, crabs, mollusks, and fish emerges. With a

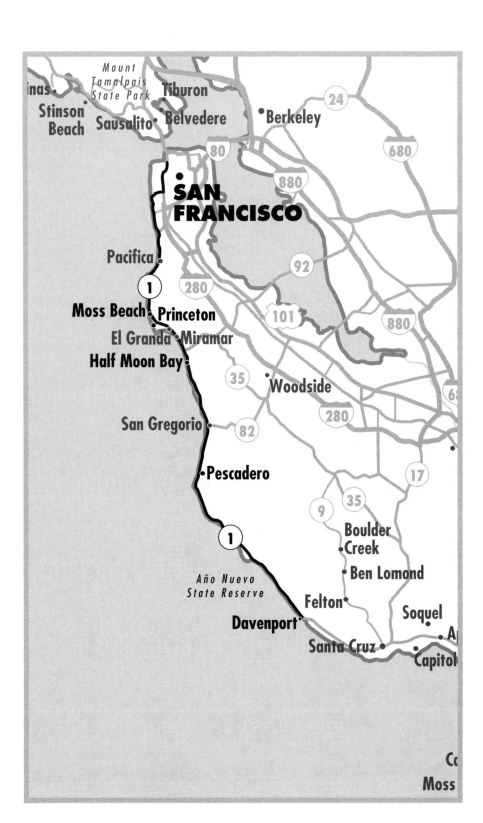

special fishing license, you can take abalone and some rockfish. For the best tide-pooling, call ahead to find out when the low tides are scheduled.

The best place to stay in Moss Beach is the **Seal Cove Inn,** a big yellow mansion in an English garden on the edge of the Marine Reserve (650–728–4114). The inn is a classic, with spacious, luxurious public rooms and guest rooms, all with garden views, wood-burning fireplaces, and traditional furnishings.

Drive south to **Pillar Point Harbor** at Princeton-by-the-Sea, a picturesque harbor busy with a fleet of more than 200 fishing boats and yachts. Here you can walk on trails to beaches and marshlands on both the north and south sides of the harbor. Pillar Point Marsh is a favorite bird-watching site. Due to the confluence of both fresh- and saltwater, and a protected environment, nearly 20 percent of all North American bird species have been sighted here.

From December through April, whale-watching boats depart from the wharf. You are almost guaranteed to see California gray whales on their 4,000-mile migration from the Arctic to Baja. **Captain John's** (800–391–8787) and **Huck Finn Sportfishing** (800–572–2934) are charter companies based at the harbor that offer regular whale-watching and fishing expeditions.

Just south of the harbor, Surfer's Beach is popular not only for surfing but for ocean kayaking, boogieboarding, sailboarding, and jet skiing. Surfers from around the world come to Maverick's off Pillar Point, where 30-foot waves breaking over a rocky reef up the ante; some say these are the biggest waves in the world. For the daily surf report, call or stop in at the **Cowboy Surf Shop** (2830 Cabrillo Highway; 650–726–0654).

Two fish markets at the harbor sell a huge variety of fresh, locally caught seafood, and there are several small cafes and bars frequented by locals who wouldn't be caught dead in the trendy downtown establishments of nearby Half Moon Bay.

LUNCH: Half Moon Bay Brewing Company, 390 Capistrano Road, Princeton By-the-Sea; (650) 728–2739, www.hmbbrewingco.com. Weekenders and locals congregate under the outdoor heaters around the fire pits and at the horseshoe bar inside to sip Mavericks Amber Ale and nutty Pillar Point Pale Ale, which are brewed on-site (call ahead for a brewery tour). Live jazz and blues bands kick off lively Friday and Saturday evenings. Top-notch fish-and-chips, chowders, an extensive seafood menu, and hearty pub food.

Afternoon

Save at least a half day for browsing Main Street in Half Moon Bay, a few blocks of buildings built early in the twentieth century that are now inhabited by upscale, country-chic shops, cafes, and galleries. Armed with a walking tour map (available at the Visitors Bureau kiosk at Main and Kelly), history buffs look for the oldest house in town—a plain and sturdy, blue and white bed-and-breakfast inn at 324 Main Street. The Zaballa House was built in 1859 by Estanislao Zaballa, prosperous owner of a large Spanish land grant, a general store, and a saloon. Around the corner at 615 Mill Street in an expanded 1900-era cottage, claw-foot tubs, featherbeds, and Victorian-era antiques are among the fancy trappings of the Mill Rose Inn. Another turn-of-the-twentieth-century landmark, the San Benito House at 356 Main Street is an antiques-filled restaurant and inn where a collection of early coastside paintings and photographs lines the walls.

At 604 Main Street, in a terra-cotta–colored enclave called **La Piazza,** are several shops and a popular bakery that serves coffee drinks and pastries in a streetside cafe (**Moonside Bakery;** 650–726–9070).

Quail Run (412 Main; 650–726–0312) is a nature-oriented emporium with elaborate bird mansions for the feathered few and butterfly gardens for kids; and the **Coastal Gallery** (424 Main in a garden alley; 650–726–3859), has rooms full of prints, oil paintings, and watercolors by regional artists. **Cedanna** is a gallery store loaded with avant-garde artisans' inventions such as iron furniture, mirrors, handmade cards, jewelry, photo frames, prints, and painted fantasies (400 Main at Mill; 650–726–6776). A marine and wildlife shop, the **Harbor Seal Company,** sells unusual sea- and bird-life toys, puzzles, soft animals, educational toys, books, and games (406 Main Street; 650–726–7418).

One of the oldest established businesses in town, **Cunha's** (448 Main Street; 650–726–4071) is a grocery with a large deli, its own line of homemade packaged gourmet foods, and, upstairs, Western boots, hats, souvenirs, hardware, and T-shirts. On the corner across from Cunha's, the city has set up a nice picnic table area.

At the north end of Main, **The Tinnery** is another indoor mall crammed with small shops and cafes, including a sushi bar, a coffee cafe, a card shop, and a gallery.

DINNER: Cetrella, 845 Main Street, Half Moon Bay; (650) 726–4090; www .cetrella.com. In a warm bistro setting with fireplaces, rustic Mediterranean cuisine, seafood, tapas; meats and poultry roasted in a wood-burning oven; cheese cave, exhibition kitchen; live music in the cozy bar. The Coastside Farmers' Market is held here in the parking lot on Saturday, April through November; local produce, fresh artichokes, plants, flowers, artisan cheeses, honey, breads, pies, herbs.

LODGING: Beach House Inn, 4100 North Cabrillo Highway, Half Moon Bay; (800) 315–9366; www.beach-house.com. Above a small beach, spacious, commodious suites with sea views from private balconies or patios, kitchenettes, sofabeds, fireplaces, soaking tubs, luxurious bath amenities and cozy flannel robes; spa services. Heated lap pool, lavish continental breakfast, evening wine and cheese.

Day 2 / Morning

BREAKFAST: Main Street Grill, 435 Main at Kelly, Half Moon Bay; (650) 726–5300. Cajun sausage, artichoke omelets, and homemade waffles and muffins. Also good for lunch: grilled sandwiches, thick milk shakes, microbrewed beers, and a jukebox.

South from Half Moon Bay along Highway 1 are a string of beaches, wildlife preserves, and two tiny historic towns. It's 15 miles to the **Pescadero State Beach,** one of the prettiest, duniest, tidepooliest places you could spend an afternoon (650–726–6238). On the inland side of Highway 1, **Pescadero Marsh** is 588 acres of uplands and wetlands, an important stop on the Pacific Flyway. More than 200 species of waterfowl and shorebirds make this a must-see for avid birders or for anyone wishing to walk the trails through the marsh. Great blue herons nest in the blue gum eucalyptus trees, egrets walk stiffly in the shallow waters, northern harriers glide above, and marsh wrens follow you around.

It's 2 miles from Highway 1 on Pescadero Road to **Pescadero,** a block or so of clapboard buildings and steepled churches, circa 1850. Peek into the few antiques boutiques and stop at **Norm's Market,** where the irresistible aroma of warm artichoke and garlic/cheese bread wafts out the door; some of the twenty-four kinds of bread are "halfbaked"—to take home, stow in the freezer, and bake later.

A half mile beyond the town on Pescadero Creek Road, park under the giant oak and get out your camera at **Phipps Ranch** (650–879–0787), a combination produce market, farm, plant nursery, and menagerie of exotic birds and farm animals. There are fancy chickens, big fat pigs, a variety of bunnies, and antique farm equipment. You pick your own berries or buy them at the produce stand.

A real sleeper of a park and campground, **Butano State Park** off Pescadero Road is a lush piece of the earth, with magnificent redwood groves freshened by creeks and ferny glades (2 miles past Pescadero, turn right onto Cloverdale Road; travel 5 miles to park entrance; 800–444–7275). From small, pretty campsites, you can walk streamside paths or take a challenging mountain hike on an 11-mile loop to the **Año Nuevo Island** lookout.

Back on the highway, proceed south; it's 22 miles to **Davenport,** where you'll have lunch. On the way is the circa 1870, ten-story-tall **Pigeon Point Lighthouse,** open for tours on weekends (650–879–2120). The hostel here offers inexpensive private and shared rooms andmarvelous views (www.norcalhostels.org). Just north of the lighthouse are beautiful beaches, tidepools, and wildflower meadows.

Proceed to the village of Davenport for lunch (36 miles south of Half Moon Bay).

LUNCH: New Davenport Cash Store Restaurant and Inn, on Highway 1, Davenport; (408) 425–1818; www.davenportinn.com. Tuck into grilled chicken sandwiches, homemade soup, omelets with homemade chorizo, big killer brownies, and fresh fruit from nearby farms. The gift shop sells guidebooks and a top-

Surfer's Beach at Half Moon Bay.

notch array of African masks, Turkish jewelry, Mexican crafts, and Santa Fe jewelry. Breakfast and brunch are very popular here on weekends and are definitely worth the wait. Upstairs is a casually comfy bed-and-breakfast. Across Highway 1 from the restaurant are a short walking path on the bluffs and a nice beach.

Afternoon

Returning north 9 miles, stop at **Año Nuevo State Reserve,** which may turn out to be the highlight of your trip on the central coast (650-879-0227 or 800-444-4445; www.anonuevo.org). On 1,200 acres of dunes and beaches, the largest groups of elephant seals in the world come to breed from December through April. A 0.5-mile walk through grassy dunes brings you to an unforgettable sight: dozens of two-ton animals lounging, arguing, maybe mating, cavorting in the sea, and wiggling around on the beach. As many as 2,500 seals spend their honeymoons here, and there's lots of other wildlife to see, too. During the mating season it is necessary to reserve spaces in guided interpretive tours (800-444-7275). At other times you can wander around on your own but are not allowed to come too close to the animals. No pets.

DINNER: Duarte's Tavern, 202 Stage Road, Pescadero; (650) 879–0464. Crowded on sunny weekends but worth the wait, Duarte's has for more than fifty years been a family restaurant serving cioppino, seafood specialties with a Portuguese accent, artichoke soup and fresh artichokes with garlic aioli, deep-fried calamari, cracked crab, abalone sandwiches, shrimp cakes, and olallieberry pie. Local ranchers belly up to the Old West–style bar. Daily breakfast, lunch, and dinner.

LODGING: Beach House Inn.

Day 3 / Morning

BREAKFAST: Half Moon Bay Coffee Company, 20A Stone Pine Road at the north end of Main Street, Half Moon Bay; (650) 726–3664. A casual place busy with locals and tourists digging into homemade pies and pastries, pancakes, burgers, sandwiches, and simple, hearty entrees. Breakfast, lunch, and dinner.

Buy a kite at **Lunar Wind Inventions** in town, and head for 3 miles of sand at **Half Moon Bay State Beach** just south of town; to get there, go west on Kelly Avenue (650–726–8820). At Francis Beach, the most popular of the three beaches here, are developed RV and tent campsites, cold showers, BBQs, picnic sites, and the ranger station. (If the campground is full, try the nice Pelican Point RV Park on Miramontes Point Road; 650–726–9100.) Water temperature is chilly, even in summer, and the surf can be treacherous, so plan to dip your toes and play on the sand.

Before you leave town, drive 3 miles east on Highway 92 and keep a sharp eye out for the right turn into **Half Moon Bay Nursery** (11691 San Mateo Road; 650–726–5392). This is a rambling, gorgeous kingdom of blooming garden and house plants, from orchids and ferns to thousands of geraniums, herbs, azaleas, camellias, climbing vines, hanging baskets, and seasonal bulbs—a veritable flower show. In wintertime, it's cozy in the main greenhouse by the woodstove.

LUNCH: On your way back to San Francisco on Highway 1, have lunch at the **Moss Beach Distillery** (Beach and Ocean, Moss Beach; 650–728–5595), said to be haunted by the Blue Lady, who wanders the nearby cliffs where she died mysteriously in the 1930s. On a spectacular hilltop overlooking a cove, with an outdoor patio and indoor dining room and bar with sea views, Moss Beach Distillery serves luscious fresh local seafood for lunch, dinner, and weekend brunch. Best place for a cocktail: in a double rocker, covered with the provided blankets, above the crashing waves of Seal Cove.

There's More

Bach Dancing and Dynamite Society, P.O. Box 302, El Granada 94018, at Miramar Beach, 2.5 miles north of Half Moon Bay; (650) 726–4143. Begun in a private home years ago, Sunday-afternoon jam sessions evolved into big-name jazz and classical concerts with catered lunches and dinners; purchase tickets in advance.

Bean Hollow Trail, 18 miles south of Half Moon Bay on Highway 1 (park at Pebble Beach or Bean Hollow State Beach); (650) 879–0832. A 2-mile bluff trail crossing six bridges. You'll see the legendary gemlike pebbles at Pebble Beach (it's forbidden to gather them), harbor seals on the offshore rocks, unique limestone formations, and sheets of blooming seaside plants such as lupines and primroses. Restrooms.

Bicyclery, 432 Main Street, Half Moon Bay; (650) 726–6000. Rentals, accessories, service.

Burleigh Murray State Park, Mills Creek Ranch Road off Higgins Purissima Road, a mile south of Half Moon Bay; (650) 726–8820. Century-old dairy barn, said to be the only one of its kind remaining in the state. Past the barn, a pretty creekside trail ambles for about a mile.

Coastside Trail. Running along the bluffs, from Mirada Road in Miramar and to Kelly Avenue on the south end of town (parking here), the flat, easy Coastside Trail promises walkers and bikers more than 3 miles of sea views, bird-watching, and beaches.

Half Moon Bay Golf Links, 2000 Fairway Drive off Highway 1, Half Moon Bay; (650) 726–4438. Stunning ocean views from every hole, steady breezes, tight fairways, and few trees call for the irons on the Arthur Hills–designed Ocean Course, which *Golf Magazine* called "a riproaring experience." Mere mortals head for Arnold Palmer's Old Course, a lovely parkland layout with a few ocean holes. The clubhouse, including the casual restaurant, has been expanded and remodeled.

Johnston House, (650) 726–0329, www.johnstonhousehmb.org. Just south of town on Higgins Purisima Road, a New England–style white saltbox stands alone in a meadow above the sea. When James Johnston came west to make his fortune in the gold rush, he built the house in about 1855 for his Spanish wife, Petra, and their family. The house is occasionally open to the public, and a breezy picnic site is always open. From this high perch you can watch fishing and pleasure boats glide back and forth and imagine how rumrunners from Canada plied this coast during Prohibition, unloading their cargos in hidden ocean coves under cover of fog.

Point Montara Lighthouse, Highway 1 at Sixteenth Street, Montara; (650) 728–7177. A short, chunky lighthouse on a high bluff, the 1875 Point Montara Fog Signal and Light Station is open to the public.

Purissima Creek Redwoods, Higgins Purissima Road, a mile south of Half Moon Bay; (650) 691–1200. On the western slope of the Santa Cruz Mountains, a redwood preserve with hiking, biking, and equestrian trails, some wheelchair-accessible trails. Wildflowers, ferny creeks, giant redwoods, maples, and alders.

Sea Horse and Friendly Acres Horse Ranches, Highway 1 at Half Moon Bay; (650) 726–2362. Ride on your own or guided rides on the beach and trails; hayrides; picnic area.

Special Events

August. Pescadero Arts and Fun Festival, Pescadero; (650) 879–0848.

September. Harbor Day at Pillar Point Harbor; (650) 726–5202. Crafts booths, music, fantastic seafood barbecue.

October. Pumpkin and Art Festival, Half Moon Bay; (650) 726–9652. Great Pumpkin Parade, entertainment, contests—carving, pie-eating, biggest pumpkin. The town is mobbed.

November. California Coast Air Show, Half Moon Bay Airport; (650) 726–3417. Antique and modern aircrafts displayed, stunning air show.

December. Harbor Lighting Ceremony, Pillar Point Harbor; (650) 726–5202. Boat owners compete with lighted and decorated boats.

Other Recommended Restaurants and Lodgings

Half Moon Bay

Best Western Half Moon Bay Lodge, 2400 South Cabrillo Highway/Highway 1; (800) 710–0778; www.halfmoonbaylodge.com. Spacious rooms with small patios or balconies overlooking gardens; some fireplaces. Large swimming pool, spa, fitness center.

Cameron's Restaurant and Inn, 1410 South Cabrillo Highway; (415) 726–5705; www.cameronsinn.com. Just south of town, eighteen European brew on tap, darts and games, pub food and pizza; a red bus with video games for kids, volleyball, and a warm welcome make this a popular English pub. Simple hotel rooms upstairs. Watch for the red phone booth!

Old Thyme Inn, 779 Main Street; (650) 726–1616; www.inntraveler.com/old thyme. A Queen Anne Victorian in an English garden on the quiet end of Main. Four-posters, fireplaces, whirlpool tubs, full breakfast.

The Ritz-Carlton, Half Moon Bay, One Miramontes Point Road; (650) 712–7000 or (800) 241–3333; www.ritzcarlton.com. Resembling a grand nineteenth-century seaside lodge, a 261-room resort on a scenic bluff with two top-rated golf courses, romantic restaurants, tennis, indoor swimming pool. Most of the ultraluxurious rooms and suites have panoramic views; some have fireplaces, window seats, and balconies. New separate deluxe guest cottages. Fifth-floor guests enjoy a private, seaview lounge with their own concierge and all-day and evening food and beverage service. In the full-service luxury spa, spa suites, yoga and exercise classes, fitness center, Roman bath, sauna, steam. A stroll around the lobby, the paneled library and the public areas of the hallways turns up a museum's worth of paintings of the coastline, and Portuguese tapestries and antique ceramics. Floor-to-ceiling windows and a telescope in the Conservatory afford dazzling views of the ocean. Take tea in the Tea Salon, complete with finger sandwiches, petits fours, and scones. In a cozy curtained nook or at a window open to the sea, enjoy dazzling California cuisine, Mediterranean dishes, and fresh seafood at Navio, a lovely, semiformal restaurant.

San Benito House, 356 Main Street; (650) 726–3425. English garden bed-and-breakfast inn built at the turn of the twentieth century. Fresh flowers throughout, twelve rooms with antiques and brass beds. European country–style restaurant with garden patio.

Miramar

Cafe Classique, corner of Granada and Seville, across the highway from Pillar Point Harbor at the stoplight; (415) 726–9775. Cappuccinos, fresh juices and monster muffins, hearty sandwiches, soups; very casual. Open early for breakfast, lunch.

Cypress Inn, 407 Mirada Road; (650) 726–6002. On 5 miles of beach, eight contemporary-design, luxury rooms and suites; sumptuous breakfasts and afternoon wine; a few steps from the beach. Fireplaces, private decks, sea views, skylights, in-house massage therapist!

Miramar Restaurant and Bar, 131 Mirada Road, 2.5 miles north of Half Moon Bay; (650) 726–9053. Lunch, dinner, and weekend brunch across the street from Miramar Beach, fresh seafood specialties, lively bar crowd, sometimes live music.

Pescadero

Costanoa Lodge and Camp, 2001 Rossi Road, P.O. Box 842, Pescadero 94060; (650) 879–2600 or (877) 262–7848; www.costanoa.com. Surrounded by beautiful parklands, Costanoa is a new idea in upscale camping—luxury tents, cabins and lodge rooms, RV and tent sites. Light breakfast, spa and sauna, bikes to rent, well-stocked general store with gourmet and deli foods to take out or eat at picnic tables. You can hike into pristine wilderness right from the camp.

San Gregorio

Rancho San Gregorio, 5086 San Gregorio Road (near Pescadero); (650) 747–0810; www.sangregorio-lodging.com. A Spanish Mission–style mansion with four delightful bed-and-breakfast rooms, some with woodstoves. Sumptuous breakfasts include fruit from the orchard, homemade crepes, scones, and muffins.

For More Information

Half Moon Bay Coastside Chamber of Commerce, 520 Kelly Avenue, P.O. Box 188, Half Moon Bay 94019; (650) 726–8380; www.halfmoonbaychamber.org.

Monterey and Big Sur

Spanish History, Wild Coastline / 3 Nights

In the late 1700s Spanish explorers arrived in force on the Monterey Peninsula, making it headquarters for their huge Baja and Alta California domains, and Father Junípero Serra built one of his largest and most beautiful missions. Then Mexico took a turn as occupier of Monterey for more than twenty years.

☐ Museums, mansions, mountains

☐ Beachcombing

☐ A golfer's dream

☐ Shopping, biking, hiking

☐ Chowder and cioppino

This rich Hispanic heritage remains in the thick-walled adobes and Spanish Colonial haciendas of Monterey. Beneath the gnarled old olive trees, in courtyard gardens planted by the early conquistadors, and beside spectacular Monterey Bay are the upscale shops, world-class restaurants, and museums that draw visitors today. Add more than twenty championship golf courses, and more than a weekend is called for on the Monterey Peninsula.

In stark contrast to the historic neighborhoods and sophisticated atmosphere of present-day Monterey, Big Sur is a sparsely developed stretch of wilderness running 90 miles south to San Simeon, a series of cliffs and river valleys hemmed in by a high mountain range on one side and a largely inaccessible seacoast. A long-time resident of Big Sur, author Henry Miller, said of the area, "It is a region where extremes meet, a region where one is always conscious of weather, of space, of grandeur, and of eloquent silence."

Day 1 / Morning

Drive south from San Francisco on Interstate 280, taking Highway 85 south to Highway 17 south to Monterey, about a two-hour drive. Take the Monterey exit; head west and turn onto Del Monte Boulevard. Pick up a walking tour map at the **Monterey County Visitor Center** (Lake El Estero at Franklin and Camino El Estero) and spend a couple of hours strolling in and out of the historic buildings and garden courtyards on the Monterey State Historic Park **"Path of History,"** a 2-mile walk that includes the grassy knolls of **Colton Hall,** at Pacific and Jefferson,

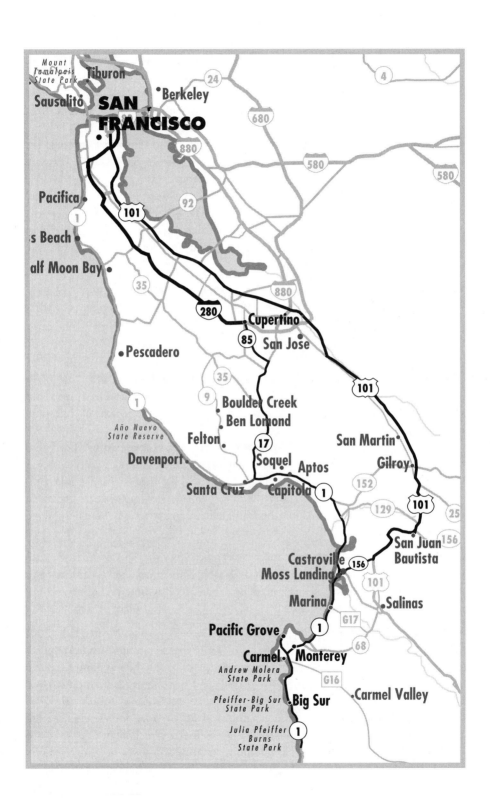

a museum in an old school. Notice the small plastered-adobe homes in back of Colton Hall, some of the first built in California. Admission to most buildings is free; guided tours cost a few dollars per person.

Part of the park complex, **Cooper Store,** on Polk Street, sells antique toys, postcards, and souvenirs. Go through the store to the museums and gardens behind; a spectacular cypress towers overhead. In the heart of the Historic District is the **Monterey Peninsula Museum of Art,** 559 Pacific Street (831–372–5477), with a fine collection of Western and Asian art and photography.

The **Maritime Museum of Monterey** at the waterfront focuses on the Monterey Peninsula's long seagoing history (831–373–2469). Priceless marine artifacts include the 16-foot-tall, 10,000-pound lens that once operated atop the Point Sur Lighthouse. When you are ready to get off your feet for twenty minutes, take in the historical film here—it's free.

LUNCH: **Abalonetti's Seafood Trattoria,** 57 Old Fisherman's Wharf, Monterey; (831) 373–1851. Sit indoors or on the wharf; calamari, Italian antipasto, pizza, seafood pasta; for forty years one of the best fish cafes on the wharf.

Afternoon

Old Fisherman's Wharf (831–649–6544; www.montereywharf.com) still smells of salt spray and caramel corn. Fishing boats bob in the harbor, seagulls squawk and wheel overhead, and sea breezes blow between slightly seedy boardwalk cafes and tourist shops.

Walk along the waterfront **Monterey Peninsula Recreational Trail** that runs from the wharf all the way along Cannery Row and around Pacific Grove, a distance of 5 miles, if you care to walk that far—or bike that far (rent a bike or a pedaling vehicle that seats four). On the way, pelicans, barking sea lions, and sea otters vie for your attention. Along the trail are drinking fountains, benches, picnic sites, and bike racks.

DINNER: **Fishwife,** 1996½ Sunset Drive, Pacific Grove; (831) 375–7107. Casual, popular, reasonably priced cafe at Asilomar Beach with sunset views. Wide variety of fresh fish, Cajun blackened snapper, salmon Alfredo, Key lime pie; reservations a must. Lunch, dinner, Sunday brunch.

LODGING: **Monterey Bay Inn,** 242 Cannery Row, Monterey; (800) 424–6242; www.montereybayinn.com. Don't let the unassuming outward appearance fool you—this four-diamond inn is a great place to stay. Newly renovated top to bottom; an unbeatable location at the south end of Cannery Row, with bay or harbor views and the sound of the surf from forty-seven guest rooms. Big glass doors lead to private balconies, where binoculars are provided for viewing sea life and boating activity. King featherbeds and plush linens; armchair sitting areas, not one but two coffeepots, high-tech amenities; rooftop, bay-view hot tub; complimentary continental breakfast. Nice, big bathrooms with double sinks and long tubs. Ask about aquarium, dinner, massage, and other packages. It's a short walk to the aquarium, walking trails, and most sights of Monterey; steps from the beach, a popular "put-in" location for scuba divers. The inn has dive lockers, showers, and a sauna on the ground floor; the Monterey Bay Dive Center is across the street.

Day 2 / Morning

BREAKFAST: Monterey Bay Inn.

A blockbuster attraction on the Central Coast is the **Monterey Bay Aquarium,** one of the largest—and some say the best—aquariums in the world. For twenty years in a spectacular location on Cannery Row at the edge of the bay, the aquarium is worth a day and some planning (886 Cannery Row; 831–648–4888; www.montereybayaquarium.org). Many visitors return year after year to view changing exhibits, enjoy annual events, and engage in some of the hands-on experiences. New are a series of visitor programs; a light-filled, easy-entry ticket lobby; and a great skywalk connecting the two wings.

Arrive early at the aquarium, especially in summer and on weekends; to avoid lines, buy tickets in advance online or at your hotel (ask about hotel packages). Check the Web site for family packages, daily and special events, tours, and feeding times. The live exhibit "cams" on the Web site will fuel your anticipation of the marine treasures on view.

In an architectural masterpiece, some 6,000 sea creatures reside here in giant tanks. The three-story Kelp Forest is the world's tallest aquarium exhibit, so huge that it feels as if you're swimming around in there with the sharks and the schools of silvery fish. The Monterey Bay exhibit is 90 feet long, full of fascinating reef life. Playful sea otters and bat rays have their own watery homes, and it's fun to watch them during feeding time. There are frequent live videos from a research submarine prowling Monterey Bay, as deep as 3,000 feet.

A million gallons of seawater behind the largest window on the planet, the Outer Bay exhibit contains species that other of the world's aquariums have not dared to exhibit, such as 10-foot-tall, 1.5-ton sunfish; pelagic stingrays; green sea turtles as big as dining room tables; vast schools of yellowfin tuna; and species of sharks too big for other aquariums.

The Drifters gallery contains the largest-scale jellyfish exhibit in the world. Otherworldly music and a dreamlike design for the jellies venue transfix viewers before the pulsing, drifting, rainbow-hued beings. The new Splash Zone is an interactive, simulated marine-environment venue for kids and toddlers.

The new Ocean's Edge exhibit comprises a rocky shore gallery and a walk-through tunnel where waves crash over your head; a large aviary; new displays for the giant octopus; and hands-on exhibits. Aquarium Adventures programs for kids include a scuba experience, Science Under Sail cruises, kayaking, and whale-watching.

A day, even a half day, at the aquarium is an intense, stimulating experience, especially for kids. Take the time to wander out onto the terraces to rest and take in the sights and sounds of the bay waters, and plan to have snacks and a meal here. Within the building, the **Portola Cafe** is an upscale restaurant (fresh seafood, pasta, appetizers, full bar service and use of Zeiss binoculars; reservations 831–648–4870); and there is the Oyster Bar and a self-service cafe (pizza, pasta, Mexican food, clam chowder in a sourdough bowl, sandwiches, and salads), all with fabulous bay views.

One of the most biodiverse marine environments in the world, Monterey Peninsula waters attract divers from all over the world to the **Monterey Bay National Marine Sanctuary,** encompassing 4,000 nautical square miles of kelp forests and rocky reefs inhabited by a miraculous variety of creatures such as leopard shark, bright nudibranchs, and hundreds more species, plus the ever-present otters, dolphins, and whales. *Scuba Diving* magazine chose Monterey Bay as the "Favorite Shore Dive in the U.S.," and the bay has also been in the top five "Favorite Beginner's Dive Destinations." The **Monterey Bay Dive Center,** 225 Cannery Row (831–656–0454 or 800–GO–SCUBA), is a PADI dive center where you can rent complete diving equipment, take a guided dive tour, and arrange to get certified as a diver.

LUNCH: **Montrio,** 414 Calle Principal, Monterey; (831) 648–8880. Euro-American urban bistro in a 1910 landmark firehouse. From the display kitchen come Dungeness crab cakes, grilled salmon with fennel ratatouille, and homemade pasta; from the wood-burning rotisserie come rosemary and garlic chicken, plus Black Angus rib eye. The wine list received an award of excellence by *Wine Spectator.* If you can't get a reservation, you can eat in the pleasant cocktail lounge.

Afternoon

Stroll about and shop on **Cannery Row** and on Wave Street, just above. At one time just a few blocks of weathered cannery buildings with funky shops and cafes, the waterfront promenade is now rampant with elegance and élan. Steinbeck and sardines were replaced by upscale boutiques and fancy hotels. The seals, otters, and sailing yachts of Monterey Bay remain.

Cannery Row Antique Mall, at 471 Wave Street (831–655–0264), is more than 20,000 square feet housing the antiques and collectibles of a hundred dealers. At 700 Cannery Row is a complex of almost three dozen shops and galleries plus a wax museum, a winery, and cafes. Located here is **A Taste of Monterey,** where you can enjoy a panoramic view of Monterey Bay, wine and food tasting, exhibits, and a multimedia show about the region (831–646–5446). What is a day by the bay without a kite? You will find lots of vivid and unique kites, flags, banners, windsocks, and toys at **Windborne Kites**, in the American Tin Cannery shopping center next to the aquarium (877–272–5483).

Shoppers and cafe-sitters are drawn to the sophisticated eateries and boutiques on 2 blocks of old Alvarado Street, downtown between Del Monte Avenue and Jefferson Street. Serious cigar smokers stop at **Hellam's,** which also holds an astonishing array of chotchkes, unique metal dolls, and arguably the world's largest collection of Zippo lighters (831–373–2816). Locals head for **Rosine's** for home-style breakfasts, lunches, and dinners, six-layer cakes, pasta, and burgers (434 Alvarado; 831–375–1400). It's **Supremos** for artichoke enchiladas and lobster burritos, in an 1850 adobe house (500 Hartnell Street behind the Cooper adobe at the end of Alvarado; 831–373–3737), and contemporary Italian food at the bistro, **Tutto Buono** at 469 Alvarado (831–372– 1880).

Drive to the Spanish Bay entrance to the **17-Mile Drive,** (831–649–8500) at Asilomar near the Fishwife restaurant; you'll pay a fee that's well worth it, even on a foggy day. Ghostly cypress forests and red lichen–painted rocks frame the many vista points. Stop and explore the beautiful beaches and many tidepools; walk or jog on the winding waterfront path. If you're a golfer, this is a chance to see three of the most famous and most difficult courses in the world.

DINNER: Sardine Factory, 701 Wave Street; (831) 373–3775; www.sardine factory.com. For nearly four decades above Cannery Row; elegant, award-winning dining in the ornate Captain's Room, a nineteenth-century drawing room with a fireplace and candlelight; or in the glass-enclosed garden Conservatory. Choose from a huge menu of seafood, from Dungeness crab cakes to cioppino; herb-crusted ahi to sand dabs; lobster, wild salmon, and prime steaks; and abalone bisque as served at President Reagan's inaugural dinner. Dress up for this special occasional restaurant, and expect perfect service; a smashing wine list and superb food in a town world-famous for its restaurants. The lounge is a hot gathering spot, with an extensive bar menu and live entertainment most evenings; stop here for drinks and appetizers or for a casual dinner. Ask about getting a peek at the medieval-style wine cellar.

LODGING: Monterey Bay Inn.

Day 3 / Morning

BREAKFAST: Monterey Bay Inn continental breakfast. Or enjoy buckwheat pancakes or huge omelets at the **Old Monterey Cafe,** voted "Best Breakfast" in the county (489 Alvarado Street; 831–646–1021; www.cafemonterey.com).

Drive south on Highway 1 to Big Sur, about 30 miles on a two-lane, winding mountain road. The brooding shoulders of the **Santa Lucia Mountains** loom to the left, and to the right it's a sheer 1,000-foot drop to a rocky, mostly inaccessible coastline pierced by the small valleys of the Big and Little Sur Rivers. Several river and forest parks are here in the **Los Padres National Forest** (831–385–5434), where you'll also find good campgrounds and walking and hiking trails. Big Sur is a banana belt, with higher temperatures than Carmel and Monterey, getting more inches of rain but also more sunny days.

You'll cross the **Bixby Creek Bridge,** also known as the Rainbow Bridge, a 260-foot-high single-spanner constructed in 1932. At **Andrew Molera State Park** (831–667–2315), the **Big Sur River** flows down from the Santa Lucias through this 4,700-acre park, falling into the sea at a long sandy beach. One of many hiking trails runs along the river, through a eucalyptus grove where monarch butterflies spend the winter, to the river's mouth, where you can see a great variety of sea- and shorebirds. For trail maps and information, write in advance to the USDA Forest Service, 406 South Mildred, King City 93930 (831–385–5434).

One of the most unforgettable ways to see Big Sur is on horseback. **Molera Horseback Tours** offers daily two-hour rides, each featuring a different perspective, such as the beach, redwood groves, mountain ridges, and sunset excursions (800–942–5486).

LUNCH: Nepenthe, Highway 1 just south of Ventana Inn, Big Sur; (831) 628–6500. The stone patios of the restaurant are perched on a magical promontory at the edge of the continent, with a bird's-eye view of a long shoreline. Just offshore are natural arches and sea stacks, rocky remnants of an ancient coastline. Try the ambrosia burger or the fresh fish.

Afternoon

Drive through **Big Sur Valley,** not a town, really, but a handful of river resorts and campgrounds on both sides of the highway. **Pfeiffer Big Sur State Park** (831–667–2315) is another place to hike, picnic, and fish in the Big Sur River. Docent-led nature walks are given in summer; one trail leads to **Pfeiffer Falls,** in a fern canyon. From the falls, climb the Valley View Trail for zowie views of the lighthouse and the Big Sur Valley gorge.

Just inside the entrance to the park, the casual restaurant at **Big Sur Lodge** overlooks the river (831–667–2315). Cottage-style lodge rooms are in big demand during vacation season. The nearby **Post Ranch Inn** (P.O. Box 219, Big Sur 93920; 831–667–2200; www.postranchinn.com) is a luxurious, visually stunning inn with fireplaces, spa tubs, a renowned restaurant, and complete privacy for guests.

Ten miles farther down the coast, **Julia Pfeiffer Burns State Park** is 2,400 acres of undeveloped wilderness. Trails along McWay Creek lead to a waterfall that plunges into the ocean (831–667–2315). The Partington Creek Trail goes through a canyon and a 100-foot-long rock tunnel to Partington Cove beach, where sea otters play in the kelp beds offshore. A popular walk in the woods is the **Pine Ridge Trail,** right off Highway 1 at Big Sur Station Visitor Center, just south of Julia Pfeiffer Burns State Park. Wild iris and columbine bloom in shady redwood glens and fern grottoes, and if you can make it 7 miles, there are swimming holes at the Big Sur River and a hot springs another 3 miles farther on. Get a topographical map and check trail conditions at the visitor center.

(If you decide to continue to southern California, take note that the two-lane Big Sur highway south from here to San Simeon crosses thirty bridges over deep canyons and stream-cut valleys—breathtaking scenery—and is unrelentingly curvy. About halfway to San Simeon, **Jade Cove** is actually a string of coves, where Monterey jade is found at low tide and following storms. It's a 0.25-mile walk down to the cove from the highway, where you are allowed to collect what will fit into your pockets.)

DINNER: Ventana Inn and Spa (Cielo), 30 miles south of Carmel on Highway 1, Big Sur; (800) 678–6500. After dark, the walk up lighted outdoor stairs through a forest is a romantic beginning to a romantic evening in the four-star restaurant, which serves lunch and dinner. Indoors, a warm, woodsy atmosphere; outdoors, a stone patio floating high above the sea.

LODGING: Ventana Inn and Spa. Rustic country-luxe, a private, quiet resort on a hillside between the sea and mountain ridges, the resort has a compound of several pine buildings, each with canyon or ocean views. High-ceilinged, wood-paneled luxury suites with fireplaces and a feeling of isolation. Decor is of stone, wood, soft earth-toned fabrics.

There are two lap pools, Japanese hot baths, sauna, and massages on your own completely private deck. Indulge yourself in the full-service spa with wraps, scrubs, massages, and exotic, soothing therapies in a glorious natural setting. The elaborate afternoon wine and cheese buffet is in the main lounge. Wild gardens abloom with native flowers and vines; oceans of clematis and jasmine pour over balconies; tree ferns create shady glades. Call ahead for a monthly listing of scheduled special events, from guided naturalist hikes to history, literary, and gardening lectures and musical performances.

Day 4 / Morning

BREAKFAST: At the Ventana Inn. Enjoy the big breakfast buffet in the sunny dining lounge, outside on a choice of several garden patios, or in your room. Fresh berries, melons, tropical fruits; homemade coffee cakes, croissants, muffins, yogurt, granola.

After a morning exploring the meadow and mountainside trails that start at Ventana Inn, head back to the Bay Area.

There's More

Golf. Bayonet & Black Horse, 1 McClure Way, Seaside; (831) 899–7271. The Bayonet and Black Horse courses here on Monterey Bay host PGA qualifying tournaments and are tough, beautiful, established layouts made playable for the average golfer by several sets of tees.

Del Monte Golf Course, 1300 Sylvan Road, Monterey; (831) 373–2700. Eighteen holes; public; oldest course west of the Mississippi.

Laguna Seca Golf Course, 10520 York Road off Highway 68, Monterey; (831) 373–3701. Eighteen holes; public.

The Links at Spanish Bay, 17-Mile Drive, Pebble Beach; (800) 654–9300. One of the "Greatest Resort Courses" and "Best Golf Resorts in America." All but four of the holes flank the sea, and, in true Scottish fashion, the course is marked by waves of low, sandy mounds; fescue grass fairways; pot bunkers; and few trees.

Pacific Grove Links, 77 Asilomar Boulevard, Pacific Grove; (831) 648–5777. Eighteen holes; public; links-style.

Pebble Beach Golf Links, 17-Mile Drive, Pebble Beach; (800) 654–9300. Legendary site of U.S. Opens, PGA Championships, and the Crosby Clambake (now the AT&T Pro-Am). Pebble rides the headlands over Stillwater Cove, as it has since 1919. The notorious combination of swirling winds and misty hazes, long tee shots over gaping crevasses, and tiny greens remains a golfing challenge equaled by few courses in the world.

Poppy Hills Golf Course, 3200 Lopez Road, 17-Mile Drive, Pebble Beach; (831) 625–2035. Eighteen holes; public.

Spyglass Hill Golf Course, Stevenson Drive and Spyglass Hill, Pebble Beach; (800) 654–9300. Semiprivate; eighteen holes.

Mazda Raceway Laguna Seca, (800) 327–7322; www.laguna-seca.com. Grand Prix auto and motorcycle races bring out huge crowds at the raceway, just north of Monterey. Come for the excitement at annual MotoGP, historic car, Grand Am, American Le Mans, and other races. Plan way ahead, and ask about hotel packages.

Monterey Bay Whale Watch, P.O. Box 52001, Pacific Grove 93950; (831) 375–4658. Three-hour winter and spring cruises to see gray whales and dolphins.

Mopeds, bikes, kayaks. Adventures by the Sea, 299 Cannery Row, Monterey; (831) 372–1807; www.adventuresbythesea.com.

Bay Bikes, 640 Wave Street, Monterey; (831) 646–9090.

Monterey Bay Kayaks, 693 Del Monte Avenue, Monterey; (831) 373–KELP; www.montereybaykayaks.com.

Monterey Moped, 1250 Del Monte, Monterey; (831) 373–2696.

Point Lobos State Reserve, 2.5 miles south of Carmel on Highway 1; (831) 624–4909. A rocky point surrounded by a protected marine environment; otters, whales, harbor seals, sea lions; scuba diving; spectacular landscape; picnicking, walking, photo snapping.

Vision Quest Ranch, 400 River Road, Salinas; (800) 228–7382; www.wildthings inc.com. On the east side of Monterey County near Salinas, see more than one hundred exotic animals and birds, which are lovingly trained for use in movie and TV filming—elephants, giraffes, bears, cheetahs, tropical birds, snakes, alligators, and dozens more creatures. The animals are very friendly and safe. Come for a tour, or stay overnight in a canvas-walled safari cabin; kids can attend a summer camp for animal education.

Special Events

January. AT&T Pebble Beach National Pro-Am; (800) 541–9091. On one of the most spectacular seaside golf courses in the world, a legendary golf tournament attracting movie stars, PGA pros, and huge crowds.

February. Masters of Food and Wine, Highlands Inn, Carmel; (831) 620–1234; www.mfandw.com. For nearly two decades, a summit featuring leading chefs from around the country and food and wine gurus. Rare wine tastings, demonstrations, gourmet dinners, special events.

March. Hot Air Affair, Monterey; (831) 649–6544. Four hundred balloons compete in events, many in the early morning. Public rides in tethered balloons and heli- copters. Skydiving exhibition.

April. Monterey Wine Festival; (800) 656–4282; www.montereywine.com. The oldest and largest California wine fest. Auction, food and cooking demonstrations, special tastings, seminars, live entertainment; held at various venues around the peninsula and the wine country.

May. Cooking for Solutions, Monterey Bay Aquarium; (831) 648–4800; www .mbayaq.org. Two days of events focusing on sustainable seafood—where to get it, what to buy, how to cook it. Celebrity chefs from around the world, wine gurus, and other luminaries are on hand (the likes of Martin Yan, John Ash, and John Cleese) for cooking demonstrations, seminars, guided farm and vineyard tours, and the incredible food/wine/special presentations "gala" in the aquarium, where the glorious sea life exhibitions are backdrops for the best of the best food and wine from area restaurants and wineries. The Saturday information fair is free with aquar- ium admission.

June. Monterey Bay Blues Festival; (831) 394–2652; www.montereyblues.com. On three stages for three days, nearly fifty blues and R&B acts, featuring the likes of the Neville Brothers, Dr. John, Ruth Brown, and Billy Preston.

July. Pebble Beach Equestrian, Pebble Beach; (831) 624–2756; www.ridepebble beach.com. An international show and competition; two weeks of spectacular jumping, dressage, and special events; wine tasting and family activities.

August. Winemakers' Celebration; (831) 375–9400; www.montereywines.com. Special tastings, food and live entertainment, auction, open houses.

Concours d'Elegance, Pebble Beach; (831) 622–1700; www.pebblebeachconcours .net. Pre- and postwar marques and contemporary marvels of the automobile world, in the stunning setting of Pebble Beach. Wear your glad rags.

September. Monterey Jazz Festival; (925) 275–9255; www.montereyjazzfestival.org. At the oldest continuous jazz fest in the world, more than 500 performers, many internationally famous, on seven stages.

October. Butterfly Parade and Bazaar, Pacific Grove. School bands and children in butterfly costumes welcome the monarchs' return to their winter home in Pacific Grove, a charming hometown event.

November. Great Wine Escape Weekend; (831) 375–9400; www.monterey wines.org. Special winery tours and open houses, winemaker dinners, discounts.

December. Parade of Lights, Pacific Grove; (831) 373–3304. Holiday floats, marching bands, dance teams, equestrian groups, and Santa Claus. After the parade, stores are open and carolers entertain.

Christmas at the Inns, Pacific Grove; (831) 373–3304. A self-guided tour of bed and breakfast inns decorated for the holidays in Victorian-era splendor; entertainment; refreshments; small fee.

Other Recommended Restaurants and Lodgings

Big Sur

Big Sur Lodge, just inside the entrance to Pfeiffer Big Sur State Park; (800) 424–4787; www.bigsurlodge.com. Casual lodge dining room with patio overlooking the river; California cuisine, pasta, local seafood; breakfast, lunch, and dinner. Cozy, simple cottages in a forest; kitchens; fireplaces; lovely views; pool.

Big Sur River Inn, Pheneger Creek; (800) 548–3610; www.bigsurriverinn.com. Eighteen rooms and family suites with balconies overlooking the river; simple, rustic accommodations. Restaurant and bar, swimming pool, general store, near state parks. Stop in for lunch and the Sunday-afternoon live concerts on the lawn above the river.

Rocky Point, 10 miles south of Carmel on Highway 1; (831) 624–2933; www.rocky-point.com. Spectacular views of the coast from the dining room and the terrace make breakfast, lunch, and dinner memorable experiences. Try the enchiladas, the crab salad, or one of the fabulous steaks.

Monterey

Hotel Pacific, 300 Pacific Street; (831) 373–5700 or (800) 554–5542; www.coastal hotel.com. Contemporary Spanish-hacienda suites with fireplaces, down comforters, private patio or balcony; continental breakfast, afternoon tea; fountains, hot tubs, and gardens.

Lone Oak Lodge, 2221 North Fremont; (831) 372–4924. Best-kept secret for inexpensive lodgings.

Monterey Plaza Hotel and Spa, 400 Cannery Row; (800) 226–6290; www.monterey plazahotel.com. A four-star, luxury hotel with top-notch restaurants, in a bayside setting with sea views from nearly every public space and from more than half of the 285 rooms (without sea views, some rooms overlook the street, busy Cannery Row). European-style full-service spa. In a lovely setting by the bay, the Duck Club Restaurant specializes in seafood and regional cuisine. Schooner's Bistro on the Bay, with an open-air bar and terrace, is for casual meals and snacks. Open to the public, big-name summer jazz concerts are held on the outdoor decks of the hotel.

Old Monterey Inn, 500 Martin Street; (831) 375–8284; www.oldmonterey inn.com. A vine-covered, 1929 Tudor mansion with patios abloom with wisteria, aromatic jasmine, and hundreds of hanging baskets and pots. Understated European country-house decor, fireplaces, elegant extras, extraordinary service. Two honeymoon cottages. Full breakfast by the fire in the elegant dining room.

Spindrift Inn, 652 Cannery Row; (800) 841–1879; www.spindriftinn.com. On the water, forty-one luxury rooms, half with ocean views, all with fireplaces, down comforters, marble baths, window seats or private balconies.

Tarpy's Roadhouse, Highway 68 and Canyon Del Rey, near the Monterey airport; (831) 647–1444. A 1920s ranch house with stone walls trailing vines on the outside, covered with art on the inside; large wine cave; garden courtyard dining; updated versions of old-fashioned comfort foods such as polenta with wild mushrooms, Cajun prawns, fresh local seafood, grilled meats, honey mustard rabbit with apples and thyme.

Victorian Inn, 487 Foam Street; (800) 232–4141. Sixty-eight charming rooms and suites, marble fireplaces, private balconies or patios, some with living rooms and kitchenettes, hot tub; breakfast buffet and afternoon refreshments; walking distance to Cannery Row and the Wharf.

Pacific Grove

Asilomar Conference Center, 800 Asilomar Avenue; (831) 642–4242; www.visit asilomar.com. Unknown to most tourists, this secluded, rustic, historic conference resort hides in a pine-and-oak forest above beautiful Asilomar State Beach. When space is available, individuals and families rent rooms and suites in thirty-two rustic buildings at very reasonable rates that include a bountiful breakfast buffet in a bright, pleasant dining room (dinner available, too). There is a heated pool, volleyball, a game room, some fireplaces, some kitchens, and easy accessibility to the wonderful tidepools and the wide, sandy beach; unsuitable for swimming. Sixty acres of dunes are traversed by a mile-long boardwalk, and a trail leads to wildflowery clifftops and stunning sea views.

Fandango, 223 Seventeenth Street, Pacific Grove; (831) 372–3456. By the fire in the dining room, on the glass-domed terrace, or on the garden patio, European country–style cuisine in a Mediterranean setting. Wood-burning grill, pasta, paella, seafood, cassoulet. Signature dishes are rack of lamb Provençal and Velouté Bongo Bongo Soup. Full bar, exceptional wine list; lunch, brunch, and dinner.

Green Gables and Grand View Inns, 555 and 557 Ocean View Boulevard; (831) 372–4341; www.pginns.com. Side-by-side Queen Anne Victorians with bay views from twenty-five rooms and cottages; exquisite period interiors, fireplaces, bicycles; elaborate breakfasts and afternoon teas. Walk to Cannery Row.

Lighthouse Lodge and Suites, 1150 Lighthouse Avenue; (831) 655–2111; www.lhls.com. In a seacoast environment of its own on Point Pinos; heated pool; thirty-one suites with ocean views, fireplaces, Jacuzzi tubs; full breakfast, afternoon refreshments. All lodge rooms include complimentary poolside barbecue each evening. Casual and quite reasonably priced.

Passionfish Grill, 701 Lighthouse Avenue; (831) 655–3311; www.passionfish.net. Line-caught local fish, slow-roasted meats, organic vegetables and salad greens from local farmers.

For More Information

Big Sur Chamber of Commerce, P.O. Box 87, Big Sur 93920; (831) 667–2100; www.bigsurcalifornia.org.

Cannery Row; www.canneryrow.com. Description of myriad pleasures of Cannery Row: accommodations, shopping, dining, outdoor recreation, events, historic sites, and more. Sign up to receive information on special packages.

Monterey County Convention & Visitors Bureau, 150 Olivier Street, P.O. Box 1770, Monterey 93942; (888) 221–1010; www.montereyinfo.org.

Pacific Grove Chamber of Commerce, P.O. Box 167, Pacific Grove 93950; (831) 373–3304.

Carmel Sunshine and Shopping

Home on the Ranch, Arts and Boutique Mecca / 2 Nights

- ☐ Cowboy days
- ☐ Tennis, golf, horseback rides
- ☐ Beach walks
- ☐ Serra's mission
- ☐ Boutique binge
- ☐ Art galleries

The Carmel River ambles over the valley floor between two mountain ranges through horse farms, ranch resorts, and meadows liberally sprinkled with spreading oaks. Just a few miles from the Pacific coast, but a world away, the tawny climate of Carmel Valley is warm and dry. Your choices are golf, horseback riding, hiking, biking, tennis, or lying in the sun by a swimming pool.

Once settled in the peace and quiet of the valley, you may find it difficult to leave, but you will enjoy forays to the ocean beaches and to the artists' colony and shopping mecca of Carmel, a square-mile village of rustic country cottages and shingled beach houses in an idyllic forest setting. Carmel's winding lanes are shaded with ancient oaks and cypress, and everyone in town, it seems, is an avid gardener. Hanging baskets and blooming window boxes are everywhere.

Shopping at the literally hundreds of boutiques and art galleries is the main activity of visitors to Carmel. Originally a Bohemian artists' and writers' colony, the town has more than one hundred art and photography galleries.

Day 1 / Morning

Drive south from San Francisco on Interstate 280, south on Highway 85, then Highway 17 south to Santa Cruz. From Santa Cruz follow Highway 1 south to Carmel Valley Road, turning east; the trip will take about three hours. You will find a large shopping and restaurant center at the intersection, and along the 12-mile route through the countryside to **Carmel Valley Village** are plant nurseries, a state park, a few winery tasting rooms, and large resorts.

About 3 miles east of Highway 1, in a beautiful setting between the foothills and a green hillside, the **Earthbound Farm Stand** is laden with organic fresh and dried fruits, herbs and vegetables, flowers, artisanal cheeses, prepared picnic foods, and homemade bakery goods. Even if buying produce is not on your agenda, stop

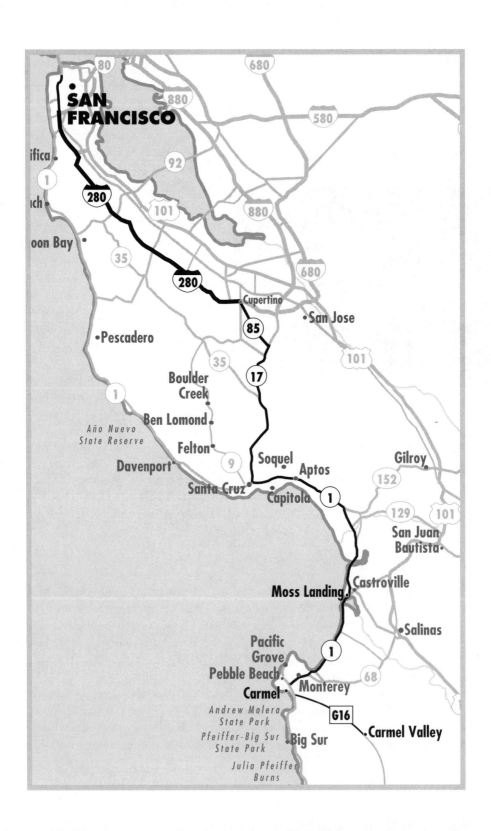

for a cold drink or a snack—and to shop for gifts. Wander the Kids' Garden, the cut-your-own herb garden, and the aromatherapy labyrinth; call ahead to join harvest walks and chef-led tours through sixty acres of garden, and to participate in garlic braiding, crafts workshops, and more events and classes (7250 Carmel Valley Road; 831–625–6219; www.ebfarm.com). This unique farm is now America's largest grower of certified organic produce.

Before you reach the village **Chateau Julien Wine Estate,** a winery with French flair, will welcome you to a soaring, peak-roofed, stone-floored Great Hall, where a blaze in the fireplace lights up the stained-glass windows (8940 Carmel Valley Road; 831–624–2600; www.chateaujulien.com). Annual art and music festivals are held in the lush gardens and the courtyard. Within the 15-inch-thick stone walls of the "chair" house, crisp *"sur lie"* Chardonnays and zesty Merlots and Cabernets age in oak barrels.

One of seven appellations composing Monterey County's diverse wine country, the Carmel Valley Viticultural Area favors the growing of Bordeaux-style varietals, in particular, Cabernet Sauvignon. Among a grouping of wineries in Carmel Valley Village, **Heller Estate** commands attention with a 15-foot-high bronze sculpture entitled *Dancing Partners,* at the entrance to a flamboyant sculpture garden (69 West Carmel Valley Road; 831–659–6220; www.hellerestate.com). The winery's motto: "Magical Wines That Dance on Your Palate."

The valley's cattle ranching heritage is recalled at **Running Iron Restaurant and Saloon**—the oldest continuously operating eating place in these parts, opened in the 1940s (24 East Carmel Valley Road; 831–659–4633). Cowboy boots and spurs hang from the ceiling, and steaks and south-of-the-border specialties are on the menu for local ranchers, winemakers, and tourists.

LUNCH: Bon Appetit, 7 Delfino Place, Carmel Valley Village; (831) 659–3559. Sit outdoors under an umbrella, watch the passing scene of the village, and enjoy bouillabaisse, paella, mesquite-grilled fresh fish, gourmet pizzas, and a notable wine list. Another top choice, the **White Oak Grill,** is famous for hearty pork-loin sandwiches and *pommes frites* with Gorgonzola (19 East Carmel Valley; 831–659–1525).

Afternoon

Stretch your legs on some of the 5,000 acres at **Garland Ranch Regional Park** with a hike, stroll, or bike ride along the **Carmel River,** across the forested hillsides, and up on the high ridges overlooking the valley (831–659–4488). An easy, flat 1-mile walk is the Lupine Loop in the lower meadow, a pleasant, wildflowery route in winter and spring, but hot and dry in summertime and fall, unless it has recently rained. The Waterfall Trail is lush with ferns, rushing streams, and beautiful falls that run winter through spring. Other trails take you to breezy hilltop meadows and ponds where birds and ducks reside.

Just a few steps from the parking lot, picnic sites beside the river are pleasant. John Steinbeck wrote in *Cannery Row,* "The Carmel [River] crackles among round boulders, wanders lazily under sycamores, spills into pools, drops in against banks where crayfish live . . . frogs blink from its banks and the deep ferns grow beside it. . . . It's everything a river should be."

Plan to arrive at your valley lodgings early enough to enjoy a late afternoon swim or a game of tennis or perhaps golf.

DINNER: Marinus at Bernardus Lodge, 415 Carmel Valley Road, Carmel Valley; (831) 658–3500 or (888) 648–9463. Amble by the jazz combo in the lobby, settle into a gold velvet banquette by the 12-foot-wide stone fireplace, and sip a glass of smoky-cherry Bernardus Cabernet while contemplating the menu. Signature dishes include portobello soup, yellowfin tuna tartare, and lobsterlike, local "spot" prawns.

LODGING: Bernardus Lodge, 415 Carmel Valley Road, Carmel Valley; (831) 658–3400; www.bernardus.com. You are greeted with—what else?—a glass of Bernardus wine at this posh Mediterranean-style retreat in a stunning mountain setting. The lodge feels like a big villa, with shady arbors and gardens, thick walls and stone terraces, a big swimming pool, tennis, boccie, and a croquet lawn. Spacious, cozy rooms have fireplaces, sofas and chairs, two-person tubs, and featherbeds with silky, imported linens. French doors open onto sunny balconies with mountain views—aaahhhh. Special services are many, including twice-daily room freshening and nightly wine and cheese in your room. A full-service beauty and health spa offers head-to-toe pampering; workout rooms; eucalyptus steam, sauna, and healthy drinks. Couples like the Vineyard Romance Experience for two, one hundred minutes of blissful privacy including crushed grape seed and red wine scrub, massage, aromatherapy, and more.

Day 2 / Morning

BREAKFAST: Bernardus Lodge.

Head west on Carmel Valley Road then just south on Highway 1 to the **Mission San Carlos Borromeo de Carmelo,** one of the most impressive in California's chain of missions (831–624–3600). Star-shaped stained-glass windows, cool colonnades, and beautiful courtyard gardens and fountains make this a good place to linger. A warren of thick-walled rooms, restored from original mission buildings, holds a magnificent museum collection of early Indian, religious, and historical California artifacts. Inside, the cathedral, cool and silent even on the hottest days, is sienna, burnt umber, and gold, with soaring ceilings and heavy wooden pews.

Continue on Rio Road 2 blocks to Santa Lucia; turn left and follow this street to the waterfront, bearing left to the north end of **Carmel River State Beach**

(831–624–4909), adjacent to **Monastery Beach** and the **Carmel River Bird Sanctuary.** Frequented by a wide variety of waterfowl and shorebirds, these two beaches are visited by fewer people than Carmel Beach. Wander over the dunes that form a "plug" for the Carmel River most of the year. Pick up driftwood and shells, or make a 4-mile round-trip run or walk. You may see scuba divers getting ready to descend into the kelp forests of the **Carmel Bay Ecological Reserve** offshore.

Monastery Beach is fine for picnicking, but heavy surf can make it unsafe for swimmers.

Four miles south of Carmel on Highway 1 is **Point Lobos State Reserve,** named for the offshore rocks called Punta de los Lobos Marinos (Point of the Sea Wolves), where sea lions lie about (831–624–4909). A rocky, forested point surrounded by a protected marine environment, the park's spectacular landscape includes several miles of trails, pebbled beaches, and one of only two naturally occurring stands of Monterey cypress (the other is at Pebble Beach). In the late 1800s, Robert Louis Stevenson called it the "most beautiful meeting of land and sea on earth."

From 6 miles of coastline, whales, harbor seals, and otters are often seen, as well as storms of pelicans, gulls, and cormorants. In the meadows mule deer tiptoe through purple needlegrass and wild lilac. Point Lobos is completely protected— the land, the marine life on the beach and in the tidepools, and the flora and fauna underwater. Not a thing may be removed or disturbed, dogs are not allowed, and visitors are required to stay on hiking trails or beaches. Sea Lion Point is accessed by an easy half-hour walk to Headland Cove, where sea lions bark and you can see the otters. Come early on weekends; guided interpretive walks are conducted by park rangers.

LUNCH: Rio Grill in the Crossroads shopping center at Carmel Valley Road and Highway 1 (831–625–5436). Southwestern-style decor and award-winning food, voted "Best Restaurant in Monterey County," make this a top choice. A wood-burning grill and an oak-wood smoker produce fresh fish, meat, and poultry specialties.

Afternoon

Adjacent to the Crossroads, **The Barnyard** (831–624–8886) is a rambling complex of fifty shops and restaurants in barnlike buildings. In every nook and cranny are riots of blooming native perennials; thousands of flowers, shrubs, and trees; and oceans of bougainvillea, rivers of begonias, and streams of California poppies.

Among the Barnyard shops, in a storybook forest at **Twiggs** (831–622–9802), are gnomes, trolls, raccoons, bunnies, twittering birds, and fantastical creatures. The fanciest store for dogs and cats you're ever likely to encounter, **Enchanted Tails** has decorated collars, stuffed animals for animals, cushy mats and sleeping baskets, and an array of treats, such as veggie hearts, liver unicorns, and banana bears (831–625–9648). Bubbling water and ringing chimes sound nice in another unique shop, **Succulent Gardens and Gifts,** which specializes in "water features"— indoor waterfalls, fountains and pools, plus wind chimes, bonsai, and garden statuary (831–624–0426).

Restaurants in the Barnyard include a pizzeria, a Japanese open-hearth grill, an English pub, and a casual sandwich place.

At the Crossroads, look for **The Jazz Store** if you are a jazz fan (236 Crossroads Boulevard; 831–624–6432). Touted as the "world's only all-jazz store," it's the offical Monterey Jazz Festival merchandise headquarters, selling an amazing array of new and vintage records and CDs, art, apparel, books, memorabilia, instruments, and more.

DINNER: Mission Ranch Restaurant, 26270 Dolores Street on the south end of Carmel; (831) 625–9040. Overlooking the Carmel River with views of the bay and Point Lobos, Mission Ranch is a place where cowboys and cowgirls kick back and eat steak, local fresh fish, and California cuisine in upscale, casual surroundings.

LODGING: Carmel Mission Ranch, 26270 Dolores Street, Carmel; (831) 624–6436. Plush, pricey rooms here are in charming former ranch buildings; some have fireplaces, living rooms, and memorabilia from Clint Eastwood's movies (he owns the place).

Day 3 / Morning

BREAKFAST: Rub elbows with the locals at **Katy's Place** (downtown Carmel, Mission Street between Fifth and Sixth; 831–624–0199), and dig into platters of French toast, eggs, and cottage fries like Grandma used to make.

Lace up your walking shoes, warm up your credit cards, and set off for a day of shopping and gallery hopping. On San Carlos between Fifth and Sixth is the visitor bureau, upstairs in the Eastwood Building, where you can pick up a walking-tour map and schedule of events (831–624–2522). If time is short, stroll down one side of Ocean Avenue and up the other. With time on your hands, wander the side streets, the courtyards, and alleyways. Even those allergic to shopping will enjoy the mix of architecture, everything from English country cottage to California Mission style.

A few notable places to visit: the **Carmel Art Association** at Dolores between Fifth and Sixth (831–624–6276), a cooperative with a wide-ranging collection of the works of top artists; the **Weston Galleries** at Sixth and Dolores (831–624–4453), where three generations of famous photographers are represented; the **Mischievous Rabbit** (Lincoln between Ocean and Seventh; 831–624–6854), a warren of Peter Rabbit–inspired treasures—hand-painted baby clothing, rabbit videos and books, carrot surprises.

Careful browsers discover gardens and shops in more than sixty courtyards; a short courtyard-tour map is available at the visitors bureau. Look for the winding path to the **Secret Garden,** on Dolores between Fifth and Sixth, to see unique statuary, a bevy of blooming baskets, and wind chimes (831–625–1131). Garden sculpture and fanciful topiaries are the specialties of **The Dovecote,** in a landmark Carmel cottage at Ocean and Dolores (831–626–3161).

L U N C H : Porta Bella, Ocean between Lincoln and Monte Verde, Carmel; (831) 624–4395. Inventive Mediterranean cuisine in the flower-bedecked Court of the Golden Bough, in the charming cottage, or on the year-round heated garden patio. Lunch, afternoon tea, and dinner. The restaurant loves your dog on the heated patio, presenting your pampered pooch with water in a champagne bucket on a napkin-covered plate.

Afternoon

In fact, the whole town is dog-friendly, with many restaurant patios open to leashed pets. Carmel Beach is one of few California beaches to allow four-legged visitors off leash. Co-owned by actress and animal rights activist Doris Day, the elegant **Cypress Inn** welcomes well-behaved pets in your room and on leash in the bar and around the hotel (Lincoln and Seventh Streets; 800–443–7443; www.cypress-inn.com). Nightly doggy biscuit turndown is among the special services.

A boutique for dogs and cats, **Diggidy Dog** at Mission and Ocean Avenues sells fabulous toys, apparel, gourmet treats, collars, and carriers. In the pet bakery, tempt your pooch with cannoli, biscotti, doughnuts, and cookies (831–625–1585). At **Mackie's Parlour Pet Boutique,** Ocean and Monte Verde, pick up a jeweled collar, homemade dog treats, and the board games Dogopoly and Catopoly (831–626–0600). In the Carmel Plaza shopping center, look for the Fountain of Woof drinking fountain.

Aviation is the theme at **Wings America,** on the corner of Dolores and Seventh (831–626–WINGS). The collection of aircraft model sculptures and specialty authentic aviation apparel is astonishing; also books, videos, and jewelry. New and antique art, decoys, and gifts with waterfowl, wildlife, and sporting dog motifs are on display at **The Decoy,** on Sixth between Dolores and Lincoln (831–625–1881).

Golf is on stage at **Golf Arts and Imports** (Dolores and Sixth; 831–625–4488)—part shop, part museum and gallery—in photos and paintings of legendary courses and collectibles and antiques. Look for a second shop at the Lodge at Pebble Beach.

Many of the inns and hotels in Carmel are historic landmarks, such as **La Playa Hotel** at Eighth and Camino Real, a pink Mediterranean mansion built in 1904 (831–624–6476). Take a peek at the luscious gardens blooming beneath a canopy of Angel's Trumpet trees. The lobby is a museumlike world of heirloom furnishings and contemporary art. Rooms are upscale traditional, with views of the sea, the gardens, or the village. Cottages are hidden in a pine and cypress grove; each has a kitchen, a fireplace, and a private terrace. With a lovely ocean-view terrace, the **Terrace Grill** here is one of the best restaurants in town for breakfast, lunch, dinner, and brunch (831–624–4010); you can dine until 11:00 P.M. in the lounge.

Before leaving town, take a late-afternoon walk on **Carmel Beach** at the foot of Ocean Avenue—truly white, powdery sand; truly memorable sunsets.

Drive north on Highway 1 to Highway 156, connecting with U.S. Highway 101 north to San Francisco.

There's More

Carmel Walks, P.O. Box 975, Carmel 93921; (831) 642–2700; www.carmel walks.com. Two-hour guided tours to hidden courtyards and gardens, storybook cottages; inside scoop on the history, the famous artists, writers, and movie stars, and the charms of Carmel, including photographer Edward Weston's photo studio, architectural landmarks, and more.

Golf. Golf Club at Quail Lodge, 8000 Valley Greens Drive, Carmel Valley; (831) 624–2770. Eighteen stunning holes for lodge guests or members of other private clubs. Luckily, you are not required to take a cart, all the better to enjoy the 840 acres of wild countryside and elaborate landscaping.

Rancho Canada Golf Course, Carmel Valley Road, 1 mile from Highway 1; (831) 624–0111. Two eighteen-hole public courses with mountain backdrop and valley views.

Jacks Peak County Park, Jacks Peak Road, Carmel Valley; (831) 647–7799. Hike in an enchanted pine forest up the trail to valley views, or take a short trek to a picnic spot.

Mission Trail Park, Carmel. Thirty-five acres of native vegetation, 5 miles of trails. Enter at Mountain View and Crespi, at Eleventh Street and Junípero, or on Rio Road across from the Mission.

Special Events

February. Masters of Food and Wine, Highlands Inn, Carmel; (800) 401–1009; www.mfandw.com. Famous chefs from around the world, more than fifty winemakers, and avid foodies gather annually at the seaside Highlands Inn for days of vertical wine tastings, culinary demonstrations, and extravagant meals.

May. Carmel Art Festival, Carmel; (831) 642–2503; www.carmelartfestival.com. Gallery Walk open house and entertainment; meet the artists at dozens of Carmel galleries; gala party and auction, sculpture in the park; four days of numerous events.

June through August. Outdoor Forest Theatre Season, Carmel; (831) 626–1681.

July. Carmel Bach Festival; (831) 624–2046; www.bachfestival.com. Internationally acclaimed; two weeks of concerts and classes.

August. Carmel Valley Fiesta, Carmel Valley Village; (831) 659–4000. Wild-boar barbecue, street dance, arts and food booths, entertainment on outdoor stages.

September. Carmel Shakespeare Festival; (831) 622–0100.

Sand Castle Building Contest, Carmel Beach; (831) 624–2522. Architects and amateurs vie for biggest, best, most outrageous sand structure.

October. Old Monterey Seafood and Music Festival, Monterey State Park; (831) 655–8070. Fresh seafood specialties, arts and crafts vendors, music, historic displays.

Other Recommended Restaurants and Lodgings

Carmel

The Cottage, Lincoln between Ocean and Seventh; (831) 625–6260. Panettone French toast for breakfast, artichoke soup and chicken stew in a sourdough basket for lunch, lemon chicken for dinner.

Highlands Inn, Park Hyatt Carmel, 4 miles south of Carmel on Highway 1; (831) 620–1234; www.highlandsinn.hyatt.com. Since 1917, wonderful accommodations at a full-service, five-star resort with glorious ocean views. The renowned restaurant, Pacific's Edge, has spectacular sea views from big windows and a California/French menu to match. Twenty-seven thousand bottles of wine in the cellar. The casual California Market cafe here is a fun place to have lunch on the way to Big Sur—a table on the deck overlooking the coast or indoors by the pot-bellied stove; pasta, salads, sandwiches. Luxurious rooms have wood-burning fireplaces, outdoor decks, or balconies. Suites have Jacuzzi tubs, kitchens, and special amenities like terry robes and large dressing areas. Heated pool, spa.

L'Auberge Carmel, Monte Verde at Seventh Street; (831) 624–8578; www.lauberge carmel.com. The longtime favorite, Sundial Lodge, has new owners and has been completely transformed into a luxurious European-style inn and restaurant. twenty spacious, romantic rooms around a garden courtyard have such special features as soaking tubs, hammered-copper sinks, designer linens, comfy seating areas, and original artwork. In the intimate twelve-table restaurant, local seafood, meats, and produce, some from the on-site organic garden, become succulent dishes—from braised artichokes to rabbit ragout, venison with sour cherry sauce, and fresh fish of all kinds; not to be missed, the chocolate-banana beignets. Take a peek in the 5,000-bottle, underground wine cellar. Parking can be difficult.

Vagabond House Inn, Fourth and Dolores; (831) 624–7738. Half-timbered English Tudor country inn; blooming courtyard gardens; elegant, traditional decor; continental breakfast.

Village Corner, Dolores and Sixth; (831) 624–3588. For more than fifty years, inside and on the patio, locals have been meeting here to complain about how Carmel isn't like it used to be. Breakfast, good sandwiches, salads; less expensive than most.

Carmel Valley

Carmel Valley Ranch Resort, 1 Old Ranch Road; (831) 625–9500. Newly renovated, a sprawling luxury resort on an oak-studded hillside overlooking a beautiful golf course and the valley. An outdoor dining and cocktail terrace overlooks a spectacular pool and gardens. Huge suites are private and quiet, secluded in the trees. Twelve tennis courts come with a full-time pro, and the Pete Dye championship golf course is one of the most challenging on the peninsula; with a clubhouse restaurant.

Cobblestone Inn, Junipero between Seventh and Eighth; (800) 833–8836. A real Carmel charmer in the English style, with stone fireplaces in each room, antiques, four-posters, and privacy. Full breakfast on the garden patio and afternoon tea by the fire. Bicycles; warm, special attention.

Quail Lodge Resort and Golf Club, 8205 Valley Greens Drive; (831) 624–1581; www.quaillodge.com. Upscale, full-service resort with a spectacular golf course at the foot of the mountains. Rooms, suites, and villas open into lush gardens; some have fireplaces. Special services at this four-diamond, four-star hostelry include an introduction to local wineries, scenic excursions, spa treatments, and golf packages. *Travel + Leisure* calls it one of the "Best Small Hotels in the World." The Covey Restaurant here is one of the best on the peninsula, a casually elegant place with views of a lake, gardens, and the hills. Swimming pool, tennis, nearby walks, and a certain relaxed luxury make this a place to hide away for a long weekend.

Riverside RV Park and Saddle Mountain RV Park, a mile off Carmel Valley Road on Schulte Road; (831) 624–9329. Tree-shaded RV sites, with valley or river views, hot showers, games, and barbecues. An attractive swimming-pool terrace has picnic tables under the oak trees.

Stonepine, 150 East Carmel Valley Road; (831) 659–2245. Old-world elegance at a circa 1920 country estate, with tennis, horseback riding, sumptuous accommodations in the château or in a guest house. Impeccable service, privacy, and unparalleled natural surroundings. You can take lessons and/or watch dressage, hunter-jumper, and sulky track activities and enjoy carriage rides, hayrides, and the golf practice course. The main château has reopened after a complete renovation of the elaborate suites and formal living and dining rooms.

Pebble Beach

Inn at Spanish Bay, 2700 17-Mile Drive; (800) 654–9300; www.pebblebeach.com. In the lee of the dark, brooding Del Monte cypress forest, the luxurious resort hotel lies a few hundred feet from the shoreline. Contemporary-design rooms and suites, each with private patio or balcony, marble bathrooms, some fireplaces, sitting rooms. One of the top tennis complexes in the country, fitness club, complete spa facilities and beauty treatments, restaurants, and upscale shops. Surrounded by the Links at Spanish Bay, the inn is a mecca for golfers who play here and at nearby Pebble Beach.

Fabulous sea views, glamorous blond Art Deco decor, and world-class Euro-Asian cuisine make **Roy's at Pebble Beach,** at the inn, a special occasion restaurant (831–647–7423).

Located at the inn, the **Ansel Adams Gallery** (831–375–7215) shows a huge collection of Adams's photos and the works of other well-known nature photographers, plus Native American jewelry and fine crafts. Camera Walks are conducted from the gallery for small groups.

The Lodge at Pebble Beach, 17-Mile Drive; (800) 654–9300; www.pebble beach.com. One of the world's great hostelries, Pebble feels like a private club. Luxury rooms and suites, all quite spacious, most with private balcony, sea or garden views, large dressing and sitting areas, some with fireplace. Guests may play golf not only at Pebble Beach Golf Links—California's most famous course—but at nearby Links at Spanish Bay, Spyglass Hill, and Old Del Monte. Pool with sea view, fourteen tennis courts, fitness club, equestrian center, several outstanding restaurants and cafes. Spectacular is too small a word to describe Pebble Beach.

Stillwater Bar and Grill, 17-Mile Drive; (831) 625–8524. At one of the world's great hostelries—the Lodge at Pebble Beach—within view of crashing waves of the Pacific and the notorious eighteenth hole of the Pebble Beach Golf Links. Fresh seafood is superb in a fresh, contemporary, casual setting; don't miss the grilled abalone appetizer.

For More Information

Carmel-by-the-Sea (visitors bureau), San Carlos between Fifth and Sixth, P.O. Box 4444, Carmel 93921; (800) 550–4333; www.carmelcalifornia.com.

Carmel Valley Chamber of Commerce, 13 West Carmel Valley Road, Carmel Valley 93924; (831) 659–4000; www.carmelvalleychamber.com.

Inns by the Sea; (800) 433–4732. Reservation services for several inns.

Monterey Peninsula Golf Packages, P.O. Box 504, Carmel Valley 93924; (831) 659–5361.

EASTBOUND
ESCAPES

Sacramento Delta Loop

Levee Towns and Old Sacramento / 1 Night

Wide, cool, and green, the mighty **Sacramento River** slides through the metropolitan capital of Sacramento and heads south, spreading out into a vast delta scattered with ramshackle river towns, where life remains slow and sweet. Boats and ferries, sailboards and houseboats ply miles of meandering waterways. Blue herons silently stalk the lagoons and sloughs, home to thousands of birds and ducks, a bird-watcher's mecca. Small towns were abandoned by the Chinese workers who built the levees a hundred years ago, but crawfish cafes, scruffy saloons, and a few inns remain for weekenders seeking quiet getaways.

You'll hang out on the boardwalks of the old port of Sacramento, where ships sailed in for supplies and refreshment in the wild days of the gold rush—as many as 800 vessels in 1849. The look and feel of forty-niner days has been re-created by the refurbishment of original hotels, saloons, restaurants, firehouses, and establishments of questionable reputation. There are upscale and down-home restaurants, paddle wheelers for river cruises, dozens of shops, and several museums highlighted by the largest railroad museum in the United States.

- ☐ Exploring the delta
- ☐ Old Town shopping
- ☐ Railroad museum
- ☐ The capitol
- ☐ Crawdads and California history
- ☐ Cruising the river

Topping off your Sacramento delta weekend is a tour of the magnificent state capitol building and grounds.

Day 1 / Morning

Drive north on Interstate 80 from the Oakland Bay Bridge for about an hour. Two miles south of Fairfield, turn east on Highway 12, past the Jelly Belly factory, through the flat cattle country of Solano County, to **Rio Vista** on the Sacramento River, a 25-mile trip.

Before crossing the Rio Vista bridge, go north along the river 2 miles to the ferry to **Ryer Island,** one of the last remaining ferries in the delta; it's free. Prowl around the island a little and take a walk or bike ride on the winding levee road to where the *J-Mack,* a cable-guided ferry, will give you a free ride across Steamboat

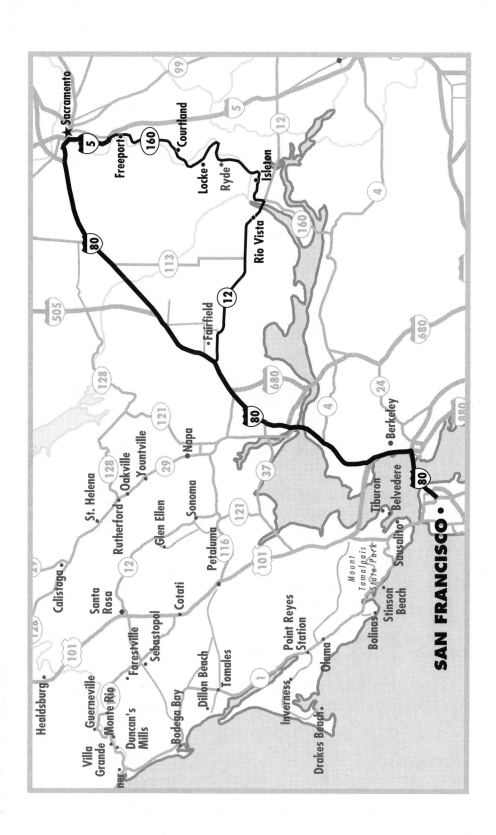

Slough to shady Hogback Park, where you can launch a boat and picnic. For information on fishing-boat and houseboat rentals and delta tours, go to www.california delta.org. Return to the bridge and take Highway 160 north, the levee road.

On the east side of the river is the **Brannan Island State Recreation Area** (916–777–6671), where campers and boaters enjoy fishing and swimming in the Sacramento and a couple of sloughs. There are tent and RV camps, boat-in campsites, a public beach, and picnic sites. Windy Cove at Brannan Island is one of the prime sailboarding spots in the state. Call ahead about guided canoe trips.

BREAKFAST: At **Isleton,** bear right at the Y to **Ernie's,** 212 Second Street (916–777–6510). Seems as though Ernie's restaurant and bar has been here forever, serving crawfish and comfort food for breakfast, lunch, and dinner.

Isleton consists of a down-at-the-heels collection of tin-front and false-front Western buildings. Antiques shops nearby are worth a browse.

You'll drive through **Walnut Grove,** a quiet community on both sides of the river, with a ghostly, empty Chinatown. At **Locke** turn right, leaving the highway, at Yuen Chong grocery; go 1 block down the hill and park. Just 1 block long, Locke is the only surviving rural community built and lived in by Chinese early in the twentieth century. Now it's a maze of creaky wooden buildings connected by a boardwalk. The **Dai Loy Museum,** open on weekends, is a spooky former gambling hall and opium den. **Al the Wop's** (916–776–1800) bar and cafe is dustily atmospheric and frequented by farmhands and fishermen. Thousands of dollar bills are tacked to the ceiling, jars of peanut butter and jelly sit on the tables, and the steak sandwiches and burgers are legendary. **Locke Ness** buys "junque" and sells antiques.

LUNCH: **Courtland Docks** at the Courtland Marina, Highway 160 at Courtland; (916) 775–1172. Burgers, salads, homemade soup, and apple pie.

Afternoon

At Freeport are several seafood restaurants and bars attracting day-trippers from Sacramento. It's just 9 miles farther to **Sacramento,** where you'll connect with Interstate 5 north, proceeding for a few minutes to the J Street/Old Sacramento exit; there are parking garages on the east side of Old Town.

Top off the day with a late-afternoon cruise on the river. The *Spirit of Sacramento* paddle wheeler departs from the L Street landing in Old Sacramento for one-hour sightseeing trips (916–552–2933).

Sacramento became a boomtown during the gold rush in the mid-1800s and was the first link in the transcontinental railroad. At the confluence of the American and Sacramento Rivers, with a deepwater connection to San Francisco Bay and the world, the fortune-seeker's town of the 1800s is now a modern metropolis and a gathering place for state representatives. Summer days average in the nineties, with many days more than a hundred degrees, but this is a city of more than a million trees and ready access to the water, so relief is never far away.

DINNER: Crawdad's River Cantina, 1375 Garden Highway, Sacramento; (916) 929–2268. On the levee near I–5; Cajun popcorn shrimp, fresh fish, steaks, salads, lively atmosphere. Several excellent marinas with restaurants and boat tie-ups are found along the Garden Highway on the north edge of the city. When Crawdad's is closed in winter, try **Joe's Crab Shack** for boiled shrimp, barbecued Dungeness crab, and music and dancing (1210 Front Street; 916–553–4249).

LODGING: Embassy Suites Riverfront Promenade, 100 Capitol Mall; (916) 326–5000; www.embassysuites.com. Walk to Old Sacramento, restaurants, shopping and museums—can't beat the location and the value. Right on the river, a soaring garden atrium and 242 spacious rooms, each with living room, kitchenette, and complimentary breakfast and afternoon happy hour; coin laundry. Patio and indoor river-view tables for American cuisine at Bistro 100; salads, sandwiches, and wood-fired pizzas in the Marketplace Cafe.

Day 2 / Morning

BREAKFAST: Fox and Goose Public House, 1001 R Street, Sacramento; (916) 443–8825. Belgian waffles, homemade cinnamon rolls, steak and eggs. For lunch here, try the bangers and mash and one or two of the many microbeers on tap.

Take Sixteenth Street into **Old Town Sacramento.** (916–264–7777; www .oldsacramento.com). Cool early morning is the best time to prowl the boardwalks, taking photos of the wooden false fronts and climbing around on antique railcars.

The **California State Railroad Museum** (916-445-6645; www.california staterailroadmuseum.org), on the north end of Old Sacramento, comprises 100,000 square feet housing three dozen locomotives and railcars in pristine condition. One of the engines weighs a mere million pounds. The Canadian National sleeping car rocks back and forth as if on its way down the track. Sound effects, snoozing passengers, and compartments that look as if they're occupied give you a taste of vintage train travel. Retired conductors in their dark blue uniforms are available to answer questions and pose for photos. New is *Small Wonders: The Magic of Toy Trains,* a century's worth of toy trains—a collection so vast, it's shown in changing exhibitions. The **Railroad Museum Gift Shop** next door has fabulous train-related toys, books, and souvenirs.

Nearby, the **Discovery Museum & History Center** (916–264–7057) features artifacts of Sacramento's historical and cultural heritage, including the 1849 gold rush.

Explore the *Delta King,* 1000 Front Street (916–444–5314; www.deltaking .com), a huge Mississippi riverboat permanently moored here at the waterfront.

Now a forty-four-stateroom hotel and restaurant, the *Delta King* has small but comfortable cabins with windows overlooking the river; the bars and restaurant have fine river views and are popular, although somewhat touristy, for brunch, lunch, and dinner. The **Visitor Information Center** is located at 1101 Second Street (916–442–7644).

From spring to fall, a bright yellow water taxi runs from the L Street landing to three marinas along the river, where you can stop and dine at waterfront restaurants (916–446–7704; www.riverotter.com).

LUNCH: California Fats, 1015 Front Street, Old Sacramento; (916) 441–7966. An offshoot of the famous Victorian-style Fat City establishment next door, jade, fuchsia, and royal blue decor seems aquarium-like as you step downstairs into the narrow dining room; subtle sounds of a 30-foot waterfall mask everyone's conversation but your own. On the menu are nouvelle Chinese specialties and fresh fish, Peking duck pizzas, grilled crab sandwiches, salads, and banana cream pie; exotic drinks include a Sacramento Slammer and Electric Lemonade.

Afternoon

A hundred or so shops await your discovery in Old Sacramento. The **Artists' Collaborative Gallery,** 1007 Second Street (916–444–3764), the best gallery in Old Sacramento, is a large space displaying paintings, ceramics, weavings, and jewelry by local artists. Navajo rugs and Native American turquoise and silver jewelry are the specialty of **Gallery of the American West,** at 121 K Street (916–446–6662).

Brooks Novelty Antiques, Firehouse Alley (916–443–0783), is a delightfully musty, crowded place, filled with old records, jukeboxes, weird TVs, radios, vintage bikes, magazines, and posters. **Visions of Eden,** 126 J Street; (916) 448–1499. The store embraces the art of graceful living; gifts for the home, garden, and bath.

Decorated to the max for every holiday and smelling like chocolate heaven, the **Rocky Mountain Chocolate Factory,** 1039 Second Street (916–448–8801), lures you in with hand-dipped ice-cream bars, caramel apples, chocolate-covered strawberries, and freshly made candy. **Fanny Ann's,** 1023 Second Street (916–441–0505), is five floors of crazily antiques-crammed restaurant and bar; it's a fun place to take the kids during the day, while an adult crowd gathers here at night.

Walk or drive the few blocks to the **California State Capitol,** Tenth and Capitol Mall (916–324–0333; www.statecapitolmuseum.com), for a tour of the remarkable double-domed building and surrounding grounds.

A guided tour provides background on the magnificently carved staircases, elaborate crystal chandeliers, marble inlay floors, historic artwork, and zillions of columns, cornices, and friezes decorated in gold. You'll learn about California lawmaking, and you may even be able to sit in on a legislative session.

The dome of the California State Capitol, completed in 1874. (©Tom Myers)

Take a tour of the grounds, or stroll around on your own through forty acres of specimen plants and trees, many planted in the 1870s. Springtime in Capitol Park brings waves of blooming camellias, azaleas, and dogwood, and rivers of tulips and daffodils. Walk between twenty-four gigantic magnolias that are more than 60 feet tall, seek out the Vietnam Memorial, and gaze up at the towering hardwoods that were planted here as saplings from Civil War battlefields.

Thanks to First Lady Maria Shriver, the old California State History Museum has a new name, a new focus, and a new high-tech, interactive environment. Now the **California Museum for History, Women, and the Arts** features more than 200 of the state's remarkable women, including today's luminaries, and the rich, overall history of the state in photographs, artifacts, an archive, and much more (1020 O Street, a block south of State Capitol Park; (916) 653–7524; www.california museum.org).

From the capitol it is just a couple of blocks to shopping malls downtown and a twenty-minute walk to Old Sacramento. A free shuttle links the K Street Mall and the Downtown Plaza with Old Sacramento. Thousands of magnificent old trees and glorious Victorian mansions line the downtown streets. Beautiful homes are found from Seventh to Sixteenth Streets, and from E to I Streets; don't miss the Heilbron home at 740 O Street and the Stanford home at 800 N Street.

It's 90 miles from Sacramento to San Francisco on I–80.

There's More

Antiques. Several large shops at Del Paso Boulevard and Arden Way and a dozen in the 800 block of Fifty-seventh Street, Sacramento. Pick up a booklet here to locate other shops in Sacramento.

Ten minutes east of Sacramento in Rancho Cordova is California's largest antiques mall, the Antique Plaza, with more than 250 dealers (off Highway 50 between Sunrise and Hazel; 916–852–8517).

Bike and Surrey Rentals of Old Sacramento, 1050 Front Street; (916) 441–0200. Get around Old Sacramento or ride 26 miles of paved bike paths on the Jedediah Smith Memorial Bicycle Trail, which follows the American River Parkway, or 23 miles of scenic pathway from Old Sacramento to Folsom Lake.

Crocker Art Museum, Third and O Streets, Sacramento; (916) 264–5423; www .crockermuseum.org. A gigantic restored Victorian sheltering the oldest public art museum in the West, European paintings and drawings, nineteenth- and twentieth-century art. Look for the blockbuster, huge painting of Yosemite by Thomas Hill. Across the street, take it easy in Crocker Park.

Grizzly Island, south of Highway 12 between Fairfield and Rio Vista (go south on Grizzly Island Road at the Sunset Shopping Center, then 9 miles to the wildlife preserve); (707) 425–3828. A relaxing place to take an outdoor break between Sacramento and the Bay Area, Grizzly Island is best in winter, when thousands of migratory waterfowl stop to feed and rest in the Suisun Marsh surrounding the island (avoid October through mid-January, which is duck-hunting season). River otters, turtles, tule elk, egrets, herons, coots, wigeons, grebes, and many more are the birds and animals you'll see in this 8,600-acre Sacramento Delta wildlife preserve .

Old Sacramento Public Market, Front Street across from the *Delta King;* (916) 264–7031. It's great fun to browse more than twenty open-air food and produce shops, flower stands, and bakeries selling Asian specialties, spices, cheese, wine, meat, poultry, and fish, plus an Italian deli and places to get walk-around snacks.

Sacramento River Train, boarding in Woodland; (800) 942–6387; www.sacramento rivertrain.com. From the farm town of Woodland, a steam locomotive pulls passenger cars through agricultural lands, about 16 miles and over an 8,000-foot-long wooden trestle to West Sacramento. You will have the chance to sample and purchase local produce at Uncle Ray's Fruit Stand. Several special-event trains during the year, including murder mystery and train robbery, Mother's and Father's Days, and more.

Southern Railroad Excursions, Front Street in Old Sacramento at the railroad depot; (916) 445–6645; www.csrmf.org. Forty-minute, 6-mile ride along the river in vintage passenger coaches or an open-air gondola pulled by a steam locomotive.

Towe Auto Museum, 2200 Front Street, Sacramento; (916) 442–6802. Travel on a sentimental journey to see more than 150 vintage vehicles.

Special Events

February. Old Sacramento Mardi Gras Celebration, under I–5 freeway between J and K Streets; (916) 442–7644. Food, music, dancing for three days.

March. Isleton Asian Festival, Isleton; (916) 777–5880. Two days of live music, ceremonial drumming, food, lion dancers, rickshaw rides, demonstrations.

April. Festival de la Familia, Old Sacramento; (916) 264–7777. Hundreds of art, souvenir, food and drink vendors, and free live Latin, Caribbean, and Native American music.

May. Grape Escapes, Crocker Park, Sacramento; (916) 808–7777. Wine tasting, food, demonstrations, and kibitzing with winemakers from eight surrounding counties.

Sacramento Jazz Jubilee, Old Sacramento and other town venues; (916) 372–5277. Largest traditional jazz festival in the world; more than one hundred bands from around the world and more than 100,000 jazz lovers dancing their feet off for three days; parade, too.

Pacific Rim Street Fest, Old Sacramento; (916) 264–7777. Asian and Pacific Islands cultures are presented in song, dance, exhibitions, and food: Lion dancers prance in the street, Japanese taiko drummers rattle your brain, and local ethnic dance and music clubs put on shows.

August. Gold Rush Days, Old Sacramento; (916) 358–3912; www.oldsacramento .com. Streets are paved with dirt, and only pedestrians (many are in costume), equestrians, and horse-drawn vehicles are permitted. Rides on covered wagons and carriages, street dramas, music and dancing, grizzled miners, ethnic villages, arts and crafts, and food. Reenactments of Pony Express, a funeral procession, squatters' riots, chuck wagon cooking, marksmanship, and more.

California State Fair, Sacramento; (916) 263–3247; www.bigfun.org. One of the biggest state fairs in the country, top-name entertainment, traditional livestock and agricultural exhibits, a carnival, rodeo, nightly fireworks, big crowds, hot summer nights.

September. Rodeo on the River, Isleton; (916) 777–5880. Western championship rodeo featuring bull riding and bronc riding, steer wrestling, calf roping, barrel racing, more competitions, and a Sunday parade.

Other Recommended Restaurants and Lodgings

Old Sacramento

The Firehouse, 1112 Second Street; (916) 442–4772. In an 1853 firehouse; eat indoors in romantic surroundings and on the garden patio; continental cuisine; voted "Best in Sacramento" and "Most Romantic."

Sticky Fingers, 1027 Second Street; (916) 443–4075. On the second floor of a vintage building, dig into ribs, chicken, and seafood. A Dixieland combo often plays on the veranda.

Sacramento

Amber House Bed and Breakfast Inn, 1315 Twenty-second Street; (916) 444–8085; www.amberhouse.com. In three restored mansions are opulent, luxurious, romantic inn rooms; Jacuzzi tubs, fireplaces; gourmet breakfast in the dining room, on the veranda, or in guest rooms; evening refreshments; bikes available. One room has a heart-shaped Jacuzzi and a waterfall!

Ernesto's Mexican Food, 1901 Sixteenth Street; (916) 441–5850. *Chile verde* and luscious *carnitas* bring folks from miles around to one of the best Mexican cafes in a town with a large Mexican population.

Leatherby's Family Creamery, 2333 Arden Way; (916) 920–8382. An old-fashioned ice-cream parlor and cafe serving light lunches, dinners, and homemade ice cream. More than forty luscious flavors in huge sundaes, shakes, and other high-butterfat treats; plus burgers, sandwiches, and salads.

Lemon Grass, 601 Munroe Street; (916) 486–4891. Wonderful Vietnamese and Thai food in a serene, contemporary atmosphere; luscious rack of lamb with hoisin-Cabernet glaze, catfish in a clay pot, award-winning traditional dishes.

Max's Opera Cafe, 1725 Arden Way at Arden Fair Mall; (916) 927–6297. This New York–style upscale deli cafe serves fabulous sandwiches, burgers, pasta, and salads, with legendary mile-high pieces of pie and cake. At night, the staff sings opera and show tunes.

Sacramento Brewing Company, Fulton and Marconi Avenues in the Town and Country Village; (916) 485–HOPS. One of the best of the many new brewpubs, with great, hearty food and a delightful European bistro atmosphere.

Sterling Hotel, 1300 H Street; (916) 448–1300. In a landmark Victorian mansion, a small luxury hotel; stunning rooms with spa tubs, room service; fine restaurant.

For More Information

California Delta Visitors Bureau; (209) 367–9840; www.californiadelta.org.

California Division of Tourism, P.O. Box 1499, Sacramento 95812-1499; (800) 862–2543; www.visitcalifornia.com. Information, brochures for travel statewide.

Sacramento Convention and Visitors Bureau, 1303 J Street, Suite 600, Sacramento 95814; (916) 264–7777; www.sacramentocvb.org.

EASTBOUND ESCAPE TWO

Gold Rush North

Forty-Niner Towns in the Sierra Foothills / 2 Nights

☐ Gold mines and museums

☐ River rambles

☐ Victoriana antiques

☐ Old West

☐ Nuggets and gems

The foothills of the California Gold Country stretch more than 300 miles along the western slopes of the Sierra Nevadas all the way to the southern gate of Yosemite National Park.

In several river corridors—the Yuba, the American, the Mokelumne, the Stanislaus, the Tuolumne, and the Merced—dozens of boomtowns exploded in population in the mid-1800s, when gold was discovered, only to be abandoned by the miners and adventure seekers when the lodes were exhausted.

Of the remaining communities still thriving today, Nevada City is the most completely original gold rush town in the state, having somehow escaped the devastating fires that plagued most of the rest of the Gold Country. More than a hundred Victorian mansions and Western false-front saloons and hotels cluster cozily together here on a radiating wheel of tree-lined streets on small hills. At an elevation of about 3,000 feet, the whole place becomes red and gold in fall, when hundreds of maples, aspens, and oaks turn blazing bright.

Once inhabited by English and Irish who worked five major mines in the area, the town of Grass Valley is honeycombed with underground tunnels and shafts. On Mill and Main Streets remain dozens of buildings built in the mid-1800s, when this was the richest mining town in the state. A block off Main, take a stroll on Neal and Church Streets to see rows of Victorian mansions and churches.

Just a few miles to the east, 1.2 million acres of wilderness in the Tahoe National Forest afford endless hiking, camping, fishing, and cross-country skiing opportunities.

Day 1 / Morning

From the Oakland Bay Bridge, drive north on Interstate 80 beyond Sacramento to Auburn; proceed north on Highway 49 to Highway 20 and Nevada City, about a three-hour trip.

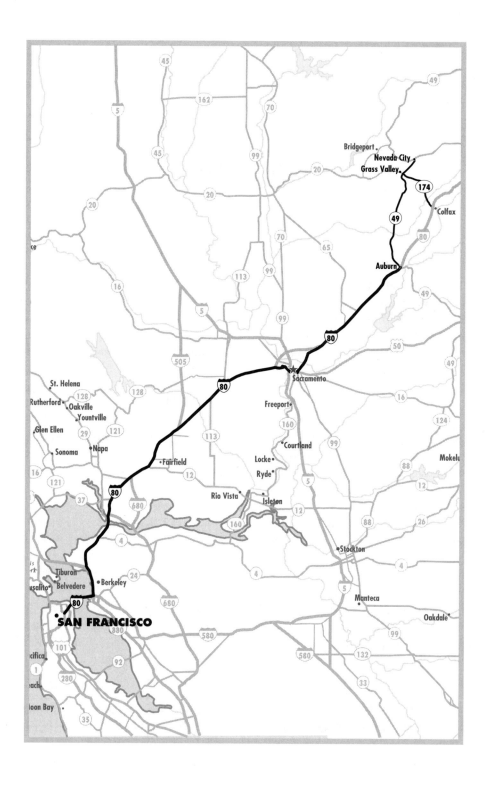

Take the Sacramento Street exit into town, parking in the lot at Sacramento and Broad. Put on your walking shoes and head across the bridge into town on Broad, the main street. Take a right down to the stone-and-brick **Yuba Canal Building** at 132 Main, built in 1850 on the banks of Wolfe Creek, where you can pick up tour maps at the **chamber of commerce.** Since early in the twentieth century, the downtown has remained lost in time, architecturally speaking, and there is much to discover within 3 or 4 blocks.

Next door, at 214 Main, the **Firehouse Museum** has two floors of gold rush and Indian artifacts.

LUNCH: Posh Nosh, 318 Broad, Nevada City; (530) 265–6064. Eat on the tree-shaded patio. Sandwiches, pasta, salads, homemade desserts.

Afternoon

The National Hotel, 211 Broad (530–265–4551; www.thenationalhotel.com), is the oldest continuously operating hotel west of the Rockies; take a look at the long bar, shipped around the Horn more than a hundred years ago. Rooms here are small and sweet, with Victorian furnishings and gimcracks: Some have balconies overlooking the street. Keep your credit cards handy. Yesterday's dusty, quaint shops are now upscale boutiques.

Tanglewood Forest, 311 Commercial Street (530–478–1223), is a fantasyland of wizards, fairies, and strange dolls. Next to the **Nevada Theatre,** the oldest theater in California, at 401 Broad, is **Utopian-Stone,** at 212 Main (530–265–6209), which specializes in gold quartz jewelry. Thousands of teddies in elaborate costumes and in furry plainness inhabit various decorated scenes in a charming circa 1860 Victorian house, the **Teddy Bear Castle Museum and American Victorian Museum;** open by appointment on weekends (203 South Pine; 530–265–5804; www.teddybearcastle.com).

At two emporiums downtown, **The Fur Traders** sells myriad leather and fur apparel, jackets, slippers, headgear, purses, boots and shoes, plus motorcycle jackets, Hawaiian shirts, and fun gift items (233 and 319 Broad Street; 530–265–2000). At **Mountain House Books,** browse for out-of-print and rare books, literature, and history relating to California and the American West (418 Broad Street; 530–265–0241).

Mountain Pastimes Fun and Games, 320 Spring Street (530–265–6692), has toys and games for grown-ups. Across the street you can taste Nevada County wines made right here at the **Nevada City Winery,** 321 Spring (530–265–9463; www.ncwinery.com). In the past couple of decades, vineyards and wineries have popped up all over the county; they celebrate in September with a Wine Fest and Grape Stomp at the Miners Foundry Cultural Center up the street.

When you reach the top of Broad Street, sink into a chair at **Broad Street Books and Espresso Bar** (426 Broad; 530–265–4204) and have a sweet treat and a cup of tea while browsing the best sellers.

The **Deer Creek Miners Trail,** perpendicular to Broad Street near the highway, is a short, easy walk along Deer Creek. Six interpretive stations describe gold prospecting in the early days, when the creek yielded a pound of gold a day.

DINNER: New Moon Cafe, 203 York Street, Nevada City; (530) 265–6399; www.thenewmooncafe.com. In a sleek, contemporary cafe, seasonal California cuisine—chicken in vermouth with sun-dried cherry balsamic honey sauce, pork chop stuffed with peaches in Marsala sauce, a fabulous rib-eye steak, and house-made pastas, with some Asian-inspired inventions. Reservations are a must.

LODGING: Red Castle Inn, 109 Prospect, Nevada City; (800) 761–4766. In a cedar forest, a spectacular four-story 1860 Victorian Gothic mansion overlooking the town, one of only two genuine Gothic Revival brick houses on the West Coast. Seven romantically decorated rooms and suites with private verandas and sitting rooms are chock-full of extraordinary and valuable antiques and art. Surrounded by an opulent, old-fashioned garden with private nooks and crannies under the trees. Arrive in time for the late-afternoon sweets and spiced tea.

Day 2 / Morning

BREAKFAST: At the Red Castle Inn. Choose from the elaborate gourmet breakfast buffet and retire to the porch, to a garden glade, or to your room. Take a stroll around the neighborhood to see pretty gardens and country homes; it's a short walk into town.

Drive south on Highway 49 to the south end of Grass Valley to the Empire Mine exit, going east on Empire Street for five minutes to reach **Empire Mine State Park** (530–273–8522), a 784-acre mining estate. The largest, deepest, and richest hard-rock gold mine in California operated here for more than a hundred years, producing $100 million in gold from 360 miles of underground channels, some 11,000 feet deep. On a tour or on your own, see an extensive complex of buildings and equipment, including part of the main shaft. A visitor center recounts the history of the mine in photos, exhibits, and films.

Sweeping lawns beneath 100-foot sugar pines surround the mine owner's home, **Bourne Cottage,** an outstanding example of a Willis Polk–designed English country manor with lovely gardens. An annual old-fashioned **Miners' Picnic** takes place in June in the park, with food, contests, gold panning, and entertainment (530–273–4667). Ten miles of trails crisscross the park. The 2.5-mile Hardrock Trail loop, which begins and ends at the park entrance, meanders beneath tall pines along Little Wolf Creek, passing mining ruins.

LUNCH: Drive back on Empire Street, across the freeway, to the first right, Mill Street, following Mill down and under the freeway to the **North Star Mining Museum** and powerhouse (530–273–4255), where a shady lawn over Wolf Creek makes a delightful picnic spot. Among antique equipment here is the largest Pelton wheel in the world, a waterwheel that produced power from the creek for the North Star Mine. A large collection of photos traces mining history; admission is free.

Marshall's Pasties is a good place to take out fresh Cornish pasties and English sausage rolls and other picnic fare. At 203 Mill Street in Grass Valley (530–272–2844), Marshall's is on the main street of town, five minutes from Wolf Creek. Introduced by early settlers from Cornwall, England, who came to work in the mines, Cornish pasties are delicious, flaky, hand-size turnover pies in which savory fillings are baked, such as potato and vegetables, ham and cheese, and fruit combinations. In forty-niner days, each miner carried a three-tiered tin lunch pail every day. The bottom was filled with tea, the pasty was placed in the middle section, and a bun on top. The miner lit a candle under his pail at the beginning of his shift, and by the time he ate, his meal was warm. Some of the best pasties in town are baked at Marshall's: broccoli and cheese, apple-figgy, sausage, and many more. (Another good place to get pasties in Grass Valley is Mrs. Dubblebee's at 251 South Auburn Street; 916–272–7700.)

Afternoon

Follow Mill Street north into downtown Grass Valley, parking near the center of town.

Step into **The Holbrooke Hotel,** 212 West Main (530–273–1353; www .holbrooke.com), the grand dame of Grass Valley since 1862. A glance in the hotel register turns up such famous guests as Presidents Cleveland and Garfield. At 114 Mill are three antiques shops. At Church and Chapel Streets, the **Grass Valley Museum** (530–273–5509) is a restored school and orphanage exhibiting gold rush artifacts, clothing, paintings, and domestic items. The fascinating cemetery on the grounds dates to 1852. The **Nevada County Chamber of Commerce,** 248 Mill (530–273–4667), is in the reconstructed home of Lola Montez, a notorious dance-hall entertainer of the 1800s. One block off Main, Neal and Church Streets are ideal to stroll and see several magnificent Victorian mansions and churches.

If you plan to spend time hiking, camping, fishing, or panning for gold on the nearby South Yuba River and environs, stop in at **Swenson's Surplus** for equipment, clothing, and supplies, including fanny packs, water bottles, rain gear, auto gear, and all the basics for gold panning (105 West Main Street; 530–273–7315).

The Jewel in the Crown at 109 West Main was voted Best Toy Store in town, a great resource for educational and scientific crafts, books, games, puzzles, and toys for kids from toddler to teen (530–477–8697). Fido will be in heaven at **Scraps Dog Bakery,** where you can pick up home-baked pet food and treats (12034 Nevada City Highway; 530–274–4493; www.scrapsdogbakery.net). Get your pooch his or her own hiker's backpack, toys, and chewies.

On the **Yuba River,** a few miles southwest of Grass Valley in **Bridgeport,** at 256 feet, the **Bridgeport Covered Bridge** is possibly the longest single-span covered bridge in the world. Mellowed sugar-pine shingles and massive, old-growth Douglas fir beams are warm reminders that buggies and mule teams once clattered across the wooden floorboards. There are nice picnic spots near the bridge, walking trails along the river, and shallow wading pools among the rocks. During much of the year, docents and rangers teach gold panning and conduct interpretive tours of the bridge (530–432–2546).

Not far from Bridgeport, **Englebright Lake** on the Yuba River is a slender piece of water with nice camping and fishing spots accessible only by boat (530–639–2342). Pleasant boat-in campgrounds have sandy beaches and trees. The shore is steep and rocky except at the campgrounds. Fishing for trout, bass, and catfish is good in quiet, narrow coves. All kinds of boats and houseboats are for rent at **Skipper's Cove Marina** on the lake (530–639–2272).

DINNER: **Kirby's Creekside Restaurant,** 101 Broad Street, Nevada City; (530) 265–3445. Above the rushing waters of Deer Creek, the outdoor deck is the place to be on a warm summer night. Inside are candlelit tables before a fireplace. Fresh fish, poultry, and meats in exotic sauces; homemade pumpkin ravioli in Chardonnay cream sauce; smoked stuffed pork chops; and more creative fare. The wine list is top-notch; live music on weekends.

LODGING: Red Castle Inn.

Day 3 / Morning

BREAKFAST: Another extravaganza of a breakfast at the inn. (If you can squeeze in a piece of pie, stop in at the **Apple Fare,** 307 Broad Street, Nevada City, 530–234–2555, and sit at a big round table with the locals.)

For a fascinating trip along the south fork of the Yuba River, take Highway 49 north from Nevada City to Tyler Foote Crossing Road, turn right, and continue to where Tyler splits to the left to Alleghany; then turn right onto Cruzon Grade Road, proceeding to **Malakoff Diggins State Historic Park** (530–265–2740), the largest hydraulic mine site in the world, a rather shocking and strangely beautiful remnant of gold mining in the 1800s, when giant waterjets, called monitors, destroyed entire mountains. Weird and colorful pinnacles, domes, and spirals, as well as a milky lake, are fringed with pines. There are reconstructed buildings and hiking trails in the park, swimming at Blair Lake, and a campground. Swimming and fishing holes on the South Yuba River and a 21-mile river corridor park are accessible near the Diggins.

Eight miles north of Nevada City on Highway 49, just before the arched Yuba River Bridge, watch carefully for the **Independence Trail** sign (530–474–4788). Easy for all ages and abilities, the trail meanders 7 miles through forests and, in some places, is dramatically suspended over the Yuba River Canyon on boardwalk bridges and flumes. You get into eye-popping scenery within a minute. The packed-dirt paths and boardwalks make it wheelchair- and stroller-accessible. There are picnic platforms along the way and ramps leading to fishing holes. Take the trail on the west side of the highway to see Rush Creek Falls and a fabulous suspended flume over a waterfall, 1 mile from the start.

On your way back to the Bay Area, take Highway 174 south from Grass Valley to Colfax, on the oldest, the twistiest, and one of the prettiest roads in the county, past horse ranches and small farms. Another pie emporium is on this road—the **Happy Apple Kitchen,** 18352 Colfax Highway, Chicago Park (530–273–2822).

There's More

Auburn State Recreation Area, Highway 49 at Auburn; (530) 367–2224; www.parks.ca.gov. Along 40 miles of the north and middle forks of the American River, trails, campgrounds, swimming, boating, fishing, biking, horseback and motorcycle riding, and white-water rafting. Boat-in campgrounds at Lake Clementine are popular for fishing and waterskiing; good swimming beaches.

Hiking. The Tahoe National Forest is 5 miles west of Nevada City. Obtain maps and information on hiking and camping at the forest headquarters office at 631 Coyote Street in Nevada City; (530) 265–4531.

Lake Spaulding, 30 miles from Nevada City off Highway 20; (916) 923–7142. A glacier-carved bowl of granite at 5,000 feet surrounded by huge boulders and a forest. Good fishing for trout, small lakeside beaches, powerboating and sailing, and a small, developed campground for tents and RVs. Nearby **Fuller Lake** has just a handful of drive-in campsites but is a lovely, quiet, small lake for fishing and boating.

Nevada County Narrow Gauge Railroad and Transportation Museum, off Highway 49, Gold Flat Road to 5 Kidder Court, Nevada City; (530) 470–0902; www.ncngrrmuseum.org. It's free to see narrow-gauge railroad cars and massive engines built between the late 1800s and early 1900s; antique stock cars, boxcars, coaches, cabooses, and more. Weekends in winter, daily in summer.

Pioneer Park, Nimrod Street on the outskirts of Nevada City; (530) 265–2521. Spend the afternoon under the trees, picnicking; playing sand volleyball, horseshoes, and tennis; or swimming in the public pool (June through August). In Grass Valley on Minnie Street, Condon Park has similar facilities, plus disc golf and walking trails; (530) 274–4390.

Scotts Flat Lake, twenty minutes from Grass Valley off Highway 20; (530) 265–5302. A nice day trip for swimming, fishing, hiking, or for camping lakeside in the national forest. The campground has developed tent and RV sites, sandy beaches, a store, and picnic areas.

Sierra Discovery Trail; (530) 265–4531. From Highway 20 take Bowman Lake Road 0.6 mile to the parking lot. Along the Bear River, a 1-mile, easy trail, partly paved, part gravel, part boardwalk, and accessible to wheelchairs and strollers, winding through a pine-and-cedar forest. Meadows are awash with wildflowers, and a small waterfall rushes year-round. Watch for water ouzels at the waterfall—they are the only American songbirds that dive into the water.

Special Events

June. Tour of Nevada City Bicycle Classic, Nevada City; (530) 265–2692.

June through July. Music in the Mountains, Nevada City; (530) 265–6124. Classical music in glorious outdoor settings.

July. Summer Nights in Nevada City; (530) 265–2692. Everyone comes in costume; fine art, classic cars, food and drink, entertainment.

August. Nevada County Fair, Grass Valley; (530) 273–6217.

September. Nevada County Wine Fest and Grape Stomp, Nevada City; (530) 272–8315.

October. Gold Rush Jubilee Crafts Fair, Auburn; (530) 887–2111.

December. Cornish Christmas Celebration, Grass Valley; (530) 272–8315. Friday night, Thanksgiving to mid-December; twinkling lights, costumed carolers and entertainers, food, wine, special events.

Victorian Christmas, Nevada City; (800) 655–6569. Four Wednesday evenings in December. Roasting chestnuts, wandering carolers and minstrels, horse-drawn carriage rides, and a walking-around Christmas tree.

Other Recommended Restaurants and Lodgings

Grass Valley

Flower Garden Bakery, next to Safeway on Neal Street; (530) 477–2253. Yummy home-baked goodies, sandwiches, and salads made with healthy ingredients in a casual cafe and coffeehouse.

Grass Valley Courtyard Suites, 210 North Auburn Street; (530) 272–7696; www.gvcourtyardsuites.com. In a garden, suites have equipped kitchens, gas fireplaces, decks or balconies, dining rooms, sofa beds, and rollaways; some have two queen beds. Small heated pool, laundry room. Continental breakfast is included, and dogs are welcome.

Sierra Motel, 816 West Main; (530) 273–8133; www.sierramotel.biz. A best-kept secret, until now. Under a landmark redwood tree, a small 1930s-era motel freshly renovated, with kitchenettes, nice bathrooms, picnic/barbecue area, and a separate cottage; reasonably priced. Big breakfast included. Walk to town.

Tofanelli's, 302 West Main Street; (530) 272–1468. Hearty American menu with huge plates of food, breakfast burritos, raspberry chicken. Breakfast, lunch, dinner, and Sunday brunch.

Nevada City

Citronee Bistro and Wine Bar, 320 Broad Street; (530) 265–5697; www.citronee bistro.com. Surprising sophistication garnering top reviews. The traditional French bistro menu: steak frites, coq au vin, burgers, and salads served in the casual front of the house. In the elegant dining room at the back, special multicourse dinners, seared ahi, veal sweetbreads, braised rabbit, and duck. Weekday lunches, dinners every day except Sunday. A wine list for the aficionado.

Kendall House, 534 Spring Street; (530) 254–0405. With a beautiful garden and swimming pool, a bed-and-breakfast inn on a quiet street within a few blocks of downtown. Large, comfortable, very private rooms with baths, plus a two-room cottage with living/dining room, fireplace, private deck, and kitchen. Full breakfast in the solarium or on the garden terrace.

Northern Queen Inn, 400 Railroad Avenue; (530) 265–5824; www.northern queeninn.com. On the south end of town; spacious, comfortable motel rooms; pool; cottages with kitchenettes; chalets on the creek; family-oriented restaurant; restored train cars and a nineteenth-century narrow-gauge engine.

For More Information

California Welcome Center, 13411 Lincoln Way, Auburn 95603; (530) 887–2111; www.visitplacer.com.

Grass Valley/Nevada County Chamber of Commerce, 248 Mill Street, Grass Valley 95945; (530) 273–4667; www.grassvalleychamber.com. In the home and museum of Lola Montez, a notorious dance-hall entertainer of the 1800s.

Historic Bed and Breakfast Inns of Grass Valley/Nevada City, P.O. Box 2060, Nevada City 93959; (530) 477–6634 or (800) 250–5808; www.innsofthegold country.com.

Nevada City Chamber of Commerce, 132 Main, Nevada City 95959; (530) 265–2692 or (800) 655–6569; www.nevadacitychamber.com. In the stone-and-brick Yuba Canal Building, built in 1850 on the banks of Deer Creek.

Placer County Visitor Information, 13411 Lincoln Way, Auburn 95603; (530) 887–2111 or (800) 427–6463.

Gold Country South

Murphys, the Wine Country,
Columbia, and Jamestown / 2 Nights

From the charming village of Murphys to the wide-open meadows of Bear Valley, then to old Columbia and rough-and-ready Jamestown, you get a lot of Gold Country in this quick escape.

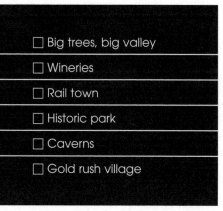

☐ Big trees, big valley

☐ Wineries

☐ Rail town

☐ Historic park

☐ Caverns

☐ Gold rush village

Wine lovers linger around Murphys, where seven top-notch wineries welcome visitors for tours, tastings, picnics, and annual events.

The most perfectly re-created gold rush town in the United States, Columbia is a living museum, with costumed performers, horse-drawn vehicles, and sights and sounds of the past that make you feel as if you've traveled back in time. Pines and maples shade the boardwalks in the hot summer months, when the place is packed with families; spring and fall are the best times to visit.

This brief warm-weather introduction to Bear Valley may encourage a return visit when the snow flies. The ski resort appeals to Bay Area residents who prefer a casual country atmosphere for their cross-country and downhill skiing.

On the way home you'll spend a morning in the rowdy little burg of Jamestown, with perhaps a ride on a steam train.

Day 1 / *Morning*

Drive from the Oakland Bay Bridge east on Interstate 580, connect with Interstate 205 east to Interstate 5 north, then Highway 120 east to Highway 49. Turn north to the Highway 4 junction, stopping in the town of **Murphys**—all told, about two and a half hours from the Bay Area.

Ulysses S. Grant and Mark Twain sat a spell on the veranda of the **Murphys Hotel,** before the locust trees became the tall umbrellas we see today. More than a dozen centuries-old buildings line the main drag, while narrow side streets are a kaleidoscope of wild country gardens, white picket fences, and ancient walnut trees shading cottages and mansions.

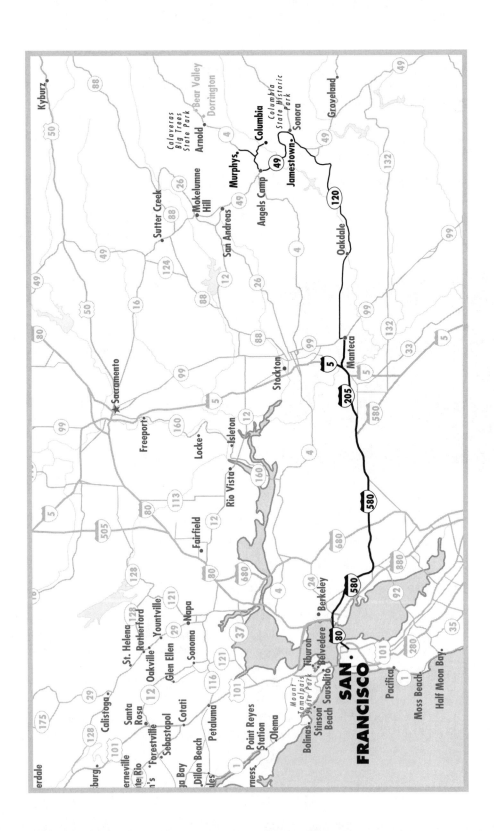

Murphys Creek runs cheerily through town, and there is a small park on its banks that's perfect for a picnic. "A Taste of Murphys" is a narrated horse-drawn wagon tour that you can take around town, on scenic back roads, and to nearby wineries (209–728–2602). The trip includes a gourmet picnic lunch creekside in Murphys Park.

LUNCH: The Peppermint Stick, 454 Main, Murphys; (209) 728–3570. Soup, salad; Miner's Bread Bowl filled with soup, chili, or beef stew; espresso, ice-cream sodas, sundaes.

Afternoon

Bullet holes in the front door of Murphys Hotel, 457 Main Street (209–728–3444), remain from the good old days when Black Bart trod the floorboards; step in for a look at the great, old, long bar, where Saturday night can be quite lively. Rooms and suites here are reasonably priced and include a substantial continental breakfast; rooms near the street can be noisy.

Surrounding the town in a rolling landscape of oak- and pine-dotted hills are a handful of premium wineries. Just a mile out of town at 1894 Six Mile Road, **Ironstone Vineyards** presents a multifaceted experience to wine, garden, and history lovers (209–728–1251; www. ironstonevineyards.com). Visitors congregate by the 40-foot-tall limestone fireplace, enjoying a collection of Western art and majestic sounds from the 1927 movie theater pipe organ. In the Heritage Museum are specimens of gold discovered locally, including the largest crystalline gold leaf nugget in the world, a forty-four pounder. On exhibit are Native American artifacts, historic photos, and mining artifacts.

Explore the aging caverns and belly up to a rococo bar dating from 1907 that was shipped around the Horn from New York. Wander the cattail-lined shores of a small lake, and browse the herb gardens. You can buy a picnic here and lounge by the lake. Colorful banks of rhododendrons and azaleas and thousands of daffodils and other bulbs burst into bloom in spring, a cause for celebration at the annual Spring Obsession festival of wine, food, art, and flowers. Another annual event is the Civil War Reenactment in October.

At **Black Sheep Vintners** off Murphy's Grade, a 1920s barn with a rusting metal roof houses the winery where voluptuous, spicy Zinfandels are made (209–728–2157; www.blacksheepwinery.com). An old wagon road, Sheep Ranch Road winds out of Murphys to a wooded valley at 1,900 feet in elevation. Here **Stevenot Winery** offers samples of its medal-winning Zinfandel, Chardonnay, and Cabernet Sauvignon in a sod-roofed former miner's cabin. In summertime, the Murphys Creek Theatre presents Shakespeare plays outdoors in the winery's amphitheater (2690 San Domingo Road; 209–728–3436).

The lovely gardens and picnic tables at **Chatom Vineyards** make this a nice place to stop at midday. The winery is built of thick rammed-earth walls (1969 Highway 4, just south of Murphys; 209–736–6500; www.chatomvineyards.com).

The harvest is celebrated each year in October at the **Calaveras Grape Stomp and Murphys Gold Rush Days,** highlighted by a raucous grape-stomping competition. In period dress or in crazy costumes of their choice, stompers climb into wooden barrels and smash twenty-five pounds of grapes at a time, while their "swappers" lean in to keep the drain clear of stems and seeds. After several rounds, sticky, drippy, and red from head to toe, the competitors repair to the massage tent, while spectators browse the tented Street Faire and indulge in barbecue, wine tasting, face painting, belly dancing, and general kicking up of heels.

DINNER: Murphys Hotel, 457 Main Street, Murphys; (209) 728–3444 or (800) 532–7684; www.murphyshotel.com. Prime rib, rack of lamb, and fried chicken are among the specialties served in the Victorian dining room. The Caesar salad is especially good, as are the homemade apple crisp and bread pudding.

LODGING: Victoria Inn, 402 Main Street, Murphys; (209) 728–8933; www .victoriainn-murphys.com. Pretty, romantic, antiques-filled rooms in a garden setting; some with fireplaces or wood stoves, spa or claw-foot tubs, balconies; spacious luxury suites and a two-bedroom cottage, too.

Day 2/ Morning

BREAKFAST: Grounds, 402 Main Street, Murphys; (209) 728–8663. Join the locals on the patio for potato pancakes, big omelets, and breakfast burritos.

Return on Highway 4, connecting with Highway 49 and Parrotts Ferry Road to **Columbia State Historic Park** (209–532–0150). When gold was discovered here in 1850, the population boomed within a month from fewer than 100 to 6,000 people, and 150 saloons, gambling halls, and stores opened up. Many Western false fronts and two-story brick buildings with iron shutters remain, inhabited by costumed proprietors who contribute to the living-history atmosphere. The state began to accumulate artifacts and restore the buildings in the 1940s. Musicians and performers are encountered on the street corners and in the restaurants and the theater; horse-drawn stages clip-clop up and down the streets; artisans demonstrate horseshoeing, woodcarving, and other vintage crafts; you can pan for gold or take a horseback ride.

A few of the many shops and restaurants: **Fallon Ice Cream Parlor** (209–533–2355), for floats, shakes, and sodas at an authentic soda fountain counter; **Matelot Gulch Mine Supply Store** has gold nuggets, rocks, guidebooks, and history books; **Columbia Candy Kitchen** (209–532–7886), where a four-generation family makes fresh taffy, brittles, fudge, and penny candy; and **De Cosmos Daguerrean** (209–532–0815), to get your tintype taken.

Columbia Candle and Soap Works in the old feed store sells freshly milled soaps in clove, oatmeal honey, rosemary, chocolate, and lavender scents, plus millions of beautiful handmade candles (209–536–9047).

LUNCH: **Columbia House Restaurant,** Main Street, Columbia; (209) 532–5134. Traditional American fare in a 150-year-old house.

Afternoon

The Columbia experience is enriched by "talking buttons" outside several storefronts; push these buttons to hear about the museum displays in the windows. Trodding the creaky floorboards of the **Columbia Museum,** at Main and State Streets, you'll see photos of the people who lived here during the gold rush, as well as huge chunks of ore, quartz, and semiprecious stones. More than $1.5 billion in gold was weighed on the Wells Fargo Express scales in this town.

Snacks, sodas, and sarsaparillas are easy to find in one of the several saloons (kids OK). Take a ride through the woods nearby on the **Columbia Stage** (209–588–0805).

Farther along on Parrotts Ferry Road is **Natural Bridges,** where Coyote Creek has created a colorful limestone cave. Walk on the streamside nature trail and consider swimming or rafting through the cave—not as scary as it looks.

No trip to the Sierra foothills is complete without a tour of one of four natural wonders, the underground caverns—Black Chasm, Mercer Caverns, Moaning Cavern, or California Caverns. Not as fearsome as they sound, each cavern consists of huge chambers connected by well-lighted walkways, platforms, and stairs designed to give breathtaking views of vividly colored limestone chambers spiked with stalactite and stalagmite formations. The atmosphere is delightfully spooky, damp, and drippy, with a constant temperature in the high fifties—refreshing in summer, when outside it may be more than a hundred degrees in the shade. Opalescent pools, spiral staircases, and striated, multistory columns and stone curtains are subtly lighted and fascinating. Mercer Caverns is near Murphys on Sheepranch Road; (209) 728–2101. View other locations at www.caverntours.com.

DINNER: **City Hotel,** Washington Street, Columbia; (209) 532–1479. Big-city cuisine in elegant gold rush–era surroundings; superb continental menu and good wine list; dinner daily, weekend lunch and brunch. You'll be surprised to find out who the chefs and wait staff are, and you will love the marinated veal chops with roast garlic risotto and shiitake Marsala sauce, the rack of lamb with garlic pine-nut crust, and the mango tart with ginger cream!

The **What Cheer Saloon** in the hotel still has the original cherry-wood bar shipped round the Horn from New England. Special vintner dinners hosted by renowned California winemakers are offered several times a year.

The hotel has ten charming, small rooms with many of the original antiques. Popular mystery weekends, with professional actors and hotel guests playing their parts all over town, are often featured.

LODGING: **Fallon Hotel,** on Washington Street on the south end of town, next door to the City Hotel and the Fallon Theatre, Columbia; (209) 532–1470.

A Victorian extravaganza of rococo wallpaper, antique furniture, and Oriental rugs.

Day 3 / Morning

BREAKFAST: Expanded continental breakfast at the Fallon Hotel.

Continue on Highway 49 through Sonora to Jamestown. (**Sonora** is the county seat and a highway junction; traffic somewhat spoils the old-town atmosphere here, although side streets, antiques shops, and historic buildings make this worth a stop if you have the time.)

Boomed and busted several times in the past 150 years, **Jamestown** retains an anything-can-happen, Wild West atmosphere, from the days when it was just a bawdy cluster of tents on a dusty road. When the gold began to rush, saloons and dance halls were erected, then hotels and homes. Dozens of antiques and curio shops line the streets, and almost as many saloons and restaurants.

Attractions include the **Railtown 1897 State Historic Park** on Fifth Avenue (209–984–3953; www.csrmf.org/railtown), a twenty-six-acre exhibit of vintage steam locomotives and passenger cars, a roundhouse, and a grassy picnic area in an oak grove. You can take a forty-minute train ride through the foothills. This is a great place for a picnic at tables or on the lawns under the aspens and maples, within sight and sound of the exciting action on the track—whistles, bells, steam, and smoke.

A stroll up and down Main Street will turn up the **Saunders Gallery of Fine Art,** at 18190 Main, in the historic 1877 **Carboni House** (209–984–4421), which shows carvings, photos, and paintings by local artists, and **Jamestown Mercantile I** and **II** (209–984–6550), two large antiques co-ops. Behind the Jamestown Hotel in the Marengo Courtyard, check out Native American art, jewelry, and baskets at **Alta California Traders** (209–984–1025). Fairies, gnomes and elves, and whimsical home and garden accessories and gifts are densely packed into **The Mossy Bog,** from frogs hiding under mushroom umbrellas to flying angels and colorful bird feeders (18145–8 Main Street; 209–527–1845).

Visitors and residents get into the spirit of the Mother Lode by dressing in period costume for annual theme events such as Old West reenactments. You can purchase or rent beautiful Victorian and Western apparel at **Dragoons** (18231 Main Street; 209–984–1848). David and Deborah Wright will outfit you in cowboy boots and hats, fancy dresses and feathered hats, beaded purses, and fringed buckskin jackets and vests. The days of the desperadoes are re-created every September at the **Jamestown Shoot 'Em Up,** when bewhiskered cowboys and wild-eyed outlaws swagger up and down the sidewalks, their six-guns smokin'.

The **Jamestown Hotel,** circa 1920, at 18153 Main (800–205–4901; www .JamestownHotel.com), is an old beauty restored to its former elegance, with a long bar and a restaurant famous throughout the region for prime rib, pepper steak, and seasonal specialties made with fresh local poultry and fresh produce. Eight rooms re-create the gold rush era, with antiques and Victorian baths. The Lotta Crabtree suite has a pink claw-foot tub, the Jenny Lind a king-size brass-and-iron bed.

When you see people panning for gold in a wooden trough on the main street (18170 Main), you are at the headquarters for **Gold Prospecting Expeditions,** where you can find out about gold panning and prospecting day trips and rafting trips on nearby creeks and rivers (209–984–4653 or 800–596–0009; www.gold prospecting.com).

LUNCH: **The Willow Steakhouse,** 18273 Main, Jamestown; (209) 984–4388. In a roadhouse built in 1862, Willow serves platters of steak of every description from filet mignon to pepper steak to London broil, plus hot and cold sandwiches. For Tex-Mex, go to the **Smoke Cafe** (18191 Main Street; 209–984–3733), in a building that is a good example of the Pueblo Revival architecture popular in the 1920s.

Afternoon

Retrace your route back to the Bay Area.

There's More

Bear Valley. An hour north of Murphys off Highway 4, in the Stanislaus National Forest, Bear Valley is a mountain meadow at 7,200 feet surrounded by dramatic granite peaks, snowcapped in winter and early spring. You can mountain bike here, walk in the pines, climb a rock, or go kayaking. Camping and fishing are popular on the river and at several alpine lakes sprinkled around Ebbetts Pass. Maps, rentals, and tours are available at Bear Valley Mountain Bike and Kayak Center (209–753–2834). Music from Bear Valley is a big annual summer festival that brings hundreds of people to hear big-name classical, opera, jazz, and theatrical performances (209–753–BEAR). Winter fun includes downhill and cross-country skiing at Bear Valley Mountain Resorts (209–753–2301), and ice skating is popular on a frozen lake. There is a nice lodge hotel; condominiums and houses to rent (209–753–2327).

Calaveras Big Trees State Park. (209) 795–2334; www.parks.ca.gov. Take a walk or a hike to see *big* sequoias. The largest trees, 1,300 of them, are found in the South Grove, a mile from the parking lot up the Big Trees Creek Trail. One giant stands 320 feet high. Winding through the park, the Stanislaus River has small beaches for swimming and developed campsites.

Special Events

February. President's Wine Weekend, Murphys; (209) 223–0350. Wine releases and library tastings, special discounts, food, and music.

April. Gunfighters Rendezvous at Railtown, 1897 State Park, Jamestown; (209) 984–3953. Gold panning, old-fashioned barbeque, musical hoedown, surprise train robberies, historical costumes.

July through August. Music from Bear Valley; (209) 753–BEAR. Big-name classical, opera, jazz, and theatrical performers.

September. Gold Fest, Angels Camp; (209) 728–1251. Gold-panning instruction and competition, forty-niner camp, Native American dance.

October. Harvest Festival, Columbia State Historic Park; (209) 532–0150.

December. Christmas Lamplight Tour, Miner's Christmas, and Las Posadas, Columbia State Historic Park; (209) 532–0150.

Other Recommended Restaurants and Lodgings

Columbia

Goldstreet Bakery Cafe, 22690 South Gold Street; (209) 532–5397. Just outside the state park; open early for breakfast and lunch. Owner Anne-Marie Holmes uses organic ingredients and local produce in healthy menu items like homemade soups, salads, and vegetarian dishes, inch-thick French toast, and fruit pastries. Breads are baked here, and juices are fresh-squeezed. Sit outside under the trees.

Harlan House, 22890 School House; (209) 533–4862. Victorian mansion renovated in 1992; three rooms with baths; full breakfast.

Jamestown

Here's the Scoop, 18242 Main Street; (209) 984–4583. Incredible banana splits, shakes, and ice-cream concoctions, plus homemade desserts, sandwiches, salads, and espresso drinks.

Historic National Hotel, 18183 Main Street; (209) 984–3446; www.national-hotel.com. In a shady garden courtyard, lunch, brunch, and dinner are among the best in town; the wine list is a *Wine Spectator* award-winner. In the elegant dining room, sophisticated dishes such as escargot, halibut with apricot glaze, steak sandwiches, and grilled trout. A historic landmark built in 1895, the hotel is a beauty. Rooms are small and quite nice; some with small baths.

Michelangelo's, 18228 Main Street; (209) 984–4830. Contemporary cafe and bar; nouvelle Italian menu, pizza, pasta.

Murphys

Dunbar House, 271 Jones Street; (209) 728–2897; www.dunbarhouse.com. Luxurious, historic bed-and-breakfast inn near Main Street; private baths; gardens; bountiful breakfast and wine buffet.

Firewood, 420 Main Street; (209) 728–3248. New in town, gourmet wood-fired pizza and Mexican food.

For More Information

Calaveras County Visitors Bureau, P.O. Box 637, Angels Camp 95222; (209) 736–0049 or (800) 225–3764; www.visitcalaveras.org.

Calaveras Wine Association, P.O. Box 2492, Murphys 95247; (800) 225–3764, ext. 25; www.calaveraswines.org. Maps and events information for Calaveras County wineries.

Jamestown Visitors Information Center, 18239 Main Street, P.O. Box 699, Jamestown 95327; (209) 984–4616.

EASTBOUND ESCAPE FOUR

Old Tahoe on the West Shore

Mansions in the Mountains / 2 Nights

The 1920s were the halcyon days of Lake Tahoe's west shore, when wealthy nabobs from San Francisco built mansions and zipped about in sleek varnished speedboats, and when wooden steamers still cruised the lake, revelers aboard. Much of this area is still privately owned; restaurants and beaches are frequented by people who've spent their vacations here for decades. The pace is slow, except in the nightspots and shops of Tahoe City. Even in the high summer season, you can doze on a quiet beach, walk and bike on silent forest trails, and poke around contentedly in a rented boat. And the rowdy, rushing Truckee River is always there for fishing, rafting, and strolling along beside.

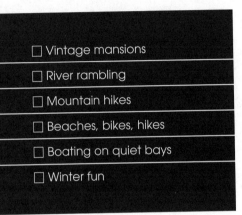

☐ Vintage mansions

☐ River rambling

☐ Mountain hikes

☐ Beaches, bikes, hikes

☐ Boating on quiet bays

☐ Winter fun

The sun shines an average of 274 days a year at Tahoe. Soft spring days are clear and wildflowery; fall is brisk, with aspen color glittering through the pines. Winter is lively at several small, inexpensive downhill and cross-country resorts and positively posh at the big ski resorts: Squaw Valley, Northstar, and Alpine Meadows.

Day 1 / Morning

From the Golden Gate Bridge, drive north on U.S. Highway 101, turning east onto Highway 37 to Vallejo, where you'll catch Interstate 80 northeast; it's a four-hour drive to the west shore of Lake Tahoe.

A lovely place to take a break is the highway rest stop at Donner Summit, at 7,227 feet, and a few miles farther you'll turn right onto Highway 89, driving 13 miles south to Tahoe City, past Squaw Valley, through the **Truckee River Canyon.** Here you get a first view of Tahoe, North America's largest Alpine lake, 22 miles long and 12 miles wide.

The paved **Truckee River Bike Path** starts at Alpine Meadows, winds along the Truckee 4 miles to Tahoe City, then takes a 9-mile route south along the lake. At some point during your west shore sojourn, you'll want to rent bikes at Tahoe City, or just walk, jog, or push a baby carriage on the path. In the low-water days of late summer and fall, the river slides quietly along. In winter and spring it boils and crashes past ice-decorated trees and snowy islands.

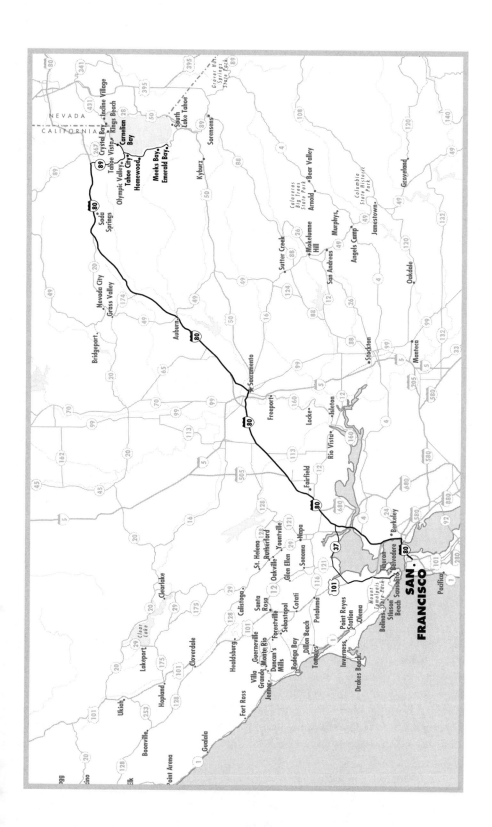

Arriving in Tahoe City, turn right at the junction with Highway 89, which turns sharply south along the western lakeshore. Cross **Fanny Bridge**—where people are always lined up, leaning over to see the trout ladder where the Truckee joins the lake—and stop at the **Gatekeeper's Cabin Museum** and lakeside park, 130 West Lake Boulevard, Tahoe City (530–583–1762), to see an exceptional collection of Washoe and Paiute Indian baskets, artifacts, and historical memorabilia.

LUNCH: Rosie's Cafe, 571 North Lake Boulevard, Tahoe City; (530) 583–8504. Ski bums and locals, families and summer vacationers are happy with burgers and sandwiches, Philly cheese steaks, prime rib, Mexican specialties, and more rib-sticking comfort food. Breakfast and dinner here, too; happy hour appetizers by the fireplace or at the lively bar.

Afternoon

Drive 9.5 miles south on Highway 89 to **Sugar Pine Point State Park** (530–525–7982) to visit one of the grand dames of Tahoe, a spectacular three-story, 12,000-square-foot Queen Anne–style summer home, the **Ehrman Mansion.** Built at the turn of the twentieth century by a San Francisco banker, the mansion still looks like the privately owned lakeside estate it once was, surrounded by sweeping lawns shaded by tall pines. Rangers give daily tours of the mansion and boathouse, imparting stories of old days on the lake. After the tour, wander around the grounds, spread a blanket on the beach, or take a walk on trails along the lakeshore. A longer hike is accessible from the large campground across the road; rangers have maps for you.

In the late afternoon, drive north on 89 to **Sunnyside Restaurant and Lodge,** 1850 West Lake Boulevard, 2 miles south of the Tahoe City Y (530–583–7200). Sunnyside has one of the best blue water and high mountain views on the lake. People-viewing is excellent here, too. Boats of every description come and go in the marina; french-fried zucchini and onion rings are tops; and once you get settled outside on the deck or inside by a lakeside window, you'll find it hard to move from the spot. Here you can rent personal watercraft, sail- and powerboats, and take a sailing lesson. Winter evenings are warm and friendly in the lounge in front of a giant river-rock fireplace. Casually elegant, small, lakefront lodge rooms and suites here have tiny balconies, some fireplaces, and include breakfast buffet.

DINNER: Chambers Landing, 1 mile south of Homewood; (530) 525–7672. Overlooking the lake on a glass-enclosed and heated terrace. Try the Moroccan lamb or fresh fish, and you owe it to yourself to have a Chambers Punch. A small bar on the Chambers pier is popular with locals. On one side of the pier is a private beach for people staying in the Chambers Landing condos (see Other Recommended Restaurants and Lodgings); on the other side is a public beach, one of the nicest on the west shore.

LODGING: Mayfield House at Lake Tahoe, 236 Grove Street, Tahoe City; (888) 518–8898; www.mayfieldhouse.com. You can walk to the shops and restaurants of Tahoe City from here, a bed-and-breakfast inn in a 1930 historic stone cottage in a delightful garden. Among the amenities in six mountain lodge–style rooms: spa tubs, sitting areas, down comforters, antiques, steam showers, and log beds. A cozy cottage has a fireplace.

Day 2 / Morning

BREAKFAST: Mayfield House, a bountiful breakfast by a roaring fire. Check your e-mail with Wi-Fi.

Now pick up picnic supplies and head south toward Emerald Bay. On the way, check out **Meeks Bay Resort and Marina** (530–525–7242), owned by the USDA Forest Service, a popular personal watercraft and water-ski beach with an unparalleled view of the lake. This is a good place for beachy activities like rowing, canoeing, and paddleboating (all rentable), or just hanging out in the sun, though all the motors create plenty of noise during summer. A little cafe serves snacks and burgers, and there are a few cottages and a 150-unit campground.

About 5.5 miles from Meeks Bay, **Emerald Bay** appears in its glittering glory far below. One of the most photographed pieces of scenery in California, the bay can be seen from several vista points along Highway 89, but you must trundle down a steep 1-mile trail (or take a tour boat) to reach the real treasure of the bay—the Scandinavian **Vikingsholm Castle** (530–525–7232), built in 1928. A cross between an eleventh-century castle and an ancient church, the mansion is considered the finest example of Scandinavian architecture in North America. Take a ranger's tour to see the extensively decorated and furnished estate home.

In the clear blue depth of Emerald Bay is California's first underwater shipwreck park. Two wooden barges from the 1930s were originally pulled by steamers, the most common form of transportation before the highway was completed. The barges were intentionally scuttled in Emerald Bay for scuba divers to explore. There are a permanent dive buoy and underwater interpretive panels at the site (530–525–7232).

At the **Emerald Bay State Park Campground** are one hundred tent and RV sites and boat-in campsites (503–525–7232). The campground is closed from mid-September until mid-June.

LUNCH: Have a picnic at Vikingsholm.

Afternoon

From Highway 89 at Emerald Bay, there is an easy 2-mile loop hike to **Eagle Falls** and beautiful **Eagle Lake,** surrounded by the sheer walls of Desolation Wilderness, where many trailheads lead into the southern part of the Tahoe National Forest.

Overlooking 22-mile-long Lake Tahoe, North America's largest alpine lake.

One of the most accessible but least known wilderness areas at Tahoe is **Blackwood Canyon,** off Highway 89 just north of Tahoe Pines. Perfect for easy walks, in-line skating, and biking, the paved road is the only development and has almost no traffic; this road is a good add-on to the shoreline bike path. Forests, meadows, and the banks of Blackwood Creek make good picnic spots. You can hike on the flat valley floor or drive up the road to the steep trails of 8,000-foot **Barker Pass,** hooking up with the **Pacific Crest Trail.** An off-road-vehicle camp and trails area are also here in the canyon (530–573–2600). A new 150-mile trail circles the lake, running along ridges and mountain tops. Access the **Tahoe Rim Trail** (775–588–0686) south of Fanny Bridge in Tahoe City; ample parking lot and well-marked trailhead.

DINNER: Gar Woods Grill and Pier, 5000 North Lake Boulevard, Carnelian Bay; (530) 546–3366. On the lake, with a zinger of a view, the glassed-in deck with heaters is a place to take your time enjoying pasta and fresh seafood. The bar is popular and lively, a good place to have an appetizer and people-watch. Sunday brunches are legendary. Try the White Chocolate Snickers Cheesecake.

LODGING: Mayfield House.

Day 3 / Morning

BREAKFAST: Mayfield House.

Explore the small town of **Tahoe City,** the action and shopping headquarters of the west shore. Boutiques are found in the **Cobblestone, Boatworks,** and **Roundhouse** malls; pine-scented breezes and lake views make shopping at the Boatworks particularly pleasant. **Sports Tahoe** in the marina mall (530–583–1990) is jammed with fabulous clothes for every season at the lake.

Tahoe City is the hub of the annual winter festival in March, **North Lake Tahoe Snow Festival,** the largest winter carnival in the western states (800–TAHOE–4–U). Fireworks at Squaw Valley start off a weekend of parades, ice carving, ice cream eating, live entertainment, and the Polar Bear Swim. More than one hundred events include the Great Ski Race—a 30K Nordic event between Tahoe City and Truckee—and the Snowboard Spectacular. It's wall-to-wall people and lots of fun.

Just north of Tahoe City is the **Watson Cabin Museum,** 560 North Lake Boulevard (530–583–8717), one of the oldest structures on the lake. Docent guides in period costumes will point out the interesting original furnishings.

LUNCH: River Ranch, Highway 89 and Alpine Meadows Road, Tahoe City; (530) 583–4264. On your way out of Tahoe City to head home, stop here for lunch and a last look at the Truckee. A small, charming hotel on the river, River Ranch offers a popular indoor/outdoor restaurant and bar, located at the south end of the Truckee bike path.

Highway 89 takes you to I–80 south and the Bay Area.

There's More

Alpine Meadows Ski Area, P.O. Box 5279, Tahoe City 96145; (530) 583–6914; www.skialpine.com. A major ski area for all abilities, priding itself on the longest season and a casual, family-oriented atmosphere. The fabulous main lodge was significantly remodeled, and new restaurants include a sushi bar, Mexican cafe, burger bar, pasta place, and bakery. Ski runs have scary names like Chute That Seldom Slides, Promised Land, and Our Father. Kids are VIPs at Kids School and Ski Camp. On the Sun Kid beginner surface lift, children just step onto a slow conveyor belt. Programs for all ages are offered for racing, snowboarding, telemark, freestyle, and just plain skiing; and there is ski instruction for people with mental and physical disabilities. Sled-dog tours from here are an exciting way to get out into the beautiful forest and snow-covered meadows.

B. L. Bliss State Park, 3.6 miles south of Meeks Bay. Mistix reservations: (800) 444–7275. One hundred sixty-eight campground sites, beautiful white-sand beach, picnics, good swimming, and a lovely 4-mile trail that leads to Emerald Bay.

Golf. Northstar, Basque Drive, Truckee; (530) 562–2490. Eighteen holes; one of the prettiest and most challenging courses at Tahoe.

Resort at Squaw Creek, Squaw Valley; (530) 581–6637. Eighteen-hole Robert Trent Jones course, surrounded by the glory of the valley.

Tahoe City Golf Course; (530) 583–1516. Nine holes.

Granlibakken Ski Area, 667 Lakeshore Drive, Tahoe City; (530) 525–2992 or (800) 543–3221; www.granlibakken.com. A perfect headquarters for summer or winter, this 160-unit condominium resort has a beginner ski and snowboard hill, Nordic skiing, developed snow play area (all for day use, too), and a big swimming pool. Rent saucers or bring your own for the groomed sledding hill. Some units have fireplaces, kitchens, lofts, and decks or patios. The complimentary hot breakfast is huge!

Hiking. Donner Lake to the Pacific Crest Trail. Drive 4 miles west on Old Highway 40 from the lake's west end; watch for the trailhead on the left. A 15-mile, strenuous hike along the ridge of the Sierra crest that descends down Squaw Valley's Shirley Canyon. Park one car at Squaw Valley's Olympic Village Inn.

Tahoe Rim Trail. For maps and information, call (916) 577–0676. From Fairway Drive in Tahoe City, you can connect with the 150-mile hiking and equestrian path that follows the ridgetops of the Lake Tahoe Basin, passes through six counties in Nevada and California, and incorporates about 50 miles of the Pacific Crest National Scenic Trail. The Tahoe Rim Trail is also accessible from several other trailheads around the lake.

Homewood Mountain Resort, 5145 West Lake Boulevard, 6 miles south of Tahoe City; (530) 525–2992; www.skihomewood. One of the most easily accessible and reasonably priced ski mountains, with big views of Lake Tahoe. A new triple chair gets you up the mountain fast. Book ahead for shuttles from around the west shore.

Kayak Cafe, in Carnelian Bay next to Gar Woods; (530) 546–9337. Cafe and kayak rentals.

Public beaches. Chambers Landing, Obexer's, Sugar Pine Point, Meeks Bay, Homewood. Just north of Tahoe City is the uncrowded beach and pier at Lake Forest; boats can be launched here, and camping is available.

River rafting. Fanny Bridge Raft Rentals, Tahoe City; (530) 583–3021.

Truckee River Rafting Center, 205 River Road, Tahoe City; (530) 583–RAFT.

Squaw Valley USA, P.O. Box 2007, Olympic Valley 96146; (800) 545–4350; www.squaw.com; snow phone: (530) 583–6955. One of the world's largest and best ski mountains, actually five peaks with thirty-four lifts and more than 9,000 acres of skiable terrain. Facilities at the Squaw Kids Children's Center are absolutely fabulous, for toddlers on up, with lessons, supervised skiing, and snow play. A second Magic Carpet step-on lift was added for easy, nonintimidating access, and the Papoose Learning Area now has deluxe lifts and expanded terrain. First-timers of all ages get free rides, rentals, and demos.

The valley is spectacular in every season. You can stay here in a luxury hotel, a reasonable lodge, a bed-and-breakfast inn, a rented condo, or a house. A 150-passenger aerial cable car accesses the High Camp complex, where you can ice skate, hike, mountain bike, swim, picnic, play volleyball and tennis, bungee jump, or just blink in amazement at the mountain surroundings. At High Camp, Alexander's is a good place to eat while enjoying the view. Ride the heated cable car to the restaurant and have dinner before you ride back down or ski down the illuminated, 3.5-mile Mountain Run.

The Village at Squaw Valley is a new complex of multistory condos, shops, and restaurants clustered around plazas, right at the foot of the mountains (888–805–5022; www.thevillageatsquaw.com). You will find Starbucks, which has indoor/outdoor fireplaces; a candle-making shop; a chocolate factory; outdoor trampolines; a fun cat and dog store; smoothies and great bagels at Mountain Nectar; and live entertainment and special events every summer weekend. Park your car and get to nearby Truckee and to destinations around the lake by free shuttle bus. Body/beauty treatments and massage are available at the glitzy new Trilogy Spa. *Tip:* look for the games arcade and a coffee counter with yummy treats in Olympic House in the older part of the village.

Sugar Bowl Ski Area, 3 miles southeast of Norden exit off I–80; (530) 426–9000; www.sugarbowl.com. Snow phone: (530) 426–3847. On the slopes of 8,383-foot Mt. Judah, express lifts and a multimillion-dollar expansion of trails and facilities make this one of the best medium-size ski resorts at the lake, and it's closer to the Bay Area by as much an hour than most Tahoe ski resorts. Among recent additions is the huge new learning center, a new Flying Carpet lift to expanded terrain for beginning skiers and boarders, and the new SnowBomb Terrain Park. You can stay right here at the Inn at Sugar Bowl; ask about winter and summer packages.

Special Events

March. North Lake Tahoe Snow Festival, Tahoe City and at several ski resorts; (530) 583–7625; www.tahoesnowfestival.com. Largest winter carnival in the western United States.

August. Tahoe Yacht Club Concours D'Elegance, Boatworks Mall, Tahoe City; (530) 583–8022. Classic wooden boats.

September. Antique and Classic Car Show, Tahoe City; (530) 525–4429.

October. Oktoberfest, Alpine Meadows Ski Resort; (530) 583–2371. Dining, dancing, and Bavarian festivities.

Other Recommended Restaurants and Lodgings

Homewood

Chambers Landing, P.O. Box 537, Homewood 95718; (530) 525–7202. On West Lake Boulevard near Sugar Pine Point. Some forty-three privately owned condos; a quiet, private hideaway in an aspen grove; lawns, views; private beach and pool. One of the nicest condo complexes at Tahoe, offering three- and four-bedroom luxury.

Meeks Bay

Sugar Pine Point State Park Campground; reservations: (800) 444–7275. Offers 175 sites.

Olympic Valley

Fireside Pizza Company, Village at Squaw Valley; (530) 584–6150; www.fireside pizza.com. Sit outside by firelight or inside for spicy appetizers and gourmet pizzas (try the pear and Gorgonzola or the portobello with goat cheese). Plain food for kids, too.

Mamasake, Village at Squaw Valley; (530) 584–0110; www.mamasake.com. Snowboarders go nuts over the wall-size screen showing eye-popping movies of extreme boarders. The sushi is expensive and really good; and there are some nonsushi menu choices like New York bagel roll, salad roll, Heads Will Roll, and more fun food.

Plump Jack Squaw Valley Inn, 1920 Squaw Valley Road; (530) 583–1576 or (800) 323–7666; www.plumpjack.com. In a charming shingle-and-stone complex near the ski tram, sixty contempo rooms with cushy comforters and comforting amenities; some suites with oversize tubs. A circular fireplace warms up the popular cocktail lounge. Pretty garden terrace with swimming pool and Jacuzzis. The upscale restaurant, with eye-popping mountain views, has one of the most exotic menus at the lake.

Resort at Squaw Creek, 400 Squaw Creek Road; (800) 3–CREEK–3; www.squaw creek.com. A 400-room luxury destination resort with a championship Robert Trent Jones golf course, shops, a tennis complex, a full-service spa, and a chairlift to ski runs and to High Camp. The terraces of three outdoor pools (and a 120-foot water slide) overlook waves of wildflowers in summer and snowy meadows in winter. Mountain Buddies is the daytime camp for ages three to thirteen, and there are special excursions for teens. Golf and ski packages. Cross-country ski from the hotel.

Squaw Valley Lodge, 201 Squaw Peak Road; (530) 583–5500 or (800) 922–9970; www.squawvalleylodge.com. Suites with one or two bedrooms and lofts, equipped kitchens, and luxurious amenities like down comforters. Park your car here and get to outdoor recreation, restaurants, and sights on foot, by cable car to High Camp, and valley shuttles. Enjoy the tennis courts and big pool, and unlimited use of a nearby health club with Nautilus equipment. Ski right out the door to the lifts!

The Village at Squaw Valley, (866) 818–6963; www.thevillageatsquaw.com. A complex of new one-, two-, and three-bedroom condos in multistory buildings are upscale and loaded with amenities, from a little kids playroom and a big-screen media room (both in the South building) to outdoor hot tubs, five fitness centers, and laundry rooms. Most units have mountain views; all have understated, contemporary decor; daily maid service, fireplaces, sofabeds in the living rooms; two or more TVs and DVDs, ski lockers, underground parking, and private balconies and are compact or spacious, depending on the number of bedrooms. Kitchens are completely outfitted. Ask about ski and summer packages.

Soda Springs

Rainbow Lodge, P.O. Box 1100, Soda Springs 95728; 677 Highway 80 at Rainbow Road exit; (530) 426–3871; www.rainbowlodge.net. Old Tahoe–style lodge, circa 1925; small, comfortable hotel rooms; good restaurant and bar. On the Yuba River near cross-country and downhill skiing, hiking, fishing.

Tahoe City

Chinquapin Resort, 3600 North Lake Boulevard; (800) 732–6721. Three miles north of town. Spacious one- to four-bedroom condos with lake views, fireplaces, fully equipped kitchens; pool, tennis courts.

Cottage Inn, 1690 West Lake Boulevard; (530) 581–4073. Two miles south of Tahoe City on Highway 89. Fifteen mountain-style cottages with Scandinavian decor, fireplaces; hearty breakfasts, sauna, private beach. Ask for a unit away from the road.

Coyotes Restaurant Latino, 521 North Lake Boulevard; (530) 583–6653. Creative Spanish tapas and Mexican food with a California cuisine style; agave wine margaritas; dinner only.

Fast Eddie's Texas BBQ, 690 North Lake Boulevard; (530) 583–0950. The best barbecue in the Tahoe Basin; lunch and dinner.

Jake's on the Lake, 780 North Lake Boulevard, Boatworks Mall; (530) 583–0188. Groovy, popular, lots of fun, right on the lake. Seafood bar and backgammon in the lounge; continental cuisine and hearty mountain food.

Tahoe Tavern, 300 West Lake Boulevard; (530) 583–4349. Near Fanny Bridge. Large complex of casual condos in a pine grove, right on the water; pool, lawns; quiet, pretty location on the edge of town.

Wolfdales, 640 North Lake Boulevard; (530) 583–5700. California cuisine with a unique Japanese flair in a century-old house by the lake; reservations essential.

Tahoe Vista

Captain Jon's, 7220 North Lake Boulevard; (530) 546–4819. French country cuisine, fresh seafood, casual elegance; one of the best restaurants at Tahoe. Cocktail lounge and lunch cafe on the lake; the dinner house has a partial view.

Rustic Cottages, 7449 North Lake Boulevard; (888) 778–7842; www.rusticcottages .com. Vintage but not so rustic cottages across the street from a public beach, with fireplaces, kitchenettes, microwaves, refrigerators, and decks. You can use the huge video library, bikes, croquet and horseshoe equipment, sleds, snow saucers, snowshoes, and barbecues. Continental breakfast and chocolate chip cookies are complimentary; dogs are okay. For this location and amenities, these small, fresh, and clean cottages are a steal.

For More Information

Caltrans Road Conditions. San Francisco: (800) 427–7623; Sacramento: (916) 653–7623.

North Lake Tahoe Resort Association, P.O. Box 1757, Tahoe City 96145; (530) 583–3494 or (888) 434–1262; www.mytahoevacation.com.

Advice: In summer and on snowy weekends, avoid driving to Tahoe on Friday afternoon or returning on Sunday afternoon, unless you've got hours to waste. Every month of the year, check the weather and road conditions. Snow can fall even in June.

EASTBOUND ESCAPE FIVE

Tahoe South

Blue Waters and Silver Dollars / 2 Nights

From the neon lights and casinos of South Lake Tahoe to lakeside beaches, boating, hiking, and historical sights, here is a nice combination of nighttime fun and days in the pure mountain air on the south side of the Tahoe Basin.

- ☐ High mountain views
- ☐ Hiking, biking
- ☐ Casino night
- ☐ Old Tahoe estates
- ☐ Beachtime

Sandwiched between Lake Tahoe and a magnificent wall of Sierra Nevada peaks, the city of South Lake Tahoe has major new development along U.S. Highway 50 and the lakefront. At Heavenly Village are two massive Marriott hotels, an ice skating rink, a movieplex, shopping, and restaurants. The new Stateline Transit Center is a hub for shuttles, buses, and trolleys that access the entire lake (www.laketahoetransit.com). Paralleling the highway and bordered by tall pines, a paved walking and biking trail, Linear Park, is a welcome addition. One of fifteen ski areas in the Tahoe basin, Heavenly Valley is accessed by a gondola to the mountaintop, year-round, from right in the middle of town. In summertime, hike, picnic, and enjoy the restaurant and view from on top of the world.

Beautiful beaches and resorts are located all along the lakeshore, from one end of town to the other. From here, it's a short drive to a tremendous variety of outdoor recreation and sightseeing destinations. Highlights of your visit might be a winter sleigh ride behind a team of beautiful blond Belgian draft horses, or a summer sail across the lake on a huge catamaran. Watch for road signs announcing snow play and ski areas, public beaches, and trailheads.

You'll get your first glimpse of Lake Tahoe, the largest Alpine lake on the continent, at Echo Summit on US 50.

Day 1 / Morning

Take Interstate 80 to Sacramento, then US 50 to Kyburz, a three-and-a-half-hour trip from San Francisco or the East Bay.

LUNCH: Strawberry Lodge, US 50, Kyburz; (530) 659–7200. Good American food and soda-fountain specialties in a restored 1940s lodge; walking trails nearby.

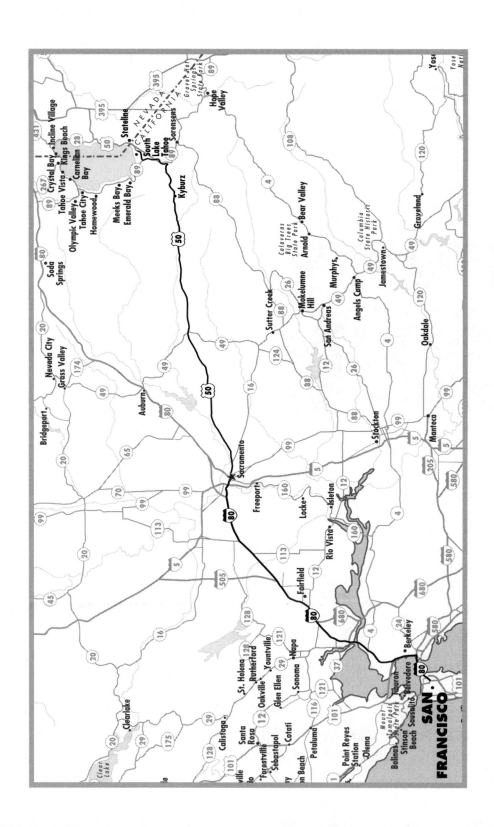

Small lodge rooms here are quiet and comfortable. You can hike, fish, swim, and cross-country ski near here in the national forest.

Afternoon

Continue to South Lake Tahoe. An exciting twelve-minute ride into the sky on the **Heavenly Gondola,** right in the middle of town, is the best way to get a bird's-eye view of Lake Tahoe on one side and Nevada's Carson Valley on the other, and hundreds of miles of high desert stretching out into the distance (between Stateline and Park Avenue; 775–586–7000). On the 10,100-foot summit, an easy 2-mile trail loops the mountaintop. There is a restaurant that serves good, but pricey, lunches, brunches, and dinners.

For a never-to-be-forgotten introduction to Lake Tahoe, take one of the big tour boats across the lake. Beautiful stern-wheelers and a catamaran cross the lake to Emerald Bay and cruise along the lakeshore (see There's More, Cruises on the Lake).

Three public beaches in town have extensive recreational facilities including playing fields and swimming pools: **El Dorado Beach, Regan Beach,** and **Connelly Beach.** At **Nevada Beach** and **Zephyr Cove** you can rent every imaginable type of water sports equipment and take lessons, take a boat tour of the lake, try parasailing, go fishing, or just lie in the sun.

A nice shopping area, the **Ski Run Marina Village,** at Lake Tahoe and Ski Run Boulevards, has specialty shops, a cafe, and an upscale lakeside restaurant.

DINNER: Llewellyn's, US 50, Stateline; (775) 588–2411. In the nineteenth story of **Harveys Resort Casino,** an elegant room with stunning views of the lake and mountains. Choose from a creative mix of French, Asian, and California cuisine. Can't get reservations here? Try **The Summit,** on top of Harrah's, a similar experience: continental dining at tables on terraced levels with breathtaking views (north end of South Lake Tahoe; 775–588–6611).

Polish up your silver-tipped cowboy boots and hit the casinos—they are open twenty-four hours. Several multistory casinos are within a coin flip of one another, some connected by an underground walkway. Big names put on big shows at **Caesars Tahoe** (like Chaka Khan, Wynonna, and David Copperfield). You can see old favorites at **Harrah's** (like Tower of Power and the Everly Brothers) and sizzling stage shows at Harveys and the Horizon.

Take a late-night break with a burger by the huge stone fireplace at the **Hard Rock Cafe** in Harveys, or dance all night at **Nero's 2000** in Caesars Tahoe.

LODGING: Lakeland Village, 3535 Lake Tahoe Boulevard, South Lake Tahoe; (703) 234–3340 or (800) 822–5969. One of the largest and nicest resorts in town is spread out along the lake on nineteen acres of pines, with a private, sandy beach; two heated swimming pools; and tennis courts. The choices here are condo or lodge units, some with fireplaces and kitchens. Shuttle buses connect with nearby ski areas and downtown.

Day 2 / Morning

BREAKFAST: The Red Hut Waffle Shop, 2723 US 50, 3.5 miles south of Stateline; (530) 541–9024. A popular retro cafe with comfy booths, a big counter, and an American comfort-food menu. A second Red Hut is located at 227 Kingsbury Grade (775–588–7588).

Toss your last few quarters into a slot machine and head south, following Highway 89, also called **Emerald Bay Road,** out of town to the south end of the lake. At 9,735 feet, **Mount Tallac** towers over a plethora of sights and things to do on the south shore. Relive the 1920s heyday of the rich and famous at the **Tallac Historic Site** (530–541–4975). Restored and open to tour are several formerly private estates, an old casino, and a hotel. Many musical and art events are held at Tallac, from jazz to bluegrass, from craft demonstrations to photo exhibits. In August the **Great Gatsby Festival** looks like the good old days, with antique boats and merrymakers in period costume.

Baldwin, Pope, and **Kiva Beaches** are accessible by bus (530–542–6077) from South Lake Tahoe; a network of hiking trails connects the beaches and the Tallac Historic Site. The popular **Emerald Bay State Park** campground has one hundred tent and RV sites and boat-in campsites. It is closed from mid-September until mid-June (530–525–7232).

At Baldwin Beach is the **USDA Forest Service Lake Tahoe Visitor Center,** where you can see exhibits of geology, animal habitat, and history; get maps and advice on trail conditions and campground availability and sign up for ranger-led interpretive walks (530–573–2600). Stroller- and handicap-friendly, the **Rainbow Trail** is a paved path that wanders past signs that explain the natural habitat; more than one hundred species of wildflowers bloom alongside the trail. The "Stream Profile Chamber" is a cross-section of a real stream filled with rushing water, fish, plants, and other wildlife. In the fall, thousands of visitors come to watch brilliant red spawning salmon wriggle their way from Lake Tahoe up Taylor Creek.

A four-hour, 5-mile, rather strenuous loop hike from here to the summit of Mount Tallac rewards trekkers with magnificent views at 9,700 feet. Trailheads are across from the road at Baldwin Beach.

LUNCH: The Beacon, east of Emerald Bay on Highway 89 at Camp Richardson; (530) 541–0630. The place to see and be seen at the beach. Watch the boats arrive and have a Rum Runner while waiting for your blackened salmon, the signature clam chowder, gourmet burgers, sandwiches and salads; pasta, fish, or steaks. Or grab food at the Camp General Store and a treat at the ice cream parlor. Live music in the summertime. Lunch, dinner, weekend brunch.

Afternoon

Go on an afternoon sail with **Woodwind Sailing Cruises** (see There's More, Cruises on the Lake) from Camp Richardson. Or take a guided horseback ride

South Lake Tahoe lies at the foot of Sierra Nevada peaks.

from here to Fallen Leaf Lake, about three hours. This is very popular, so reserve ahead. Fallen Leaf Lake is accessible by road off Highway 89 and makes a wonderful day trip. With Camp Richardson as headquarters, you can hike around the lake, swim, and picnic, barbecue, or launch a boat (see Other Recommended Restaurants and Lodgings).

DINNER: **Riva Grill,** 900 Ski Run Boulevard at Ski Run Marina Village, South Lake Tahoe; (530) 542–2600. Overlooking the lake, Riva serves California cuisine in a vintage wooden boat interior with outdoor deck. Steaks, seafood, Mediterranean food.

LODGING: Lakeland Village.

Day 3 / Morning

BREAKFAST: **Ernie's,** near the Y, 1146 Emerald Bay Road, Stateline; (530) 541–2161. Down-home American food for breakfast, lunch, and dinner; where the locals go.

Drive north from South Lake Tahoe to near the junction of Highways 28 and 30, about twenty minutes, to **Spooner Lake.** You can take a short hike around a small lake and enjoy the mountain meadows, fish for trout, picnic, and, in wintertime, cross-country ski (rentals available); this is a great place for beginning skiers. The trailhead for the moderately strenuous, uphill, 10-mile hiking and mountain biking Flume Trail to Marlette Lake is here. Spectacular views of the lake and surrounding mountains are the reward at the top, especially in the fall when the aspens are blazing yellow. You can see vestiges of a huge system of wooden flumes, which were built in the mid-1800s to move water from the lake to the booming silver mining towns of Virginia City and Carson City, on the east side of the mountains.

Mountain bikers ride up the trail to the lake, then down the mountain on the other side to Incline Village, a 14-mile ride. To obtain a Tahoe area mountain-biking brochure, call the Tahoe Douglas Chamber of Commerce, (775) 588–4591, or the South Lake Tahoe Chamber, (530) 541–5255.

Another place to mountain bike, right above South Lake Tahoe, is on Heavenly's bike trail network; new bikes and equipment can be rented (877–243–0003).

LUNCH: Sprouts Natural Foods Cafe, 3123 Harrison Street at US 50 and Alameda, South Lake Tahoe; (530) 541–6969. Grab a luscious Tahoe Turkey sandwich to go, or sit at the counter or outside to enjoy a veggie burrito, a fruit smoothie, and some homemade soup. A very, very popular place.

Heading home, retrace your route on US 50.

There's More

Casinos. Caesars Tahoe, US 50, Stateline; (775) 588–3515 or (800) 648–3353; www.caesars.com. Four hundred forty rooms, most with whirlpool tubs.

Harrah's Lake Tahoe, US 50, Stateline; (775) 588–6611 or (800) 427–7247; www.harrahstahoe.com. Five hundred suite-style rooms, each with two bathrooms; a four-star, four-diamond hotel.

Harveys Resort Hotel, US 50, Stateline; (775) 588–2411 or (800) 427–8397; www.harveystahoe.com. Seven hundred rooms, each with lake or mountain view.

Horizon Casino Resort, US 50, Stateline; (775) 588–6211 or (800) 648–3322; www.horizoncasino.com. Five hundred rooms and suites, Olympic pool.

Cruises on the Lake. MS *Dixie II,* 5 miles north of South Lake Tahoe on US 50, Zephyr Cove; (775) 588–3508. This beautiful paddle wheeler was once a cotton barge on the Mississippi in 1927, then a floating casino at Tahoe, when it sank and was raised and converted into a tour boat.

Tahoe Queen, 9090 Ski Run Boulevard, South Lake Tahoe; (530) 541–3364;

www.hornblower.com. Huge, beautiful paddle wheeler; day and evening trips to Emerald Bay. Ski cruises to Tahoe City, too.

Woodwind Sailing Cruises, Zephyr Cove Marina, South Lake Tahoe; (775) 588–3000; www.sailwoodwind.com. A fifty-passenger, 41-foot trimaran with a glass bottom, indoor/outdoor seating. Also a catamaran that sails out of Camp Richardson.

Golf. Edgewood Tahoe Golf Course, US 50 at Stateline; (775) 588–3566. Eighteen holes; the site of major tournaments; the most challenging course at the lake. Located behind the Horizon Casino.

Tahoe Paradise Golf Course, on US 50 in Meyers; (530) 577–2121. Eighteen-hole course.

Heavenly Ski Resort, 4004 Ski Run Boulevard, South Lake Tahoe; (775) 586–7000 or (800) 243–2836; www.skiheavenly.com. One of the biggest ski resorts in the world with one of the highest skiable summits in the United States. Nearly eighty runs get an average of 360 inches of the white stuff a year. On the Nevada side, hundreds of miles of high desert stretch out into the distance. On the California side you have the phenomenal experience of feeling as though you are skiing right into the lake. If your legs can take it, start from the top of Sky Express and ski non-stop 5.5 miles.

Hiking. Desolation Wilderness. Hundreds of lakes, thousands of acres of outback, many trails. Easy accessibility makes it extremely popular; best off-season. For an 11.4-mile loop day trip, take the Glen Alpine trailhead at the end of Fallen Leaf Lake Road, hiking to Lake Aloha.

Round Lake, 6.4-mile loop to a neato swimming hole. Take Highway 89 south out of Meyers; 3.6 miles before Luther Pass is roadside parking on the north, trailhead on the south.

Tahoe Rim Trail. Trailhead information: (775) 588–0686. A 150-mile trail around the lake.

Kirkwood Meadows, Highway 88 at Carson Pass, P.O. Box 1, Kirkwood 95646; (209) 258–6000; www.kirkwood.com. Thirty-five miles east of South Lake Tahoe; at 7,800 feet, highest base elevation in the Tahoe area means a long ski season and top snow conditions for downhill and Nordic skiing. Kids and fun-loving adults are towed up the slopes of Slide Mountain Tube Park for an exciting tube run down. Condos, lodge rooms, and rental houses make Kirkwood a major vacation destination in summertime, when the meadows turn to rippling waves of wildflowers. Biking and hiking trails and lake and stream fishing are popular. The Mountain Club is a deluxe condo hotel with one- and two-bedroom units with lofts, and Snowcrest, a condo complex at the base of the lifts. Snazzy boutique shops, restaurants, and an ice rink are new additions. Nearby at the summit of Carson Pass, Caples Lake attracts trout anglers, canoers, sailboarders, and swimmers. Trails lead into the Mokelumne Wilderness.

Upper Truckee River Marsh. (530) 542–5580. Take an idyllic, 4-mile self-guided kayak paddle on the Upper Truckee River, starting at the US 50 bridge to the lake and down to Ski Run Beach. The river meanders quietly through meadows and forest, and you will likely see waterfowl; beautiful marshlands with water lilies and other aquatic plants. Rent kayaks and canoes at SunSports at the Ski Run Marina.

Special Events

March. Torchlight Parade and Fireworks, Kirkwood; (209) 258–6000.

June. Train Parade, South Lake Tahoe; (530) 644–3761. Annual mile-long historic wagon train brings the Old West to life. Hundreds of people dressed in period costume in wagons, stagecoaches, or on horseback—mountain men, scouts tracing the original route of the Pony Express.

Valhalla Renaissance Festival, Tallac Historic Site; (530) 542–4166. An old English country "faire" with knights in combat, archery contests, jugglers, magicians, dancers, plays, period music, food vendors, crafts, psychic readings, and more. Wear costumes to the festival!

June through July. Lake Tahoe Sailweek, Tahoe Keys Marina; (800) AT–TAHOE. Sailboats from across the country converge for a weeklong series of races.

June through September. Valhalla Summer Festival of Art and Music, South Lake Tahoe; (530) 542–4166. Concerts and exhibits in and around historic mansions.

July. Rhythm and Brews Festival, Tallac Historic Site; (530) 541–4975. Live bands and the beers of forty western breweries.

August. Great Gatsby Festival, Tahoe Keys Marina, Tallac Historic Site; (530) 546–2768. Antique and classic wooden boat show, Roaring Twenties living history.

Other Recommended Restaurants and Lodgings

Hope Valley

Sorensen's Resort, 14255 Highway 89; (530) 694–2203 or (800) 423–9949. In a pine-and-aspen grove on the west fork of the Carson River, rustic, nice cabins have homespun country decor, brass beds, woodstoves, some kitchens. The cafe serves great home-cooked, hearty meals. A variety of special events and classes are offered, from llama treks to fly fishing, star watches, birding, hikes, and more. At the nearby Hope Valley Outdoor Center, you can rent winter and summer sports equipment of all kinds and sign up for hikes, kayak trips, and ski tours (530–694–2266; www.hope valleyoutdoors.com). A popular place for families; reservations are necessary weeks and sometimes even months in advance. Kids fish in the small stocked pond for trout. An old logging road leads from here into the Toiyabe National Forest, with views of a jagged range of mountains. Ask about the guided hike on the Emigrant Trail.

South Lake Tahoe

Black Bear Inn, 1202 Ski Run Boulevard; (800) AT–TAHOE or (877) 232–7466; www.tahoeblackbear.com. Lodge and cabins in a wooded acre, luxurious interiors with fireplaces, full breakfast.

Camp Richardson, P.O. Box 9028, South Lake Tahoe 96158; (530) 541–1801. Just east of Emerald Bay on Highway 89. A favorite family summer vacation resort for decades, with small, simple rooms in a cavernous main lodge and cottages to rent. There are a marina, a sandy beach, riding stables, restaurants, a 300-unit campground, a "trading post," and a general store. The camp makes a convenient headquarters from which to set off on horseback or on foot into Desolation Wilderness. Paddleboats, personal watercraft, and other water toys are rented at the marina. Cross-country ski and snowshoe trails are open in winter, with rentals, lessons, and tours. Kayak Tahoe here rents boats for self-guided and guided lake tours (530–544–2011).

A new children's activity camp offers supervised winter and summer play for guests of the camp and of Harrah's Casino Hotel. Breakfast and steak-dinner guided horseback rides from Camp Richardson to Fallen Leaf Lake are fun; they take about three hours and are very popular, so reserve ahead.

Embassy Suites Resort, 4130 Lake Tahoe Boulevard; (800) 924–9245; www .embassytahoe.com. Luxury suites; Old Tahoe–style architecture; full breakfast and cocktail hour are free. Indoor pool and spa, sundeck, workout room, seasonal packages; shuttle to airport, Heavenly Ski Resort, and casinos.

Forest Inn Suites, 1 Lake Parkway; (530) 541–6655 or (800) 822–5950. One- and two-bedroom suites with equipped kitchens on five acres of forest with pools, spas, and health club; shuttle to Heavenly Valley Resort.

Scusa! on Ski Run, 1142 Ski Run Boulevard; (530) 542–0100. Load up on fresh pasta with seafood, hearty calzones, or pizza. A casual, popular place.

Tahoe Keys Resort, 599 Tahoe Keys Boulevard; (530) 544–5397; www.cal tahoe.com. Homes and condos for rent. You can fly into the international airport and be there in ten minutes. Some of the amenities: indoor and outdoor swimming pools, a health club, bicycles, outdoor games, a playground, a private beach, ski shuttles, powerboat rentals, parasailing, personal watercraft, boat launching— in other words, vacation central.

Womack's Texas Bar BQ, 4041 US 50; (530) 544–2268. A cozy little spot serving what could be the best barbecue outside Texas: baby back ribs, Louisiana gumbo, red beans and rice, peach cobbler, and sweet potato pie.

For More Information

California State Campgrounds, P.O. Box 942896, Sacramento 94296-0001; (916) 653–6995 or (800) 777–0369; www.cal-parks.ca.gov.

Lake Tahoe Accommodations, 2048 Dunlap Drive, #4, South Lake Tahoe 96150; (530) 544–3234 or (800) 544–3234. Condo and home rentals.

Lake Tahoe Visitors Authority, 1156 Ski Run Boulevard, South Lake Tahoe 96151; (800) AT–TAHOE; www.virtualtahoe.com. Use this number to book reservations, get tickets to events and casino shows, buy airline tickets, and hear about weather and road conditions.

Road conditions and ski reports: (415) 864–6440 or (800) 427–7623.

EASTBOUND ESCAPE SIX

Tahoe North

Peaceful Pines and a Western Town / 2 Nights

The Washoe Indians called it *Tahoe,* or "Big Water." Twenty-two miles long and 12 miles wide, Lake Tahoe is 1,600 feet deep and "clear enough to see the scales on a cutthroat trout at 80 feet," according to Mark Twain. Surrounded by snow-frosted mountains and dense evergreen forests, the translucent blue water is hypnotic and cold, very cold. Legends tell of Indian chiefs in full regalia and women in Victorian garb floating motionless and frozen at the bottom of the lake.

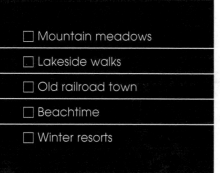

☐ Mountain meadows

☐ Lakeside walks

☐ Old railroad town

☐ Beachtime

☐ Winter resorts

On the north shore are less traffic, less honky-tonk, and a more residential atmosphere. Fewer beaches and restaurants, too, but some of the best. A handful of small casinos add spice.

The old miners' and loggers' town of Truckee, still rough-and-tumble after all these years, makes a fun stop on your way to the lake.

Day 1 / Morning

From the Oakland Bay Bridge, drive north on Interstate 80 to Sacramento; it's a four-hour drive to the north shore.

At Donner Summit, just past Baxter, stop at the **Emigrant Gap Viewpoint** on the west side of I–80. Looking out over hundreds of miles of high country, you see the tremendous tilted block of the Sierras, sloping shallowly toward the west. Glacial canyons are gouged out of the granite, and the Yuba and Bear Rivers have cut their own valleys. Pioneers winched their wagons down into the Bear Valley from here at 4,000 feet, then dragged themselves back up to Washington Ridge on the opposite side of the valley, the most difficult section of their journey to a new life in the West.

Beyond the summit of Donner Pass, take a rest stop at **Donner Memorial State Park** (530–544–3053), a camping, picnicking, and snow play area at 5,950 feet, with a short, pleasant walking trail. The **Emigrant Trail Museum** features the Donner party tragedy and the building of the railroad through the Sierras in the 1800s. You'll see train tracks, running along rugged mountainsides above Donner Lake. Taking the Amtrak train from Oakland to Truckee is a relaxing way

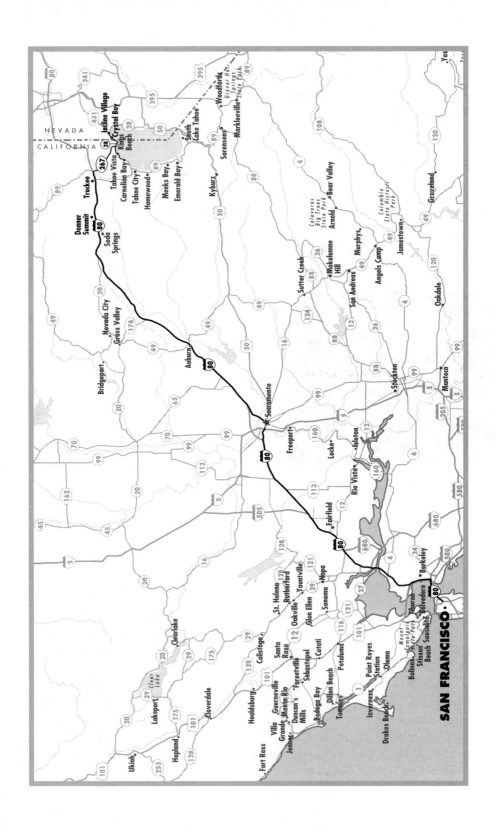

to get to Tahoe; parties of skiers have fun doing this in wintertime, and the scenery—wow!

Donner Lake, 3 miles long, is a smaller, quieter, less developed version of Tahoe, and many vacationers prefer it. You can camp, launch a boat, rent a cabin, fish, hike, ski, and enjoy the crystal blue waters. **Donner Lake Village Resort** rents lodgettes, studios, and one- and two-bedroom condos (916–587–6081). There are nearly thirty public piers on the north side for fishing and boating. Shoreline Park offers bank fishing and a pier, boat launching, picnic sites, and swimming. On the west end, a swimming area is supervised by lifeguards.

Below the lake, in Coldstream Canyon, is an easy mountain-bike trail. On the west end of Donner Lake is a trailhead for the **Pacific Crest Trail.** From here you can take a strenuous 15-mile hike along the ridge of the Sierra crest, descending down into Squaw Valley's **Shirley Canyon.** On the opposite side of I–80 is a leg of the **Donner Lake Rim Trail,** a route that now encircles the lake.

Continuing on I–80, take the Central Truckee exit into Truckee a rollicking railroading, logging, and ice-harvesting headquarters in the 1800s. The picturesque main street is lined with Western wear and outdoor-equipment stores, restaurants and saloons in brick and stone false-front buildings facing the railroad tracks, and the 1869 depot where Amtrak trains blast into town daily. In May, Truckee steps back in time with a weekend of gunslinger reenactments, gold panning, strolling musicians, and storytelling (www.truckee.com).

At **Bud's Sporting Goods and Fountain,** sit on a stool at the mirrored soda fountain and have a cherry Coke or an ice-cream soda, then shop for fishing gear. Across the street, the train station houses the visitor center, where you can browse a huge array of brochures and maps and get sightseeing and outdoor recreation advice for the North Tahoe area.

LUNCH: Andy's Truckee Diner, next to the railroad tracks and Highway 267, Truckee; (530) 582–6925. An authentic 1940s diner moved from Pennsylvania, open twenty-four hours with a huge all-American menu. Got an appetite? Try the chicken-fried steak, a juicy burger, a hot turkey sandwich, or a Philly cheesesteak, with a thick shake followed by a banana split.

Afternoon

Proceed east out of Truckee on Highway 267 through the **Martis Valley,** passing **Northstar** (see There's More) as you climb up Brockway Summit—a short but icy ascent in winter—on your way to the stoplight at Kings Beach. Stop here and jump in the lake, then take a left onto Highway 28, crossing into Nevada at Crystal Bay; it's five minutes to **Incline Village.**

If there is a secret hideaway at Tahoe, it's Incline Village, a small community of gorgeous homes and condos sprinkled on the shores of the lake and across steep mountainsides, with breathtaking views. Traffic-free and quiet, Incline has many virtues, such as the small, excellent ski resort of Diamond Peak; two Robert Trent Jones golf courses; two of Tahoe's loveliest beaches; and one elegant casino hotel.

Incline's private beaches, and a beautiful recreation center with a pool, playground, and tennis courts, are available only to those who rent, own, or stay at selected hotel and motel accommodations in Incline. Renting a condo or house is the way to go here, and it can be as cost-effective as a resort or a motel. When you make your arrangements for accommodations, be sure to ask about getting an "IVGID" card from the Incline Village General Improvement District, which will admit you and the family to the beaches and the rec center.

A small, exquisite beach park, **Burnt Cedar Beach** (702–831–1310), has a big heated pool, a lifeguard, a snack bar, a kids' playground, shady lawns for lounging, picnic tables, barbecues, shallow water for wading, deep water for swimming, and a killer view. **Ski Beach,** in front of the Hyatt Regency Lake Tahoe, has many amenities, and it's long enough for a morning walk.

Park at the east end of Lakeshore Drive at the Hyatt and walk back along the lake. The paved sidewalk runs for several miles, past the beaches and lovely homes— perfect for jogging, baby carriage–pushing, walking, and biking. Giant sugar pine cones are scattered liberally about, free for the taking. The gardens and the architecture are interesting sights in themselves.

Have a sundown cocktail at the **Lone Eagle Grill** (775–832–1234), a stunning wood-and-granite bar with a massive river-rock fireplace, a floor-to-ceiling view of the lake, and an elegant restaurant. You may find it difficult to leave here.

DINNER: Cafe 333, 333 Village Boulevard, Incline Village; (775) 832–7333. On the patio or indoors; a casual, upscale place with a creative menu: walnut-crusted chicken with Gorgonzola pesto sauce, seared fresh salmon with sun-dried tomato coulis, and heartier dishes, plus a great wine list. Breakfast, brunch, lunch, and dinner.

LODGING: Hyatt Regency Resort, Spa, and Casino Lake Tahoe, 111 Country Club Drive at Lakeshore Drive, Incline Village; (775) 832–1234; www .laketahoe.hyatt.com. A 460-room, full-service hotel and casino. "Old Tahoe" lodge–style interiors, lakeside cottages, health club, pool, tennis, and shuttles to major ski resorts. Among the several upscale eating places are the indoor/outdoor restaurant on the beach with a lively bar, a twenty-four-hour-a-day cafe, and an Italian/Asian fine restaurant. A recent multimillion-dollar expansion and renovation added the Spa Terrace, a three-story wing with luxury balcony rooms, a glitzy full-service Stillwater Spa, new swimming pools, outdoor fireplaces, and beautiful public areas by the lake.

This evening, lurk around the Hyatt, even if you're not a gambler. You can lounge in front of the big fireplace and people-watch, or plunge in and throw some money away. *Tip:* Play the slot machines at the ends of the aisles, near the center of the room; payoffs occur on the most visible machines.

Day 2 / Morning

BREAKFAST: **Wildflower Cafe,** 869 Tahoe Boulevard, Incline Village; (775) 831–8072. Rub shoulders with skiers (snow or water) and construction workers at the counter or at a wooden table and have a Paul Bunyan–size breakfast of waffles or eggs and potatoes. Next, stop at **Grog & Grist Market and Deli,** located at Highway 28 at Northwood, (775) 831–1123, and pick up some picnic fare to enjoy later.

If tennis is your game, you will be glad to know that Incline has the largest concentration of top-quality tennis facilities at the lake, with twelve professional courts at the **Lakeside Tennis Club,** Highway 28 at Ski Run Boulevard (775–832–4860), and seven courts at the **Incline Village Recreation Center,** 980 Incline Way (775–832–1310). As an "IVGID" guest at the rec center, you can come in for the day and use the indoor Olympic pool and fitness facilities, as well as the child care.

You can launch a boat at Incline Beach (775–831–1310) or at Sand Harbor (775–831–0494). Rentals of ski boats, paddleboats, canoes, and kayaks are available at **Action Water Sports** on the beach in Incline (775–831–4386).

For a day of hiking and exploring in the mountains, drive east on Tahoe Boulevard to Country Club Drive and turn left, then right at the top of the hill onto Highway 431, also known as the Mount Rose Highway.

Dominating the mountain skyline on the north shore is Mount Rose, above Incline. From the scenic overlook on Highway 431, almost the entire 22-mile-long lake gleams below, rimmed by the Sierras on the west and the Carson Range on the east. Seven miles beyond the lookout point is **Tahoe Meadows,** at 8,600 feet, a series of huge meadows where you can enjoy miles of cross-country skiing and summertime hiking, easy or strenuous. The meadows are crisscrossed with small streams and crowded with wildflowers most of the year. Tahoe Meadows Whole Access Trail is a wide, 1.3-mile loop designed for persons in wheelchairs and baby strollers.

Just beyond Tahoe Meadows, **Mount Rose Campground** is nice and cool in midsummer and often has tent and RV sites available when campgrounds near the lake are full (775–882–2766). Stop here for fresh water and restrooms. You can walk from the campground to the top of the mountain and the Tahoe Meadows trail system.

LUNCH: Have a picnic here or take it back down the mountain to Tahoe Boulevard, going east out of Incline on Highway 28 a few miles to **Sand Harbor State Park** (775–831–0494), which is picturesque, with two white-sand beaches, tree-shaded picnic spots, and lake and mountain views—the most beautiful beach park at the lake.

Afternoon

The annual Music and Shakespeare Festival and reggae, Dixieland, and Country Western concerts are held at Sand Harbor in summer. On a clear summer night, you'll watch the sun go down over the lake while you sit on a blanket sipping wine. The lights go down, the stars come out, and magic begins on stage (530–583–9048).

Between Incline and Sand Harbor on the lakeshore highway, you may notice clusters of parked cars. There are a number of small beaches and fishing spots along this shoreline, including a nude beach. After an afternoon dip in the lake or a dip in the Burnt Cedar pool, or perhaps a nap, drive to **Crystal Bay,** at Stateline (five minutes west of Incline on Highway 28), and go into **Cal-Neva Lodge** (800–225–6382), the high-rise hotel casino at Stateline. It's one of the oldest casinos on the lake, made famous by a former owner, Frank Sinatra. Off the lobby, the Indian Room is a vast, beam-ceilinged lounge with a big boulder fireplace and a fascinating collection of early Tahoe artifacts, bearskins, and bobcats.

As the sun starts to set, continue on Highway 28 to **Gar Woods,** 5000 North Lake Boulevard, Carnelian Bay (530–546–3366), for cocktails or tea; this is one of a handful of restaurants located right on the lake.

DINNER: Big Water Grille, 341 Ski Way, at the top of Incline Village; (775) 833–0606. With views of the world from 7,000 feet; California cuisine in an elegant setting. Lunch, dinner, weekend brunch.

LODGING: Hyatt Regency Lake Tahoe.

Day 3 / Morning

BREAKFAST: The Original Old Post Office, 5245 North Lake Boulevard, Carnelian Bay; (530) 546–3205. Down-home cooking, with monster-size breakfasts starting at 6:00 A.M. every day.

Before heading back to the Bay Area, play a round of golf on one of Incline's falling-off-the-mountain golf courses; play tennis on one of the town's twenty-six courts; or head to the beach.

On Highway 28, within a few minutes' drive of Incline, is a string of beaches and small villages attuned to the tourist trade, including **Crystal Bay, Kings Beach, Tahoe Vista,** and **Carnelian Bay.** At Crystal Bay a few casinos are clustered. Kings Beach has huge arts and crafts fairs on summer weekends and a golf course that turns into a snowmobile park when the snow flies. **Kings Beach State Recreation Area** is a wildly popular, long, sandy beach buzzing with summertime activity, with game courts and watercraft rentals. **North Tahoe Regional Park,** at the end of National Avenue off Highway 28, is a great place for beginning cross-country skiers, on nearly 7 flat miles of groomed tracks, plus a snow play hill. When the snow melts, stop off here to take a short walk on the tree-lined trails or have a picnic or a barbecue (775–546–7248).

The thin, clear mountain air allows Lake Tahoe's crystalline water to reflect the sky above.

There's More

Boreal Ski Area, I–80 at Donner Summit; (530) 426–3666. A reasonably priced, nonintimidating choice for new skiers, and the view from the top of Sunset Boulevard run is dazzling. Night skiing is popular, especially in the illuminated terrain park; all-day lift tickets are valid for night skiing. On groomed sledding lanes at Playland Park, rent mini-snowmobiles and sleds. Admission is free at Boreal's Western American Ski Sport Museum, where ski history from the 1850s to the present is depicted in photos, displays, and vintage movies.

Diamond Peak Ski Resort, 1210 Ski Way, on Highway 431 above Incline Village; (775) 832–1177; www.diamondpeak.com. A medium-size ski resort with spectacular lake and mountain views from downhill and cross-country trails. Intermediates and beginners are happy here; expert skiers will head for larger resorts. Unlike higher elevation resorts, the snow is less dependable—call ahead. The good news: somewhat lower prices, casual atmosphere, fewer people. Formerly a popular out-of-bounds area, with its own quad chair, The Chutes is now a developed plunge of 1,500 vertical feet of nine expert and seven advanced runs; and a new six-passenger quad accesses the East Bowl. Ski, snowboard, and cross-country lessons and clinics.

Fishing. Giant kokanee salmon, released into the lake by accident in 1940, lurk below rocky ledges on the north shore, along with several species of trout. Crystal Bay is the best spot to catch them.

Golf. Incline Championship and Executive Courses, Incline Village; (775) 832–1144. Completed in 2005, remodeling of the golf courses and a brand-new clubhouse and restaurant with outdoor lakeview deck, two pro shops, and new practice areas. The lower course doubles as a cross-country ski area used primarily by residents, but you can rent skis in town and ski here, too.

Old Brockway Golf Course, North Lake Boulevard at Kings Beach; (530) 546–9909. Nine holes; inexpensive and easy.

Two spectacular new courses near Truckee, both with restaurants and complete practice facilities. Coyote Moon Golf Course (10685 Northwoods Boulevard, Truckee; 530–587–0886). Old Greenwood is a Jack Nicklaus signature course (12011 Old Truckee Airport Road, Truckee; 800–754–3070; www.oldgreenwood.com). A good resource for golf throughout the Tahoe basin: www.golfthehighsierra.com.

Northstar-at-Tahoe, between Truckee and Lake Tahoe on Highway 267; (800) 466–6784; www.northstarattahoe.com; snow phone: (530) 562–1330. In a glorious mountain and forest setting, one of the largest all-year vacation resorts at the lake, the Northstar complex includes a golf course; equestrian, mountain-biking, and hiking trails; shops, a deli, and a grocery; several bars and restaurants; beautiful pool and tennis complexes; and many condos, lodge rooms, and houses to rent. You can settle in here for a vacation and never need a car, getting around on the forest paths and the resort shuttles. In summer, chairlifts take hikers and bikers up to 100 miles of marked, mountaintop trails. There is a busy schedule of activities and events all year, including guided nature hikes, orienteering, and sports and fishing classes. Extensive new additions in 2005: luxury condominiums, delis, cafes, shops, bars, and restaurants; a high-speed quad chair; family terrain park, snowboard learning center, an ice skating rink, a mountaintop restaurant, and outdoor leisure areas.

The ski mountain is about equally beginning, intermediate, and advanced, and free ski clinics are offered to all ages. Snow play is state-of-the-art here, with snowscoots, snowbikes, and snowsliding toys; tubing; and the Zorb, a 9.5-foot clear plastic sphere that rolls downhill with a passenger inside. At night, on weekends, and on holidays, Polaris Park is an illuminated snow playground with music. The sunny

Summit Deck on the top of Mount Pluto is lively and fun for casual lunches and snacks.

Royal Gorge, near Donner Summit, off I–80 and Old U.S. Highway 40; (800) 500–3817; www.royalgorge.com. In the Sierra National Forest, the largest Nordic ski area in the nation, voted the best in North America. Spend the day on the trails, or ski to the lodge and stay overnight. You can rent everything here, including pulk sleds, with which to pull small children. Lodge accommodations include meals and trail passes, or you can stay at Sugar Bowl or Rainbow Lodge and connect directly to Royal Gorge trails; free shuttle bus to and from Sugar Bowl. Warming huts with snacks available are scattered throughout the trail network.

Tahoe Donner Ski Area, 897 Donner Pass Road, Truckee; (530) 587–9444; www .skitahoedonner.com. A small, friendly, reasonably priced Nordic ski resort with a day lodge, restaurant, lots of flat meadow trails for beginners, and a nearby snow play area.

Special Events

June. Gigantic Arts and Crafts Fair at Kings Beach; (530) 546–2935.

July. North Lake Tahoe Symphony Association Summer Music Series; (775) 832–1606. Sunday-afternoon concerts.

July through August. Music and Shakespeare at Sand Harbor; (530) 583–9048. Beautiful outdoor amphitheater.

Other Recommended Restaurants and Lodgings

Incline Village

Austin's, 120 Country Club Drive; (775) 832–7728. A casual, friendly place serving hearty, Texas-style food, three meals a day. Bring your appetite for Mountain Man Omelet, pork chops and steak sandwiches, buttermilk fries, chicken-fried steak. Stick around for the homemade pie.

Club Tahoe Resort, 914 Northwood Boulevard; (800) 527–5154. Two-bedroom town houses sleeping six; simple decor, fireplaces, fully equipped kitchens, laundry, linens, tennis, racquetball, pool, sauna, ski shuttles.

Inn at Incline, 1003 Tahoe Boulevard; (775) 444–6758. Motel units in a forest set-ting; indoor pool, sauna, spa. Continental breakfast, some kitchens.

Kings Beach

Steamer's Beachside Bar and Oven, 8290 North Lake Boulevard; (530) 546–2218. One of the most popular pizza restaurants on the north shore, with an outdoor patio on the beach. Try the calzone!

Soda Springs

Rainbow Lodge, P.O. Box 1100, Soda Springs 95728, off I–80 at Rainbow Road exit; (530) 426–3661. Historic thirty-room hotel, restaurant, bar. Like an old chalet in the Alps, beside a rushing bend in the Truckee River. Small, country-style inn rooms are fresh with comforters and brass beds. Cross-country ski from here right onto Royal Gorge trails.

Tahoe Vista

Le Petit Pier, 7238 North Lake Boulevard; (530) 546–4464. In the French country tradition; a small, elegant place on the lake with a world-class wine list and nouvelle cuisine. Sundown cocktails in the lakeside bar.

Truckee

Donner Lake Village Resort, 15695 Donner Pass Road; (530) 587–6081; www.donnerlakevillage.com. Moderately priced, comfortable accommodations, from lodgettes sleeping four to town houses sleeping six. Right on the lake with great views, a private marina, and boat rentals.

O.B.'s, 10046 Donner Pass Road; (530) 587–4164; www.obstruckee.com. Good, hearty food in a historic, museum-like building adorned with old photos, barnboard walls, and artifacts of old Truckee. Get into a cozy booth and order chili, burgers, wraps, steak sandwiches, and more stick-to-your-ribs lunches and dinners; do not miss the mud pie and the old-fashioned apple pie.

For More Information

BRAT Resort Properties, 120 Country Club Drive, Incline Village, NV 89452; (888) 266–3612; www.bratresort.com. Rental condos and houses, with ski and vacation packages.

Incline Village Visitors Bureau, 969 Tahoe Boulevard, Incline Village, NV 89451; (775) 832–1606; www.gotahoe.com.

North Lake Tahoe Resort Association, P.O. Box 1757, Tahoe City 96145; (530) 583–3494 or (888) 434–1262; www.mytahoevacation.com.

Truckee Donner Chamber of Commerce, 12036 Donner Pass Road, Truckee 96161; (530) 584–2757; www.truckee.com.

Vacation Station, P.O. Box 7180, Incline Village, NV 89452; (775) 831–3664. Homes and condos to rent.

FARTHER AFIELD
ESCAPES

Shasta Cascade

Mountain Majesty, Rivers, Lakes, Timberlands / 2 Nights

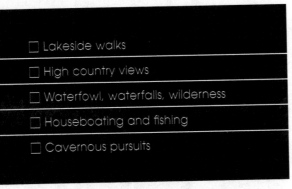

- ☐ Lakeside walks
- ☐ High country views
- ☐ Waterfowl, waterfalls, wilderness
- ☐ Houseboating and fishing
- ☐ Cavernous pursuits

One in a chain of Cascade Range volcanoes, Mount Shasta is a frosty, 14,162-foot presence that seems to take up half the sky in Siskiyou County. The mountain presides over vast timberlands and wilderness areas freshened with lakes, rivers, and streams, offering a paradise for hikers, anglers, summer- and winter-sports enthusiasts, and just plain lovers of high-country scenery.

On a weekend in the Shasta area, you may fall under the magic spell of the mountain and return again to see it streaked with lightning in a summer thunderstorm or transformed into a frozen white wave in winter.

Your route along Interstate 5 follows the mighty Sacramento River—wide, cool, and green; fringed with overhanging trees; plied by fishing boats and water-skiers.

Day 1 / Morning

From San Francisco it's 325 miles to Redding. Take Interstate 80, connecting with Interstate 505 above Vacaville; then take I–5 north to Redding. Bordering the valley are the crumpled eastern foothills of the Coast Range and the distant peaks of the Sierra Nevada; the peaks of the Klamath Mountains and the Cascades emerge in the distant north and east. The Sierra Nevada ends; the Cascades begin.

LUNCH: Take the Central Redding/Highway 99 exit into town; turn left on East Street to **Buz's Crab Stand, Seafood Restaurant, Market, and Deli,** at 2159 East Street; (530) 243–2120. A fun, eclectic, sea-related casual setting for chowder, fish-and-chips, salmon burgers and crab cakes, cioppino, and myriad seafood dishes, salads, and sandwiches. You can also purchase fresh fish, condiments, and fixings to take away.

A major attraction in Redding, **Turtle Bay Exploration Park** is marked by a new landmark in Redding, a soaring, ultramodern pedestrian bridge over the

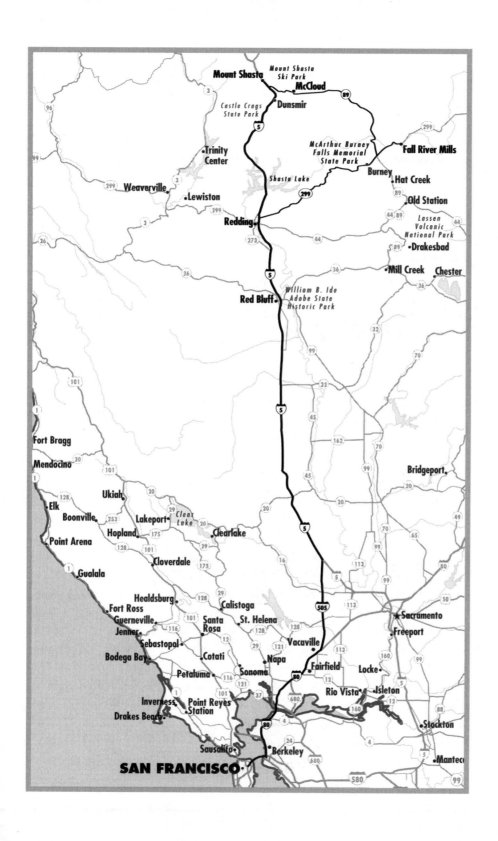

river, 200 feet high and 710 feet long. The glass deck is suspended from a dazzling white tower, and at the end of the bridge is a glass-walled cafe. The park is focused on the Sacramento River watershed, its natural sciences and resources, art, culture, and human history (intersection of Highways 299 and 273; 530–243–8850 or 800–887–8532; www.turtlebay.org). Explore the Museum of Art and History and the Natural Science Museum; wander the butterfly house and the sprawling botanical gardens. Stroll on 220 acres of paved walking trails through oak savanna and wetlands to see otter ponds, a raptor exhibit, and botanic gardens in the arboretum.

From the north end of the bridge, you can set off on 20 miles of walking or biking on the Sacramento River Trail, a tree-shaded path along the riverbank.

Afternoon

It's 23 miles beyond Redding on I–5 north to **Shasta Lake,** one of the best fishing lakes in California, fed by the Sacramento, McCloud, Pit, and Squaw Rivers. At an elevation of 1,000 feet, surface water reaches eighty degrees in summer, perfect for houseboating and waterskiing.

Take the Shasta Caverns Road exit, driving 2 miles to **Lake Shasta Caverns** (530–238–2341), a dramatic natural wonder. The tour includes a fifteen-minute boat ride across the lake to a wooded island, where groups of about twenty people are guided into a series of giant chambers, up and down hundreds of stone steps. The atmosphere is delightfully spooky, damp, and drippy—a constant fifty-eight degrees, refreshing in summer, when outside temperatures can reach more than one hundred degrees. Multicolored columns, 20-foot-high stone draperies, stalactites and stalagmites, brilliant crystals, and unusual limestone and marble formations are subtly lighted and fascinating.

It's 38 miles from the caverns to the town of **Mount Shasta,** in the shadow of the mountain and almost completely surrounded by the **Shasta National Forest.** Motels line the road into the town, an overnight stopping point for travelers on their way to the Northwest. The old-fashioned town has shady streets, a few shops and outdoor gear stores, and a handful of good restaurants.

DINNER: Mount Shasta Resort, 1000 Siskiyou Lake Boulevard, Mount Shasta; (530) 926–3030 or (800) 958–3363; www.mountshastaresort.com. A popular, comfortable restaurant with great views of Mount Shasta. Wide variety of hearty American fare, steaks, pasta, grilled chicken, and fish. Book ahead for weekends and holidays.

LODGING: Mount Shasta Resort. In a pretty wooded setting near walking trails and lakes. Settle into a studio room or one- or two-bedroom chalet with fireplace, sofabed, fully equipped kitchen, spacious living room, and deck. The golf course here is spectacular and challenging, and there are also tennis courts. Ask about ski and golf packages.

Day 2 / Morning

BREAKFAST: Lily's, 1013 South Mount Shasta Boulevard, Mount Shasta; (530) 926–3372. Hearty all-American breakfasts and gourmet specialties like polenta fritters and giant omelets. At lunch and dinner, California cuisine, Asian specialties, and even enchiladas.

Off Siskiyou Lake Boulevard are the **Sisson Museum** and **Mount Shasta Fish Hatchery,** 1 North Old Stage Road (530–926–5508), with displays of the history, geology, and climate of the mountain. Walk around to see the hatching and rearing ponds.

Drive 3 miles south on Stage Road to **Lake Siskiyou,** surrounded by dazzling mountainscapes and a tree-lined shore. **Lake Siskiyou Camp Resort,** 4239 West Barr Road, Mount Shasta (530–926–2618 or 888–926–2618; www.lakesis.com), is one of the prettiest multiuse camping and RV facilities in California. You can even rent a fully equipped trailer for use on-site. Walk around the 430-acre lake, lounge on the beach and swim, launch a boat, or rent water toys, kayaks, canoes, pedalboats, sailboats, and fishing equipment. A store, snack bar, outdoor movies, and playground are also found here. The resort was recently expanded and refurbished to include a larger marina, new lakeside cabins, and a new gift shop and general store. A newly developed 7-mile walking and cycling trail encircles the lake.

At the end of W. Barr Road, **Gumboot Lake** is a tiny, shallow bit of icy water stocked with trout and surrounded by meadows, mountains, and forests. Bring a picnic and an inflatable raft or a canoe.

To see one of the clearest, prettiest lakes in the Sierras and take an easy walk or a strenuous hike, continue on West Barr Road, and go left on Castle Lake Road to the parking area for **Castle Lake;** (530) 926–4511, one of the most easily accessible alpine lakes in northern California. Within a few minutes' easy stroll you can be in an idyllic, seemingly isolated wilderness setting. Walk along the lakeshore through the forest, putter around in the creek, fish in the lake, launch your skiff or kayaks, have a picnic, or set up your tent. The water here is pure and clear, and the fishing and (chilly) swimming are great. For a 3-mile round-trip moderately strenuous hike, take the trail to the left of the lake near the stream, along the lakeside, and up to 5,900 feet. Bear to the right up another 100 feet to **Heart Lake,** a small gem that warms up in summer. One of the best photo ops of Mount Shasta is on Castle Lake Road, about 0.5 mile before the parking lot. The road is plowed all winter for ice fishing. For maps and information on area trails and hiking Mount Shasta, go to **Fifth Season,** North Mount Shasta Boulevard (530–926–3606), or **Shasta Mountain Guides,** 1938 Hill Road (530– 926–3117).

LUNCH: Michael's, 313 North Mount Shasta Boulevard, Mount Shasta; (530) 926–5288. Italian specialties and continental dishes, homemade pasta, soups, sandwiches, burgers. Try the deep-fried zucchini or the teriyaki turkey sandwich. Lunch and dinner.

Afternoon

From Mount Shasta take Highway 89 east around the base of the mountain into the **Shasta National Forest** and **McCloud River Valley.** Two miles south at the first exit is **Mount Shasta Board and Ski Park** (530–926–8600), with ski runs at 5,000 feet. Here you'll find downhill and cross-country skiing; a day lodge, restaurant, and ski school. Among the advantages of skiing here are the reasonable cost, the lack of lift lines and crowds, and a carefree drive up on I–5, which is seldom encumbered with enough snow to require chains. In summer, take the lift up to the mountaintop, hike around, picnic, and take the lift back down, or bring your mountain bikes up on the lift (you can rent them here) and pedal the excellent trails, ending up back at the lodge. Wildflowers in spring and summer and fall colors are legendary. There are frequent concerts and festivals in the beautiful outdoor amphitheater, and you can buy hot food to eat here on the sunny deck or cold picnic fare to carry away. A 24-foot climbing tower is safe for all ages and abilities, and there is also a free multimedia exhibit about the formation of Mount Shasta.

For more cross-country ski trails, watch for **Bunny Flat, Sand Flat,** and **Panther Meadows** off Highway 89. Marked trails for beginners and intermediates are maintained by the USDA Forest Service (530–926–4511 or 530–926–3781). Restrooms and parking are available only at Bunny Flat, which is also a snow-play area.

Seventeen miles farther on Highway 89, at Fowlers Campground, the **McCloud River Falls** is a side trip well worth taking (530–964–2184). Accessible by car, the three falls on a 2-mile stretch of river plunge into deep pools perfect for swimming. The third cascade has picnic tables above and a ladder that divers use to jump into the pool.

It's about an hour's drive over 4,000-foot Dead Horse Summit to **McArthur-Burney Falls State Park** and **Lake Britton** (530–335–2777). The big attraction here is two million gallons of water a day tumbling over a misty, fern-draped, 129-foot cliff. Take the 1.5-mile hike down into a forest fairyland gorge where wild tiger lily, maple, dogwood, black oak, and pine decorate the streamside; the loud rush of the falls and the stream intensifies the experience. It takes about a half hour for the fit and fast, an hour for amblers and photographers, and two hours for waders, anglers, and walkers who take offshoot trails. Good trout fishing can be had in the deep pool at the foot of the falls and in the 2-mile stream above and below.

At 9-mile-long Lake Britton are camping and RV sites, not too private. Accessible by boat (rentals here), with a terrific swimming hole at its foot, **Clark Creek Falls** is a jet of frigid water crashing into the lake. Crappie, bass, and catfish bite all season; some of the best fishing is downstream from the lake at the outlet of Pit River.

Head back to McCloud, on Highway 89.

DINNER: McCloud Guest House, 606 West Colombero Drive, McCloud; (530) 964–3160. In the old-fashioned dining room of a glorious 1907 Victorian mansion, yummy dinners of steak, chicken, fresh fish, and homemade pasta in the American tradition are served. Upstairs, five nice guest rooms with antiques and four-poster beds.

LODGING: McCloud Hotel, 408 Main Street, McCloud; (530) 964–2822 or (800) 964–2823. Fourteen spacious rooms and suites, some with Jacuzzi tubs and four-poster beds, all delightfully decorated with antiques; queen or twin beds. A place to linger by the fireplace in a big armchair, the lobby is cozy and outfitted with comfy furnishings, games, and books. Arrive in a pre–World War II car, and you get a discount! Expanded continental breakfast and afternoon tea.

For dinner, amble over to one of two dance halls in town to join in the square dancing; open May to September.

Day 3 / Morning

BREAKFAST: At the McCloud Hotel.

Just north of Highway 89 on Highway 299, Fall River Mills is headquarters for fishing and hiking in the northern Lassen River valleys. There is golf to be had at the **Fall River Valley Golf Course,** west of town on Highway 299 (530–336–5555). Open May through October, the **Fort Crook Museum,** in town (530–336–5110), has exhibits of pioneer history, Indian artifacts, and several historical buildings.

Take Highway 299 west to I–5 and south to Red Bluff.

LUNCH: Raging Fork Riverfront Grille, 500 Riverside Way near I–5, Red Bluff; (530) 529–9453. A casual place with a deck on the river; steaks, chicken, pasta, fish, sandwiches, burgers, soups, and daily specials.

Afternoon

Just north of Red Bluff is a lovely spot on the river, **Ide Adobe State Park,** 3040 Adobe Road (530–527–5927), cool and shady, with giant oaks, lawns, picnic tables, and historical displays. You can fish here, but swimming in the fast current is not advisable.

Head south to the Bay Area.

There's More

Backpacking. The Shasta-Trinity National Forest offers exceptional backpacking. The Pacific Crest Trail is accessed west of Mount Shasta at Parks Creek, South Fork Road, Whalen Road, and at Castle Crags State Park. Wilderness permits and maps

222 FARTHER AFIELD ESCAPE ONE

are available at Mount Shasta Ranger District, 204 West Alma Street, Mount Shasta; (530) 926–3606.

Castle Crags State Park, 6 miles south of Dunsmuir off I–5; (530) 235–2684. A 6,000-foot granite fortress of giant pillars and monster boulders; good trout fishing in several streams; 2 miles of the Sacramento River; swimming, hiking, rock climbing. Get maps at the park office and amble up the sun-dappled Indian Creek Nature Trail, a 1-mile loop. The Vista Point loop is 5 view-filled miles. The Crags Trail to Castle Dome is 5.5 strenuous miles up and into the Castle Crags Wilderness; the Pacific Crest Trail is accessible from here.

Golf. Lake Shastina Golf Resort, 5925 Country Club Drive, Weed; (916) 938–3201.

Mount Shasta Resort Golf Course, 1000 Siskiyou Lake Boulevard, Mount Shasta; (530) 926–3052. Eighteen spectacular holes with mountain views.

Hedge Creek Falls Park, Dunsmuir Avenue at Mott Road in Dunsmuir; (800) 474–2782. From a nice picnic spot, take a 0.25-mile, steep hike down to a lovely fall spilling over a massive stone cliff festooned with ferns. Stand inside the big cave to peer out through the water curtain.

Houseboats. With a shoreline of 365 miles, Shasta is very popular for houseboating. Boats range from 15 to 56 feet long and sleep four to twelve people; they're easy to navigate and may include air-conditioning, TV, and washers and dryers. Rentals at twelve houseboat marinas cost $1,000 per week and up.

Antlers Resort and Marina, P.O. Box 140, Lakehead 96051; (916) 238–2553. Houseboat rentals, cabins, and water-sports equipment.

Bridge Bay Resort, 12 miles north of Redding, Bridge Bay exit off I–5, 10300 Bridge Bay Road, Redding; (530) 275–3021 or (800) 752–9669; www.seven crown.com. Under a big bridge over the lake, a full-service marina with houseboat rentals, cabins, ski boats, patio boats, personal watercraft, and a clean, simple motel with a swimming pool and some kitchens—a great headquarters for plying the lake or trying out a houseboat. The houseboat rental company, Seven Crown Resorts, is one of the largest and oldest of its kind. They have rental operations also at Digger Bay on Shasta, and in the California Delta and other states.

Jones Valley Resort, 22300 Jones Valley Marina Drive, on the Pit River arm of Lake Shasta; (916) 275–7950; www.houseboats.com. Specializes in luxury houseboats with gourmet galleys, fancy entertainment systems, and flying bridges.

Lassen Volcanic National Park. East of Redding and Red Bluff, three park entrances (main park headquarters at 38050 Highway 36, just east of Mineral; 530–595–4444). On a 35-mile drive over the 8,000-foot summit, you can see snow-covered peaks and crystalline lakes, woodlands, meadows, streams, and the largest "plug dome" volcano in the world. Camping, hiking on 17 miles of the Pacific Crest Trail, nonpowered boating, cross-country skiing, and snowshoeing. Near the north entrance, Manzanita Lake is a postcard-perfect, evergreen-surrounded lake with dazzling views of the mountain. Easy 1.5-mile hike around the lake; campsites are pretty and private. Near the southwest park entrance, at Bumpass Hell, boardwalks lead to hot springs, steam vents, mudpots, and other eerie manifestations of the earth's hot insides. The Devastated Area Interpretive Trail is a quarter-mile path through a lush forest of lodgepole pines and aspens, breathtaking in the fall. To get to the beautiful 30-foot cascade of Kings Creek Falls, meander 1.5 miles one-way through meadows and forests.

McCloud Railway Shasta Sunset Dinner Train; (800) 733–2141; www.mctrain .com. Elegant dinners in restored vintage dining cars pulled by a 2,000-horsepower locomotive through spectacular scenery below Mount Shasta, Castle Crags, and the Trinity Alps.

Mossbrae Falls, off I–5. Take the Dunsmuir Avenue exit; go to Scarlett Way down the hill and over the river and the railroad tracks. A forty-minute easy walk along the river brings you to magical 70-foot-high falls.

Railroading. The Blue Goose, P.O. Box 660, Yreka 96097; (916) 842–4146. Take a three-hour trip on the historic short-line Yreka Western Railroad from Yreka to Montague. A 1915 Baldwin engine pulls cars over the river through beautiful ranchlands of the Shasta Valley with views of Mount Shasta—the train may be attacked by bandits! You get time in the quaint burg of Montague to have lunch, shop, and take a horse-drawn wagon ride, then return to the Yreka Depot, where model trains and railroad memorabilia are on display.

Redding Big League Sports Complex; (530) 225–4485 (from I–5, take the Highways 678/44 exit east nearly 4 miles to Old Oregon Trail, and go north 1.3 miles to the entrance on Viking Way; 530–223–1177). Fenway Park, Wrigley Field, and Yankee Stadium are replicated in ¾-scale, and batting cages, an indoor multi-sport field house, sand volleyball courts, playgrounds, a family restaurant, and walking trails are among the facilities at this new sports center.

Shasta Dam, off I–5 just north of Redding, on Shasta Dam Boulevard (a half-hour drive on summer weekdays, longer on weekends); (530) 275–4463. Walk out on the rim of the second-tallest concrete dam in the United States. Take a look at historic photos and watch a short film in the visitor center. The guided tour into the dam involves an elevator ride that kids younger than about age eight may find scary.

Sweetbriar Falls, 8 miles south of Dunsmuir. Take the Sweetbriar exit off I–5. Park on the west side of the railroad tracks and walk across the bridge to see feathery falls surrounded by ferns and trees. Photos are best in late morning.

Special Events

April. Sacramento River Festival, Dunsmuir; (530) 235–2012.

May. Shasta Art Fair and Fiddle Jamboree, Redding; (800) 874–7562.

July. Dunsmuir Railroad Days; (530) 235–2177. Since 1940 a celebration of historic railroad days; parade, barbecue, jazz festival.

McCloud Lumberjack Fiesta; (530) 964–3124. Fishing tournaments, parade, barbecue, entertainment, lumberjack show.

October. Heritage Days at McArthur-Burney Falls State Park; (530) 335–2111. Large crowds turn out for Native American dancers, musicians, pioneer crafts, square dancing, fiddlers.

Mount Shasta International Film Festival, Mount Shasta; (530) 926–5186, www.shastafilmfest.com. From more than 20 countries and the United States, independent features and documentaries; celebrity appearances, food and wine events.

Other Recommended Restaurants and Lodgings

Dunsmuir

Cafe Maddalena, 5801 Sacramento Avenue; (530) 235–2725. In a fresh, knotty-pine interior, Mediterranean bistro-style food for dinner, Thursday through Sunday. Wine bar; Spanish mackerel, steamed mussels, pork tenderloin, fresh pasta, and more creative dishes influenced by the cuisines of Spain, France, Italy, and North Africa; wine bar.

Railroad Park Resort, 100 Railroad Park Road; (530) 235–4440. Restaurant and motel in antique railroad cars; pool, spa. Good jumping-off point for exploring and hiking in Castle Crags. Also, RV park, campground, cabins.

Mount Shasta

Mount Shasta KOA Campground, 900 North Mount Shasta Boulevard; (530) 926–4029. A grassy, gardeny place for RVs and tents; animal corrals, camping cabins, store, pool, playground.

Mount Shasta Ranch, 1008 W. A. Barr Road, five minutes from Lake Siskiyou; (530) 926–3870; www.travelassist.com/reg/ca121s.html. In a beautiful country setting, a bed-and-breakfast with spacious rooms and suites in a circa 1920 ranch house, cottages, and a carriage house; gigantic common living room and game room, full breakfast. Children are quite welcome in the carriage house.

Strawberry Valley Inn, 1142 South Mount Shasta Boulevard; (530) 926–2052. Lovely landscaped grounds and shade trees make this reasonably priced motel a winner; some rooms have two beds, and there are two-room suites. A huge breakfast buffet is served on a sunny patio or by the fireplace.

Trinity Cafe, 622 North Mount Shasta Boulevard; (530) 926–6200. Surprisingly sophisticated in a little laid-back town, seasonal California cuisine and updated bistro food with a great wine list. Go for the wild salmon, handmade buffalo mozzarella, duck prosciutto, cassoulet, or the succulent lamb shanks.

Redding

Hilltop Inn, 2300 Hilltop Drive; (800) 221–6100. A very nice motel with spacious rooms, swimming and wading pools, complimentary continental breakfast, and two reasonably priced restaurants.

Jack's Grill, 1743 California Street; (530) 241–9705. In a casual, noisy, hometown atmosphere. Sixteen-ounce steaks, deep-fried prawns, big plates of good old American food; dinner only.

For More Information

Mount Shasta Visitors Pavilion, 2 blocks east of the I–5 central exit at Lake and Pine Streets; (800) 926–4865.

Redding Convention and Visitors Bureau, 7777 Auditorium Drive, Redding 96001; (800) 874–7562; www.visitredding.com.

Shasta Cascade Wonderland Association, 1619 Highway 273, Anderson 96007; (530) 365–7500 or (800) 474–2782; www.shastacascade.org.

Yosemite

The Big Valley and Wawona / 3 Nights

Native Americans called it Ahwahnee, or "Deep, Grassy Valley." John Muir saw it as a "great temple lit from above." You'll wax poetic in Yosemite Valley when a setting sun paints a shining 4,000-foot curtain across the face of Half Dome and glitters like a crown on snowcapped peaks.

□ Waterfalls and wildflowers

□ Historic hotels

□ Hetch Hetchy

□ Trailside picnics

□ Mountaintops, monoliths

□ Sequoia groves

Americans have camped and hiked below the granite monoliths of Yosemite Valley since before Abraham Lincoln dedicated the valley and the Mariposa Big Trees to the state in 1864; sixteen years later, the national park was created.

Today Yosemite Valley is an international tourist attraction, jam-packed with visitors in summertime. Eighty percent of them stay in the valley, where most of the public facilities and the best-known postcard views are found; nevertheless, it's just 1 percent of the park.

Fall is a good time to come. Kids are back in school, and the Merced River becomes a stream of molten gold, bright maples reflecting in its chilly waters. Crisp breezes rustle hauntingly through the aspen groves. In spring the wildflowers are a riot of color, and the valley's famous waterfalls are at their booming best. Nowhere in the world are so many high falls concentrated in so small an area as the 7 square miles of Yosemite Valley. And a winter weekend at Yosemite can be unforgettable, whether you cross-country ski on silent forest trails or view a white wonderland through the tall windows of the old Ahwahnee Hotel.

The southern part of the national park, called Wawona, is the place to go in midsummer, when the valley is crowded with cars and people. The wilderness is silent, except for the crunch of your own footsteps and the prattle of Steller's jays.

Day 1 / Morning

Drive from the Oakland Bay Bridge east on Interstate 580 to Interstate 205 east to Interstate 5 north to Highway 120 east, connecting with Highway 99 north to

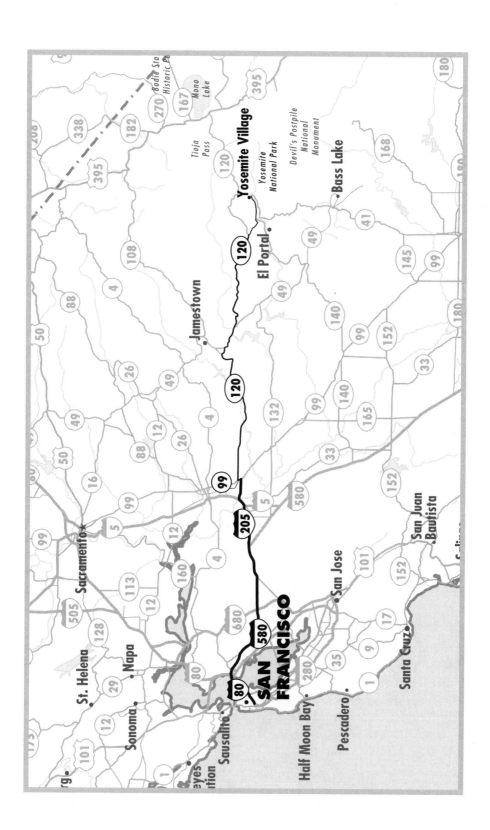

Manteca, then Highway 120 east to the Big Oak Flat entrance to **Yosemite National Park,** a four-hour drive. The highway narrows here, ducking under huge overhanging boulders before emerging above the boiling Merced River into the valley, at an elevation of 4,000 feet.

To help plan your trip and find out about events, activities, and seminars held throughout the year, read *Yosemite Today* online (www.nps.gov/yose); this is the free tabloid that is handed to you at the park entrance gates. You can also download the *Yosemite Guide,* which provides more general information. The park is open year-round, 365 days a year, twenty-four hours a day. Reservations are not required to enter the park; private vehicles are always welcome. The park entrance fee is $20 per vehicle and all occupants. Summertime midday temperatures in the park, particularly in the valley, may top ninety degrees, and the sun is intense at this elevation, between 3,000 and 4,500 feet.

At the **visitor center,** at **Yosemite Village** in midvalley (209–372–0299), get information and advice from Park Service rangers; make reservations for guided walks, hikes, classes, live theater, and musical programs events. Watch slide shows and films, browse the exhibits and the excellent bookstore for guidebooks, posters, videos, and maps. You will find a handy courtesy phone with which to make lodging reservations. Sightseeing in the valley is best done on foot, on 9 miles of bike trails, or by tour bus or free shuttle bus—in other words, without your car.

If you plan to take an extensive hike or backpack trip, stop at the **Wilderness Center** next to the post office, where you will find wilderness permits, maps, and information (209–372–0740; www.nps.gov/yose/wilderness).

If you are first-time visitors with only a day to spare, take the two-hour, 26-mile valley floor narrated tour to see the main attractions, in an open-air tram or enclosed motorcoach.

LUNCH: Degnan's Deli, Cafe, or Pizza Loft in Yosemite Village; (209) 372–8454. In the deli, custom-made and premade deli sandwiches, salads, snacks, espresso drinks, and other beverages to take out. The cafe serves gourmet sandwiches, homemade soups and pastries, soft-serve ice cream, burgers, and light meals. A fireplace and valley views make the upstairs pizza and pasta place a cozy spot.

Afternoon

Jump on the shuttle bus and tour the valley. At stop #7 walk a short path to the base of **Yosemite Falls,** three cascades dropping 2,425 feet, the third highest waterfall in the world. As of 2005, an extensive area at the base of the falls has been completely transformed to the tune of $13.5 million, with restoration of habitat, new footpaths and nature trails, benches and alcoves—all creating a much-improved, tranquil environment. New interpretive exhibits showcase natural history and Native American culture.

For an hour's easy walk in the meadows around **Mirror Lake,** with wonderful views of Half Dome and Mount Watkins, get off at stop #17. The **Tenaya Zig Zags/Snow Creek Trail** is a little-used, 3.5-mile route to the rim of the valley, beginning east of Mirror Lake—not an easy hike, but views are eye-popping.

You can leave children at **Happy Isles** at shuttle stop #16 for free one-hour walks and talks on nature, birds, and forest lore. Happy Isles is the start of several trails, including the 1.5-mile (one-way) **Mist Trail** to **Vernal Falls,** an exciting route but too strenuous and slippery for kids younger than age seven or eight. This is the most popular hike in the valley because the rewards are a breathtaking close-up view of the falls dropping over a 317-foot cliff, plus knockout vistas of many peaks, domes, and water cascades.

Now that you're warmed up to Yosemite, go into the **Ansel Adams Gallery** (209–372–4413), near the visitor center; since 1902 the place has been a camera store and gallery of signed Adams photos, prints, and posters of the valley in its seasonal raiments. Free two-hour photography workshops with professional teachers are conducted here. There are also Sunrise Camera Walks from Yosemite Lodge (209–372–0299).

DINNER: **Ahwahnee Hotel Dining Room,** Yosemite Village at midvalley; (559) 252–4848 or (209) 372–1488; www.yosemitepark.com. With a 24-foot-high ceiling and baronial chandeliers, the 130-foot-long dining room is world famous for its beauty and views through the sky-high windows. A pianist plays for dinner, and the food is better than it has ever been in the history of the hotel—top-notch California cuisine and a good wine list, plus choices that kids like. The dining room is elaborately decorated and glowing with candles and merriment every Christmas season, when the medieval-style Bracebridge Dinners are held. Gala Vintners' Holidays and Chefs' Holidays are popular in the wintertime.

LODGING: **Ahwahnee Hotel,** (559) 252–4848. Standing gloriously aloof in a woodland setting, with granite cliffs rising behind, the Art Deco hotel is in perfect shape, with painted beams, decorated floors, and stained-glass windows faded into subtle Indian colors. Sofas, armchairs, and fabulous old Oriental rugs are arranged by a huge fireplace in the Great Lounge. Built in 1927, the place still has a halcyon-days atmosphere and is museum-like, enriched with paintings, photos, and priceless Native American baskets. When fall leaves blow along the footpaths and wood smoke curls silently into a twilight glow, the spirit of summers past comes alive at the Ahwahnee. The gift shop is a good place to shop for souvenirs and books. Light meals are served on the outdoor terrace, and afternoon tea in the Great Lounge. You can walk or bike from here, or take the shuttle, to all valley sights.

Rooms have been redone and they are fabulous, with king beds, cushy fabrics, upscale mountain- and Indian-theme decor, sitting areas, and huge windows with spectacular views. Now that the food and the accommodations are the tops, the Ahwahnee lives up to its spectacular outdoor setting and atmospheric interiors.

A view of Bridalveil Fall from Wawona Tunnel.

Day 2 / Morning

BREAKFAST: An American breakfast in the Ahwahnee Hotel Dining Room.

Purchase picnic goodies and set off on the 32-mile drive on Glacier Point Road to **Glacier Point,** atop the sheer southern wall of the valley. Some 3,200 feet above the valley, the view is of several waterfalls, **Half Dome, El Capitan,** and other famous pinnacles, and the Merced River snaking along. With binoculars you may see climbers making a several days' ascent to the dizzying 2,850-foot summit of El Capitan. A vertical wall of granite four times as large as Gibraltar, "El Cap" is a memento of glaciers that tore off and ground into little pieces great sections of mountain. The faint thundering sound you hear in springtime is **Nevada Falls,** 2 miles away.

At Glacier Point are a 150-seat granite amphitheater, campfire programs and ranger talks, viewing terraces, and a beautiful stone-and-timber building where food and gifts are sold. In wintertime the building is a bunkhouse for guided cross-country ski tours. The "Stars Over Yosemite" experience here on weekend nights gives you a chance to see the incredibly starry sky and the moon-washed monoliths through an astronomer's telescope.

A relaxing way to get to and from Glacier Point is on a narrated bus tour that runs three times a day from the valley. You can also take a hikers' bus to Glacier Point and walk down to the valley, 4.8 miles, a three- to four-hour hike. Robust climbers trek to the top of Half Dome by hiking the John Muir Trail or Mist Trail to Little Yosemite Valley, where they camp overnight. The next day, the climb is made with the aid of cables that were permanently installed on the 8,892-foot monolith in 1919. Every year more than 10,000 people climb Half Dome.

Along Glacier Point Road are several memorable stops to make. **Dewey Point,** at 7,385 feet and overlooking **Bridalveil Fall** and El Capitan, is accessible by a beautiful 7-mile round-trip trail just west of Bridalveil Campground. According to the time of year, the path may be bordered with sky-blue lupine, Indian paintbrush, or 6-foot-tall rose-colored fireweed. Crossing a footbridge over a creek, bear left around **McGurk Meadow,** where mule deer graze in grasses sprinkled with shooting stars and goldenrod.

To reach **Mono Meadow** and **Mount Starr King View,** park 2.5 miles beyond Bridalveil Campground and take the trail east, dropping for 0.5 mile to the meadow, continuing to a spectacular view 1 mile farther on: 3 miles round-trip.

LUNCH: Have a picnic on top of the world at Glacier Point or on a nearby nature trail.

Afternoon

Explore some of the 800 miles of hiking trails in the Yosemite backcountry or amble along the banks of the Merced River, trying your luck at trout fishing. Lie about on a sunny beach or take a swim in the river or at the Ahwahnee. Rent kayaks, rafts, and life jackets at Curry Village. If you've become fascinated by the history and geologic wonders of the park, you may wish to get in on one of the many seminars, lectures, theater presentations, and tours offered throughout the year.

Head west out of the valley, dropping south on Highway 41 to the southern part of the park, called Wawona. Wilderness trails for hiking and horseback riding are largely deserted, and you can fish and swim in the Merced River, play tennis and golf, and snowshoe or downhill and cross-country ski in wintertime.

Before you arrive at the Wawona Hotel or your campground, take the tram or walk up to see the **Mariposa Grove,** where the 209-foot, 300-ton Grizzly Giant, the 290-foot Columbia, and hundreds more 2,000-year-old giant sequoias stand in all their magnificence in the largest of the three magnificent sequoia groves in the park. You can hop off at tram stops and wander the trails, or proceed to the vista point overlooking the Wawona basin. In the museum are exhibits about the big trees and other flora of the Sierras. Take the tram down, or walk the 2.5-mile, easy downhill route beneath fragrant cedars and pines. In wintertime, the snowshoe trail to the grove is a wonderland.

DINNER: **Wawona Hotel**, Highway 41, 7 miles west of the south entrance to the park; (559) 253–5635; www.yosemitepark.com. Open for all meals and Sunday buffet brunch, the beautiful Victorian dining room offers California cuisine and American comfort food; don't miss the fresh trout, the pine-nut pie, and the summer barbecues outdoors on the lawn. Full bar, good wine list. Call ahead for dinner reservations.

LODGING: Wawona Hotel. Riding the edge of Wawona Meadow like an aging, but still glistening, white ocean liner, the oldest resort hotel in the state was built in the 1870s and is in fabulous shape. Rooms in vintage buildings and cottages have been redone in sumptuous fabrics, with armoires, antiques, and nice bathrooms with amenities. Call ahead to check on the winter schedule; the hotel may be closed on some weekdays. Evenings by the fireplace in the lobby parlors are sweet, while a honky-tonk pianist plays and spins tales of old Yosemite; take a look at the vintage photo collection. There is a beautiful, small pool, sweeping lawns, rockers on the veranda, and a nine-hole golf course. Ask about free shuttles to the valley, to Badger Pass, and to the Mariposa Grove.

Day 3 / Morning

BREAKFAST: Wawona Hotel.

Across from the hotel, stroll the 3-mile, flat path around **Wawona Meadow** through the pines and the wildflowers; you can cross-country ski on the meadow, too. From here you can hike to **Chilnualna Falls,** a steep 8-mile round-trip through a forest to a spectacular jetting avalanche of water.

Small beaches and swimming spots are easily accessible on the south fork of the **Merced River** as it runs through Wawona. Costumed docents re-create the period of 1890 to 1915 at the **Yosemite Pioneer History Center,** a compound of historic buildings, a covered bridge, authentic furnished log cabins, a jail, and stagecoaches. In June the **Pioneer Wagon Train,** headquartered here, is an elaborate procession with riders in costume, campfires, and historic presentations.

Head out of the park to the **Yosemite Mountain Sugar Pine Railroad** (56001 Highway 41; 559–683–7273; www.ymsprr.com). Plan a couple of hours to ride the train, picnic, and enjoy the beautiful forest. An eighty-four-ton, vintage Shay locomotive, the largest ever built for a narrow-gauge track, pulls open cars 4 miles through forestlands into Lewis Creek Canyon. It's exciting to climb aboard at the tiny station while steam rolls out from under the huge engine and black smoke belches into the sky. Keep your eyes peeled for train robbers! A conductor spins tales of when the railroad hauled timber out of the Sierras. June through September, a "Moonlight Special" excursion ends with a steak barbecue and live music around a campfire. There is a very nice restaurant and the Narrow Gauge Inn on the property (www.narrowgaugeinn.com).

With more time on your hands, stop in **Oakhurst** to browse the many art galleries. On the north end of town at **Gallery Row** (40982 Highway 41; 559–683–3375) are several top-notch fine art galleries, including a National Park Gallery.

From Oakhurst, take Highway 49 west to Mariposa, and Highway 140 to Merced, heading north on Highway 99 to I–205 and I–580 to the Bay Area.

There's More

Art Activity Center, Yosemite Village; (209) 372–1442. Free outdoor art classes are offered in watercolor, sketching, and mixed media (kids under twelve must be accompanied by parent or guardian). Here is a small, well-stocked shop selling artists' materials and equipment, including top-quality paints, brushes, paper, pens and pencils, and children's art kits.

Bridalveil Fall. Near the Highway 140/Highway 41 junction, a short, paved trail leads to the base of the fall—a miraculous, wispy sheet of water floating 620 feet to the valley floor. The fall flows year-round and is often decorated by rainbows. In springtime, turn around for a view of Ribbon Fall, the highest single fall in the park, at 1,612 feet. On a hot day, cool your feet in the icy creek.

Complimentary shuttle-bus service is provided year-round throughout Yosemite Valley. In summer it also runs from Wawona to the Mariposa Grove and between Tenaya Lake and Tuolumne Meadows Lodge. In winter, buses run from valley hotels to the Badger Pass Ski Area.

Curry Village Lodge, shuttle stop 14 at the east end of the valley. Take a slow stroll around the great old lodge to view vintage photos and charming artifacts from early days in the park. Sit a spell by the fireplace in a hickory-branch rocker, play a game at a birch-bark table, or get a beer from the bar across the way and relax on the veranda in an Adirondack chair. Open from 8:00 A.M. to 10:00 P.M.

Dog Lake is the closest lake to Tuolumne and the warmest of the chilly lakes at this altitude. It's a 1.5-mile one-way trek, a little steep at first but easy enough for all ages, and there's good swimming and fishing at the end.

Events, Activities, Tours. Year-round, daytime and evening talks and slide shows, classes, guided walks and hikes, fireside gatherings and old-fashioned campfires, and theater presentations, all showcasing the natural and cultural history of Yosemite. Learn about the secret life of bats, see through the eyes of a Buffalo soldier of the 1900s, meet John Muir, take a wilderness survival class, learn to use a digital camera. Some are free and require no preregistration; others are fee-based with advance sign-up. Ask at the visitor center and Yosemite Lodge; see *Yosemite Today* for schedules, and get information online at www.yosemitepark.com and www.nps.gov/yose.

Mirror Lake. Take the popular, scenic half-mile walk on a paved path to a small, glassy lake for fabulous views of Half Dome. The wildflowery trail around the lake takes an hour or so.

Rafting. Ahwahnee Whitewater Expeditions, P.O. Box 1161, Columbia 95310; (209) 533–1401. Rafting on the Merced, Tuolumne, Stanislaus, and Carson Rivers.

Tuolumne Meadows, at 8,600 feet, is the largest open meadow in the Sierras at the subalpine level, bordered by the snow-fed Tuolumne River and surrounded by peaks and glacier-polished domes. The nearest access is by Tioga Road near the town of Lee Vining, on the northeasern side of the park, a road that is closed for about half the year due to snow. You can also take the beautiful drive up from the valley (also closed during wintertime).

A hub for backpacking trails, 2.5-mile-long Tuolumne Meadows may sparkle with frost or be awash in purple nightshade, golden monkeyflowers, and riots of magenta lady-slipper orchids. You can drive to the rustic Tuoloumne Meadows Lodge (209–252–4848) and the Tuolumne Meadows Campground (800–365–2297), the largest in the park, with 325 sites; the most desirable sites are on the east side near the river. Campfire programs are held most nights. Within walking distance of the campground are a grocery store, stables, and a restaurant that serves substantial American fare. Tent cabins with woodstoves are located in a picturesque setting near the river.

A variety of guided walks begin at Tuolumne Meadows (209–372–0263). The "Night Prowl," an after-dark caravan around the meadow, turns up great gray owls, spotted bats, and other nocturnal denizens of the High Sierras.

Between Tuolumne and the valley off Tioga Road, **White Wolf,** a summertime-only headquarters for backcountry trails, has rustic tent cabins, a "first-come" campground, store, stables, and a lovely old clapboard dining hall that serves simple meals all day.

Wawona Golf Course. Opened in 1917, this gorgeous nine-holer rolls on easy terrain bordered by towering cedars and pines; clubs are available to rent in the pro shop; (209) 375–6572.

Winter fun in Yosemite. Although frosty white on the clifftops and often in the valley, winter weather is usually mild. The valley gets about 29 inches of snow, Badger Pass Ski Area about 180 inches. The outdoor skating rink at Curry Village is a cozy place to be, with a warming hut, skate rentals, hot drinks, and views of Half Dome. Badger Pass is the oldest ski school in the state and still one of the best, with low prices for everything (209–372–8430; www.badgerpass.com). Except on holiday weekends, you won't wait in lift lines; the dining decks and all facilities are just steps away from the lifts and school meeting places. On the great new 100-yard-long snow tubing hill, two-hour tubing sessions are scheduled twice a day for

$9.00 per person, including equipment. You are not permitted to use your own tubes or sliding devices, and a parent must accompany children ages ten and younger.

Take the shuttle bus from your accommodations up the (sometimes icy) hill to Badger. There are six lifts to the 8,000-foot summit. Nordic skiing on 350 miles of trails and roads, and 23 miles of machine-groomed track and skating lanes. A two-hour, ranger-guided, narrated snowshoe hike is only $3.00, including equipment. There is a popular overnight ski hike to a rustic lodge, including meals. Junior Snow Ranger program, winter field trips for photographers and artists. Snow-play areas at Crane Flat on state Route 120 and just outside the southern entrance on state Route 412 near Fish Camp.

Yosemite High Sierra Camps Saddle Trips; (209) 372–1445. Four- and six- day saddle trips to camps between 7,150 and 10,300 feet. Camps are 8 miles apart, and each provides tents, beds, linens, and blankets. Breakfast and dinner are served in a heated dining tent. Groups are limited to ten people and are accompanied by an experienced guide. Personal belongings are carried on a pack mule.

Special Events

January through February. Chef's Holidays, Ahwahnee Hotel and Yosemite Lodge; (559) 253–5676. Demonstrations, seminars with prominent chefs, gala banquets.

February. Yosemite Renaissance, Yosemite Valley Visitor Center; (209) 372–0299. National juried art show with Yosemite as the theme; paintings, photography, sculpture, lithography.

March. Vintage Days; (559) 253–5676. A three-day showcase of the glamour, style, and cultural significance of the Roaring Twenties with themed special events, speakeasies, live Big Band concerts, fox-trot and tango dance lessons, and a period clothing fashion show.

November through December. Yosemite Vintners' Holidays; (559) 253–5676. Banquets and seminars with prominent vintners. Presentations in the Great Lounge at the Ahwahnee are open to park visitors free of charge.

December through January. The Bracebridge Dinners, in the Ahwahnee Hotel Dining Room; (559) 253–5676. The Renaissance is re-created at elaborate performances and monumental banquets.

Other Recommended Restaurants and Lodgings

Accommodations in the national park at the Ahwahnee Hotel, Yosemite Lodge, Wawona Hotel, White Wolf Lodge, Curry Village, and Tuolumne Lodge and in campgrounds and cabins can be arranged by calling (559) 253–5635 or by writing to Delaware North Parks and Resorts at Yosemite, 5410 East Home Avenue, Fresno 93727. You can also check availability and make reservations online at www .yosemitepark.com. By the end of 2004, the four-diamond Ahwahnee, the Yosemite Lodge, and Curry Village were all extensively renovated and outfitted in great new interior furnishings, amenities and decor, mattresses, carpeting, and much more. Yosemite Lodge now has TV, and wireless Internet access is available in many areas—not your grandpa's Yosemite! Sustainable and organic menu choices have been integrated into most menus.

The Curry Village area of the valley offers a variety of accommodations, from tent cabins to hotel rooms and loft rooms sleeping six or more; all are clean and quite basic; some can be noisy. Nearby, Yosemite Lodge (now called Yosemite Lodge at the Falls) has hundreds of units from hotel-type rooms with balconies to rustic cabins, with or without baths, in a compound that includes a cafeteria, restaurants, post office, gift shops, swimming pool, outdoor theater, and tour desk; free nightly programs.

Camping: Although they are crowded in the high season, and sometimes noisy with road traffic and RV generators, North, Upper, and Lower Pines campgrounds are convenient to walking and biking throughout the valley and to most public facilities and trailheads. Many valley campers prefer North Pines—it is a little more isolated than others and is shaded by tall pines. Sites near the river are the first to go, so make your reservations well in advance. You can bring an RV up to 40 feet to some, not all, campgrounds. A fast way to check campsite availability year-round, is on the Web at www.yosemitesites.com. Hot showers are available to the public twenty-four hours a day at Curry Village and Housekeeping Camps; a small fee includes towel and soap.

A compromise between accessibility to the valley and a quieter, prettier place to camp is found at Bridalveil Creek Campground, 25 miles from the valley on the Glacier Point Road at an elevation of 7,200 feet. Each of the one hundred tent and RV sites here and at other higher-elevation camps are provided with "bear lockers," secure boxes where your food can be kept safe from black bears.

Food Court at Yosemite Lodge, (209) 372–1274. The cafeteria of old is now an attractive food court with a tree-shaded patio and umbrella tables; you can charge purchases to your lodgings. Freshly made choices include prepacked lunches and custom deli sandwiches; vegetarian and meat-based entrees, ethnic dishes, and specialty sauces at the pasta station. Seafood, fruit and veggie salads, a grill station for hamburgers, garden burgers, and chicken and fish sandwiches; and a hot and cold breakfast station. At the bakery-dessert station are muffins, bagels, Danish, cakes and pies, and espresso drinks.

Housekeeping Camp, midvalley; (209) 252–4848. Like to camp but not sleep in a tent or on the ground? The camp has 266 tent cabins sleeping up to six with concrete walls and floors and canvas roofs; each has a fire ring. With electricity, no phones or plumbing; the cabins are close together, with minimal privacy. Facilities include a central bathhouse, a laundry and a small grocery store. Bring your own linens or sleeping bags, cooking equipment, dishes, and food.

El Portal

Yosemite View Lodge, Highway 140 near the Arch Rock entrance; (800) 321–5261; www.yosemite-motels.com. The closest to the park with the nicest accommodations, this is a large motel with balconies or patios overlooking the Merced River. Rooms are spacious and attractive, with mountain lodge–style furnishings; some with kitchenettes, fireplaces, sofabeds, and whirlpool tubs. Gorgeous new suites were recently added with oversize in-room spa tubs overlooking the river. Indoor and outdoor swimming pools, a convenience store and gift shop, a pizza place and a small restaurant and cocktail lounge, and a new river walk. In the lobby, Yosemite Guides is the place to find out about guided tours in and around the park. From here, take a shuttle bus into the valley.

Fish Camp

Tenaya Lodge, 1122 Highway 41; (877) 322–5492 or (800) 514–2167; www.tenaya lodge.com. In a sun bowl surrounded by forested mountains, a 244-room, destination resort hotel, five minutes from the south entrance to the national park. From here you can hike, bike, take a sleigh ride, cross-country ski, and horseback ride or take a variety of guided tours into and around the park. Decorated with Indian artifacts Western-style furnishings, the casual yet luxurious hotel has newly updated, spacious rooms with sitting areas, sofabeds, and windows that open to the view and the scent of the pines. Two restaurants, cozy bar, sunny dining terraces. Some ground floor rooms are available for guests and their dogs. Indoor and outdoor swimming pools, rental bikes, shuttles into the park. A full-service spa offers steam, sauna, whirlpools, a nice array of workout equipment, and a staff of therapists for massage and health and beauty treatments. Among special events are barbecue evenings starting with horse-drawn wagon rides to the cookouts, with campfire singing and marshmallow roasting with cowpokes. Five- to eleven-year-olds are supervised all day at Camp Tenaya.

For More Information

Delaware North Parks and Resorts at Yosemite. 5410 East Home Avenue, Fresno 93727; (559) 253–5635; www.yosemitepark.com. Accommodations and campground reservations and packages, tours and programs, general park information.

Traveler's Information; www.yosemite.com. Lodging, dining, attractions, things to do, maps and general information about the areas surrounding the national park; park information, too.

Yosemite Association, P.O. Box 230, El Portal 95318; (209) 379–2646; www .yosemite.org. Extensive calendar of outdoor adventures led by top rangers, scientists, and naturalists, from tours to multiday trips; a big online bookstore.

Yosemite National Park, P.O. Box 577, Yosemite National Park 95389; (209) 372–0200; www.nps.gov/yose. Trip planning, tours, programs and events, nature and cultural information.

Advice: Hikers and campers should keep in mind that sudden storms are not uncommon in Yosemite any month of the year. Weather changes rapidly in the Sierras, and snow can fall as early as September.

INDEX

National Hotel, Nevada City, 168
Natural Bridges State Beach, 114
Nature Conservancy Uplands
    Nature Preserve, 92
Nepenthe, 136
Nero's, 197
Nevada City, 166–69, 171
Nevada City Winery, 168
Nevada Theatre, 168
New Brighton Beach, 113
New Davenport Cash Store
    Restaurant and Inn, 124
New Moon Cafe, 169
Nick's Cove, 101
Niebaum-Coppola Estate
    Winery, 29
Norm's Market, 124
North Lake Tahoe Snow
    Festival, 189
North Star Mining Museum,
    169–70
Northstar, 207
North Tahoe Regional Park, 210
Noyo Harbor, 79
Noyo River, 79

O

Oakhurst, 233
Oakville Grocery, 30, 44
Oat Hill Mine Trail, 42
Oceania, 113
Odyssey, 89
Old Coast Hotel, 79–80
Old Fisherman's Wharf, 132
Old Monterey Cafe, 135
Old Sacramento, 159–61
Olema, 99, 104

Olive Press, 14
O'Neill Coldwater Classic, 110
Open Water Rowing, 89
Options, 4
Original Old Post Office, 210
Out of This World, 76
Overland Sheepskin Company, 27

P

Pacific Blues Cafe, 27
Pacific Crest Trail, 188, 207
Pacific Edge Indoor Climbing
    Facility, 110
Pacific Wave, 110
Papa Birds, 80
Patch, The, 17
Peppermint Stick, The, 177
Pescadero State Beach, 124
Pescadero, 124
Petri's, 89
Pfeiffer Big Sur State Park, 136
Phipps Ranch, 124
Pierce Ranch, 102
Pigeon Point Lighthouse, 124
Pillar Point Harbor, 122
Pine Ridge Winery, 30
Pioneer Park, 41
Pioneer Wagon Train, 232
Point Arena, 68, 71–72
Point Arena Lighthouse, 69
Point Arena Public Fishing Pier, 68
Point Lobos State Reserve, 147
Point Reyes Headlands, 102
Point Reyes Lighthouse, 102
Point Reyes National Seashore,
    97–99
Point Reyes Seashore Lodge, 100

About the Author

Karen Misuraca is a travel and outdoor writer based in Sonoma, in the heart of California's Wine Country. When not exploring the High Sierras, kayaking on the California coast, or golfing, she writes travel books and contributes articles to a variety of publications, including *Alaska Airlines* magazine, *Odyssey, Yoga Journal, San Francisco* magazine, *Physicians Travel & Meetings Guide,* and others. She is the author of *The 100 Best Golf Resorts of the World, The California Coast, Our San Francisco, Insiders' Guide Yosemite,* and *Fun With the Family Northern California.*

Karen has written about golf in Ireland, ancient cities in Jordan, waterborne safaris in Africa, and adventure travel in Central America and Vietnam. She is accompanied on some of her journeys by her three daughters, a lively contingent of grandchildren, and her partner, Michael Capp, an international broker of architectural products.